# MASTERING

### THE

# PROCESS

ALSO BY ELIZABETH GEORGE

FICTION

*A Great Deliverance*
*Payment in Blood*
*Well-Schooled in Murder*
*A Suitable Vengeance*
*For the Sake of Elena*
*Missing Joseph*
*Playing for the Ashes*
*In the Presence of the Enemy*
*Deception on his Mind*
*In Pursuit of the Proper Sinner*
*A Traitor to Memory*
*A Place of Hiding*
*With No One as Witness*
*What Came Before He Shot Her*
*Careless in Red*
*This Body of Death*
*Believing the Lie*
*Just One Evil Act*
*A Banquet of Consequences*
*The Punishment She Deserves*

SHORT STORIES

*I, Richard*

YOUNG ADULT

*The Edge of Nowhere*
*The Edge of the Water*
*The Edge of the Shadows*
*The Edge of the Light*

NON-FICTION

*Write Away: One Novelist's Approach to Fiction and the Writing Life*

ANTHOLOGY

*Crime From the Mind of a Woman (Ed.)*
*Two of the Deadliest (Ed.)*

# MASTERING

## THE

# PROCESS

*From Idea to Novel*

## Elizabeth George

HODDER &
STOUGHTON

First published in Great Britain in 2020 by Hodder & Stoughton
An Hachette UK company

1

Image 19 by Anastasiya Lobanovskaya, courtesy of Pexels.
Image 20 by Vincent Tan, courtesy of Pexels.
All other images courtesy of the author.

A CIP catalogue record for this title is available from the British Library

Hardback ISBN 978 1 529 39081 0
Trade Paperback ISBN 978 1 529 39082 7
eBook ISBN 978 1 529 39084 1

Printed and bound in Great Britain by Clays Ltd, Elcograf S.p.A.

Hodder & Stoughton policy is to use papers that are natural, renewable
and recyclable products and made from wood grown in sustainable forests.
The logging and manufacturing processes are expected to conform to the
environmental regulations of the country of origin.

Hodder & Stoughton Ltd
Carmelite House
50 Victoria Embankment
London EC4Y 0DZ

www.hodder.co.uk

*For my Sistahs:*
*Gail*
*Karen Joy*
*Jane*
*Nancy*

Writing, I'd seen, demands a ferocious, all-consuming commitment, a refusal to be distracted.

Pico Iyer,

'The Man Who Told Futures'

# Contents

# MASTERING

—— THE ——

# PROCESS

# Prologue

When *Write Away* was first published in 2004, I had no thought of writing a follow-up volume to it. But after a number of years during which I taught writing courses and appeared at writers' conferences, I began to see that creating a process book that used one of my novels as an example of each step of my own process might prove useful to people who are interested in novel writing or in how this one individual writer approaches the complicated task of putting together a British crime novel.

Let me first explain how I developed my process for creating a novel.

When my first to-be-published novel was acquired by Kate Miciak at Bantam Books, I waited anxiously for an editorial letter. I knew enough about the craft of writing and the world of publishing to understand that it's a rare occurrence for a novel to be accepted and then published without editorial input. So I understood that my work on *A Great Deliverance* wasn't complete. What I didn't see was that my work on *A Great Deliverance* was *far* from complete. The editorial letter I received from Kate three and a half months later was nine pages long, comprising twenty-two paragraphs. The twenty-two paragraphs consisted of nothing but questions. It was my job to answer these questions somehow in whatever way I saw fit within the body of the novel as I revised it. Looking back, I recall that creating the answers

to these questions added in the vicinity of one hundred pages to the manuscript.

It was a task that I didn't wish to repeat. So once I had completed it, I
studied Kate's letter to see how I could avoid having to do so much editor-
requested work on my next novel. From my study of the letter, I saw that
there were two areas towards which Kate directed most of her questions.
One was towards a fuller examination of place, and the other was towards
a fuller exploration of character.

So I asked myself: In my next novel, what can I do to illustrate place
with more depth and verisimilitude? How do I make my characters more
real? The answers that I developed gave me the first two elements of what
ultimately became my process.

Initially, I came to understand that I would have to examine far more
closely any setting I wished to use in the future. These were the days before
the Internet, so the onus was on me to come up with a way to make place
jump out for the reader. I did this by upping the quality and intensity of
every prewriting activity I engaged in to understand a place when I was in
England trying to decide where to set a novel. That meant making more
copious notes about what I saw in every location, taking far more photographs, learning the flora and the fauna of any area in which I might wish
to set a scene, recording all sensory impressions of a place, conducting interviews when necessary. I would also need to purchase brochures and
books, Ordnance Survey maps, road atlases of the individual areas and
hundreds of postcards. I would have to learn the architectural style and the
building materials of any county I was investigating, as well as the geology
and the topography. I would have to listen carefully to people speaking
around me. I would have to watch carefully people living their lives around
me. From all of this, I would then create a setting, and I would do this in
*advance* of any writing of the novel itself. In this way, when I placed a character in a scene of the book, I would have notes and photographs and maps
and booklets to use in order to make the location real for the reader. If

necessary, I would create my own map of the location, especially if I wasn't using a place that actually exists or if I was combining several places into one for the purpose of my story.

Second, I would have to create my characters in advance. Once I had the kernel of the story (which quite often emerges from my experience of the place in which the story will occur), I would need to people that kernel with the various individuals who logically would be involved in the tale I wanted to tell. Since I write crime novels, this peopling of the story would begin with the victim and the killer and would spread out from there. But creating the characters in advance couldn't mean just knowing that there would be – for example – five generic suspects, a generic killer and a generic victim. Additionally, creating them in advance couldn't mean I was merely giving them names and ages. Those pieces of information wouldn't make them real to my editor or, actually, to me either.

So I decided I'd become my characters' psychologist, social worker, historian, medical doctor, psychiatrist, religious adviser, guardian angel, omnipresent observer, parent, sibling, confidant, best friend, worst enemy, etc. In doing this, I would eventually know my characters better than they could ever know themselves because, in effect, I was the god who was creating them from nothing. I would mould them into real people in a document that I could turn to throughout the writing of the novel, and from this document I'd learn how each of them would act, how they would react, how they would speak, what their biases were, what they needed in life, what they wanted from life, what their agendas were, what their attitudes looked and sounded like, and what their hidden psychopathologies were.

After I did both the setting activities and the character activities, then and only then would I start the novel. This became the process I used when I wrote my second British crime novel, *Payment in Blood*.

The setting came from a trip I took to the Scottish Highlands and from the great house in which my husband and I stayed. It stood on quite a large property, and once I had a decent wander around the area, I realised that

I could use it as the primary location for the book because it had all sorts of intriguing spots: an overgrown family graveyard, a misty loch and an isle in the loch just to name three. Other locations also came from that trip, specifically the scenes in Hampstead and the chase scene that became the climax of the book.

Obviously, I wasn't going to 'create' Hampstead. It exists, so it had to be rendered as it truly is when it came to writing the novel. Thus, I would need notes, maps and photographs to make that setting real. The Scottish setting, as I've indicated, I would base upon the great house in which we stayed as well as the land surrounding it, but I would need to map the property, and I would need to create the architectural exterior and interior of the house.

Additional locations that I'd use were places with which I was already familiar, as I'd stayed in that general area of London many times when travelling there over the years: South Kensington, Chelsea and Belgravia. These were the spots – in close proximity to each other – where four of my five continuing characters would live: Lady Helen Clyde in South Kensington; Simon St. James and his wife, Deborah, in Chelsea; and Thomas Lynley in Belgravia. I'd already found specific streets and squares in which these individuals would have their homes. I'd prowled around enough – including staying there for five weeks one summer – that I thought I'd be able to render each neighbourhood realistically, specifically Onslow Square, Eaton Terrace and Cheyne Row.

In doing all of this and then forging ahead with the novel itself, I ended up with what I thought was a manuscript that was going to address all of Kate's concerns. I did manage to address a number of them, for my second editorial letter was only two pages long instead of nine. It comprised nine paragraphs instead of twenty-two. That told me that I was on the right track, and if I expanded my approach for the third novel, there was a good possibility that I could create works requiring very little editor-requested revisions once I'd written a satisfactory draft. That would never be my first draft (no one has ever seen a first draft of one of my novels). But it would be a draft that I had taken as far as I felt I could without commentary or reaction from someone else.

How to expand the approach was the question. It seemed to me that I had the process of creating characters down fairly well, but there was more I could do on setting. Kate had not had any questions or concerns about the plot or the structure of the scenes, and she was fine with the dialogue. So it seemed to me that broadening my understanding of the setting, of the culture, of the traditions, and – perhaps most important – of policing was going to be worthwhile.

For my third novel – *Well-Schooled in Murder* – I decided to take on the challenge of writing about a British boarding school with the authority of someone who had actually attended one, which was as far from my personal experiences as an American Catholic schoolgirl as one could get. To meet the challenge, I began by locating British boarding schools that would allow me to visit while they were in session. And then I did just that, ultimately spending time at four.

The plot of the novel rose directly from those visits I made. Headmasters, teachers and pupils – understanding why I was there – were enthusiastic about helping. Since a pupil was the designated victim, I was shown myriad places where a young person could meet an untimely end at the hands of another student or a faculty member or one of the non-teaching staff. I attended classes, was shown hidden spots where young people got into mischief, learned the vocabulary of the English boarding school world, and eventually came face-to-face with a young boy – called in to meet the headmaster for attempting to run away from the school to visit his mother, who was in the hospital – who would, in the novel, become Matthew Whateley, the child whose body is found behind the wall of the country churchyard in which the poet Thomas Gray is buried.

I had piles of information when I returned home. I used it to create my own British boarding school. I wrote the prospectus for the school; I mapped out the school grounds; I named the dormitory buildings; I placed it in West Sussex. This was, by far, the most extensive preliminary location work I'd yet done. Once I had it completed, I went on to create the characters. Once they were real, I added a new step to the process: the running plot outline, which I would write one section at a time and which would guide me through the plot and assist me when it came to keeping every detail straight.

When I had a draft that I was satisfied with – it was at least my third – I sent it to Kate. My work paid off. She accepted it without revisions and sent it off to the copy editor.

Thus my process was born, a process to which I've added elements as I've seen their usefulness to me. That's the crucial part: *as I've seen their usefulness to me.* What's useful to me isn't necessarily going to be useful to anyone else, but for people for whom writing by the seat of the pants creates roadblocks and dead ends instead of thoroughfares, there might be something in these following pages that proves worthy of trial.

One might argue that I'm attempting to give you a 'recipe' for writing a novel when, in reality, no recipe exists. One might also argue that I'm telling you that if you only do exactly as I'm advising you throughout this volume, you will indeed write a publishable piece of fiction. However, what I actually want to do is show you how a particular process that I've developed over time works for me. You can certainly follow the steps I'll be describing in order to discover if they work for you. You can follow some of them and reject others. You can modify or tweak them in any way that meets your needs. You can reject them all and go your own way. But those three final words – *your own way* – constitute the point I'll be trying to make. You'll find the writing itself much more joyful if you develop a way to go about it.

Some writers use a process journal to do this.

Some writers like to construct a novel out of a series of scenes written in no particular order, stringing them together logically only when the entire story seems to have been told.

Some writers like to plunge into a moment of drama and then see what comes out of it.

Some writers come up with a plot and then use index cards and post them on a wall, shuffling until they have an order that best reflects what they want their novels to be about.

What I do is what I'll be describing in this book, a process that has served me well throughout the creation of twenty-two of my twenty-four novels. As illustration of my process, I'll be using one of my novels for all of my examples: *Careless in Red*. It isn't necessary that you read or that you have read the book, but you might find it helpful to grab a copy in the event that you want to read further in a scene or a section from which I'm merely taking a few paragraphs. It's up to you. However, do take note of the fact that there will be spoilers throughout, so if you hate spoilers and want to read the novel in advance of learning about the process I followed in creating it, please do.

As you read *Mastering the Process*, then, the only requirement is that you keep your mind open. As I always tell my writing students, take what you like and leave the rest.

# CHAPTER 1

# Research

*Eliminating the Fear of the Blank Page*

There's some sense in arguing that writing can't be taught, especially if one sees writing as purely art with no craft behind it to serve as a foundation. For art is the result of the impulse to create, and an impulse can neither be taught nor learned. An impulse just *is*. The result of that impulse is always in the eyes of the beholders who judge it and find it . . . well, any number of things: magnificent, inventive, idiotic, exceptional, mundane, vulgar, awe-inspiring, moving, nauseating. Name the reaction and someone will have had it. Tracey Emin's bed on display at the Tate Modern in London is, I believe, a good example of the impulse to create. To some people it's art; to others it's an immense joke that Emin is playing upon the public.

The truth is that there is very little that we can call 'pure' art, something arising from an impulse to create but having nothing besides impulse serving as its foundation. Most art is based on a fundamental knowledge of craft, and craft is what an artist puts to work in order to create a piece of art. It is this – craft – that can be both taught and learned.

For example, should one wish to become a sculptor, there is something to be learned about working with stone before one bangs out the *Pietà*. It helps to understand *how* the old masters painted before slapping *The Night*

*Watch* onto canvas. Someone working in bronze learns about moulding clay or the lost wax method first and *then* goes on to *The Burghers of Calais*. One might want to learn exactly *how* to blow glass before expecting to be the next Dale Chihuly. All of this is craft, and craft is what we use as a foundation for art. In writing, an understanding of craft is what we use to develop process. In writing, process is what we follow to write a novel.

Essentially, by developing and utilising a process, we eradicate our fears of the blank page and eliminate the chaos of the thoughts that are produced by our mental committees. We trick our minds into believing that there *is* actually a recipe for novel writing.

For me, this trickery begins with research, and the research comprises not only the background information I need in order to write with some degree of authority about various subjects that may or may not come up in my novel but also an experience and an understanding of the place in which the novel is going to be set so that locations can be rendered with accuracy. These days, some of this can be done via the Internet, especially when it comes to preliminary information that might well fuel the story. But for me, most of it needs to be done in person, in the actual setting, especially when the setting can inspire plot elements that I wouldn't have considered had I not been there to prowl around.

By travelling to a location, I'm able to examine the broad landscape in which the novel is going to occur. This landscape is filled with countless details – equating to countless possibilities – that I can't see using Google Earth. My job while in the location is twofold: I'm choosing from among myriad details those that will illuminate the story; I'm also looking for a score of places that can be used as individual settings for scenes in the novel. While doing this, I try to take into the examination of place absolutely no preconceived notion about *how* anything I see might be used. I simply look for places that shout 'story' to me. Upon seeing them, I make no determination about where in my novel each place will fit or even if a place will fit at all. I just see the place as a story possibility and add it to my storehouse of collected knowledge about a location.

Here is what I knew when I went to Cornwall to do the research for *Careless in Red*:

In one of the previous novels – *With No One as Witness* – the wife of my central character (Thomas Lynley) is murdered in a completely senseless street crime in London.

Crushed by grief, Lynley has returned to his family home in Cornwall, having resigned from his job in London with the Metropolitan Police.

Because his mother, brother, sister and niece live there in the home to which he has decamped and because of their deep and overt concern for him, he comes to feel that he must get away, in order to deal privately with his sorrow.

To do this, he embarks on a walk along the South-West Coast Path in Cornwall. This will take him from the vicinity of Lamorna Cove in Cornwall where his home is, around Land's End, and north to Minehead in Somerset, a distance of more than two hundred miles.

That was what I knew. That was all I knew. Because of my choice of location, I had also decided that the novel would touch upon surfing in some way. This meant that most, if not all, of the locations chosen as individual settings would probably be along the coast of Cornwall rather than inland.

Since Lynley is experiencing not only terrible grief but also the need somehow to get through it, I was looking for settings in Cornwall that would be appropriate to the tone of melancholy that I wanted to depict. This meant that, because Lynley was going to be on the South-West Coast Path, I was going to have to walk parts of the path myself in order to see if there were specific places where I could visualise him, finding locations that would serve my purpose of establishing both tone and atmosphere. I knew that the description of place and the depiction of Lynley's reaction to place would help in doing this. The critical part was finding a spot that would also be useful in launching the crime story at the heart of the novel.

Thus, my job was to make certain that I understood what the environment was like through a personal experience of it so that I could then use it with confidence, rendering with verisimilitude the action within every scene. That meant going to Cornwall at approximately the same time of year that Lynley would be there.

If you examine Image 1 and Image 2, you'll see two of the photographs I took while on location in north Cornwall. It was the month of March when I was there, the wind was blowing fiercely from the Ural Mountains, the temperature was hovering in the vicinity of thirty degrees, and the weather alternated between fog and rain. I would have been hard-pressed to find a better environment to photograph and to record impressions if I wanted to achieve an atmosphere of melancholy and a tone of grief.

IMAGE 1

IMAGE 2

At the time, I wasn't sure how or if I could use either of these pictures of this place. But given my experiences walking various sections of the South-West Coast Path, I developed the opening of the novel, which would take place a month later than the month during which I made my explorations:

He found the body on the forty-third day of his walk. By then, the end of April had arrived, although he had only the vaguest idea of that. Had he been capable of noticing his surroundings, the condition of the flora along the coast might have given him a broad hint as to the time of year. He'd started out when the only sign of life renewed was the promise of yellow buds on the gorse that grew sporadically along the cliff tops, but by April, the gorse was wild with colour, and yellow archangel climbed in tight whorls along upright stems in hedgerows on the rare occasions when he wandered into a village. Soon foxglove would be nodding on roadside verges, and lamb's foot would expose fiery heads from the hedgerows and the drystone walls that defined individual fields in this part of the world. But those bits of burgeoning life were in the future, and he'd been walking these days that had blended into weeks in an effort to avoid both the thought of the future and the memory of the past.

He carried virtually nothing with him. An ancient sleeping bag. A rucksack with a bit of food that he replenished when the thought occurred to him. A bottle within that rucksack that he filled with water in the morning if water was to be had near the site where he'd slept. Everything else, he wore. One waxed jacket. One hat. One tattersall shirt. One pair of trousers. Boots. Socks. Underclothes. He'd come out for this walk unprepared and uncaring that he was unprepared. He'd known only that he had to walk or he had to remain at home and sleep, and if he remained at home and slept, he'd come to realise that eventually he would will himself not to awaken again.

So he walked. There had seemed no alternative. Steep ascents to cliff tops, the wind striking his face, the sharp salt air desiccating his skin, scrambling across beaches where reefs erupted from sand and stone when the tide was low, his breath coming short, rain soaking his legs, stones pressing insistently against his soles . . . These things would remind him that he was alive and that he was intended to remain so.

Thus, one location along the South-West Coast Path gave me the opening I needed for the novel. But an overall depiction of place, while offering me a broad landscape for the book, was going to need to move from the wide vista we see in the third paragraph to the specific setting in which this first scene occurs.

In Image 3 and Image 4, you can see exactly what I saw: the deadly fins of slate that constitute much of the coastline; the South-West Coast Path itself in a photo taken from above it. In Image 5 you have a much more intimate look at the path.

IMAGE 3

In the paragraphs from *Careless in Red* that follow, you can see how these photos were used in the creation of the narrative. What I'm attempting to do is bring in details that not only influence the shading of tone but also begin to attach the reader to the character on the path. It's the reader's interest in and caring about a character that will keep her reading.

He was struggling in the wind to the top of a cliff, climbing from a V-shaped cove where he'd rested for an hour or so and watched the waves slamming into broad fins of slate that formed the reefs in this place. The tide was just beginning to come in, and he'd noted this. He needed to be well above it. He needed to find some sort of shelter as well.

Near the top of the cliff, he sat. He was winded, and he found it odd that no amount of walking these many days had seemed sufficient to

IMAGE 4

build his endurance for the myriad climbs he was making along the coast. So he paused to catch his breath. He felt a twinge that he

IMAGE 5

recognised as hunger, and he used the minutes of his respite to draw
from his rucksack the last of a dried sausage he'd purchased when he'd

come to a hamlet along his route. He gnawed it down to nothing, re-alised that he was also thirsty, and stood to see if anything resembling habitation was nearby: hamlet, fishing cottage, holiday home, or farm.

There was nothing. But thirst was good, he thought with resignation. Thirst was like the sharp stones pressing into the soles of his shoes, like the wind, like the rain. It reminded him, when reminders were needed.

Going to the place and experiencing it eliminates the need for me to create a setting from my imagination. (When it comes to setting, I have virtually no imagination to speak of, I'm embarrassed to say.) The many places I visit whenever I do location research allow me to consider spots where characters are going to be placed into conflict, or forced to act, or challenged to be different, or faced with an aspect of themselves that was previously unacknowledged or even unknown.

IMAGE 6

IMAGE 7

Images 6 and 7 offer me the opportunity to deepen the sense of place for the reader, inviting her understanding of the inherent dangers Lynley will encounter while simultaneously serving as an indication of what is soon to come. Image 6 shows the reader the height of one of the cliffs so that she can anticipate what's possible should anyone fall from it. Image 7 depicts the absolute danger of wandering too close to the edge, where the ground is unstable and apt to break off, sending a walker to his death.

So far in my location research, then, what I photographed ended up giving me an entrée into my novel. It provided a sense of place, and it suggested that hiking along the South-West Coast Path was not only a logical activity for Lynley to engage in after the violent death of his wife but also something that was going to place him where he needed to be in order to come across a crime. What the crime would be, I didn't know at this point, but my research in Cornwall was going to introduce me to the police, to surfers, to surfboard makers, to a cider maker, and to sea cliff climbers. I was relying upon my conversations with them to come up with an idea that could be developed into a book.

As I've indicated, there are occasions in my observations of place when I see something that I know for certain I will use in the novel. The moment I see it, I don't always know *how* I will use it, but I do know that, because of its qualities or its specific details or its quirkiness or its unexpectedness, it will find a place in the narrative. So I photograph it. Images 8 and 9 serve as good illustrations of this.

I had gone to the general location of the cottage in the distance because

IMAGE 8

IMAGE 9

the cove in which the cottage sits was one of the spots along the coast that gave me access to the beach. I'd read about the cove in one of my guidebooks before leaving the US. In Image 8, you can see my rental car in the small car park above the beach. I had climbed from there up the South-West Coast Path to photograph the valley in its entirety. On my way along the lane to the beach, I had passed the cottage you can see in the distance. I found its isolation intriguing, but I wasn't sure how I might use it in my story. Its isolated presence, however, told me there were possibilities.

In Image 9 you have a much better sense of the cottage and, more important, of its immediate environment. I had walked back to it along the lane at this point and crossed over the wooden bridge in the foreground, climbing a short distance up another section of the South-West Coast Path in order to take a photograph both of the building and the meandering

brook that bypasses it on its way to the sea. I realised upon a closer inspec-
tion of the place and its surroundings that it was demanding to be part of
the novel. So I got closer and prowled around.

What came from the hiking, prowling and photographing was what
follows from *Careless in Red*. This selection comes soon after Lynley's seeing
a lone surfer as he's walking on the path. He's wondered what the surfer is
doing, out on the waves in such bad weather.

His inadequate meal finished, he resumed his walk. The cliffs were friable in this part of the coast, unlike the cliffs where he'd begun his
walk. There they were largely granite, igneous intrusions into the landscape, forced upon ancient lava, limestone and slate. Although worn
by time, weather and the restless sea, they were nonetheless solid
underfoot, and a walker could venture near the edge and watch the
roiling sea or observe the gulls seeking perches among the crags. Here,
however, the cliff edge was culm: slate, shale and sandstone, and cliff
bases were marked by mounds of the stony detritus called clitter that
fell regularly to the beach below. Venturing near the edge meant a
certain fall. A fall meant broken bones or death.

At this section of his walk, the cliff top levelled out for some one
hundred yards. The path was well marked, moving away from the
cliff's edge and tracing a line between gorse and thrift on one side and
a fenced pasture on the other. Exposed here, he bent into the wind, and
moved steadily forward. He became aware that his throat was painfully dry, and his head had begun to fill with a dull ache just behind his
eyes. He felt a sudden bout of dizziness as he reached the far end of the
cliff top. Lack of water, he thought. He would not be able to go much
farther without doing something about it.

A stile marked the edge of the high pasture he'd been following, and
he climbed it and paused, waiting for the landscape to stop swimming

in front of him long enough for him to find the descent to what would be yet another cove. He'd lost count of the inlets he'd come upon in his walk along the undulating coast. He had no idea what this one was called, any more than he'd been able to name the others.

When the vertigo had passed, he saw that a lone cottage stood at the edge of a wide meadow beneath him, perhaps two hundred yards inland from the beach and along the side of a twisting brook. A cottage meant potable water, so he would make for that. It wasn't a great distance off the path.

He stepped down from the stile just as the first drops of rain fell. He wasn't wearing his hat at the moment, so he shrugged his rucksack from his shoulders and dug it out. He was pulling it low onto his forehead – an old baseball cap of his brother's with 'Mariners' scrolled across it – when he caught sight of a flash of red. He looked in the direction from which it had seemed to come, and he found it at the base of the cliff that formed the far side of the inlet beneath him. There, a sprawl of red lay across a broad plate of slate. This slate was itself the landward end of a reef, which crept from the cliff bottom out into the sea.

Notice that Images 6 and 7 became the first part of this section. Information from my research into the geology of the area provides details of the place.

Images 8 and 9 gave me the momentum I needed to move the story forward. I saw the cottage; Lynley sees the cottage. Seeing the cottage, I decided I would use it somehow. Seeing the cottage, Lynley decides to go there for potable water.

Because it begins to rain, he pauses to put on his hat, and this is when he sees what will be the crime in the book. During my research at this point, I still didn't know what the crime was going to be, nor did I know

Lynley would see the crime occur at this precise moment. All of that came later, once I looked at my pictures and my notes and evaluated exactly how I could use them.

You might find it interesting to know that none of the places photographed so far are anywhere near each other. Part of the pleasure of the post-research process is to put things together in order to mould them into story.

Consider Images 10 and 11, which come from my prowling round the cottage itself.

The more I saw of the place, the more I *knew* I would use it because it prompted questions, always a good omen when constructing a novel: Who lives here? Why does this person live in such isolation? Is this a permanent home? Is it for holidays? Is there anyone inside at this point in time?

Moments after Lynley sees the cottage, decides to descend to it for

IMAGE 10

IMAGE 11

water, and then witnesses what will be the crime in the novel, Daidre Trahair is introduced to the reader and at least some of the questions about the
cottage begin to be answered:

A light rain was falling when Daidre Trahair made the final turn down
the lane that led to Polcare Cove. She switched on the windscreen
wipers and created a mental note that they would have to be replaced,
sooner rather than later. It wasn't enough to tell herself that spring led
to summer and windscreen wipers wouldn't actually be necessary at
that point. Late April was so far being as notoriously unpredictable as
usual and while May was generally pleasant in Cornwall, June could be
a weather nightmare. So she decided then and there that she had to get
new wipers, and she considered where she might purchase them. She

was grateful for this mental diversion. It allowed her to push from her mind all consideration of the fact that, at the end of this journey south, she was feeling nothing. No dismay, confusion, anger, resentment or compassion, and not an ounce of grief.

The grief part didn't worry her. Who honestly could have expected her to feel it? But the rest of it . . . to have been bled of every possible emotion in a situation where at least marginal feeling was called for . . . That concerned her. In part it reminded her of what she'd heard too many times from too many lovers. In part it indicated a regression to a self she thought she'd put behind her.

So the nugatory movement of the windscreen wipers and the resulting smear they left in their wake distracted her. She cast about for potential purveyors of auto parts: In Casvelyn? Possibly. Alsperyl? Hardly. Perhaps she'd have to go all the way to Launceston.

She made a cautious approach to the cottage. The lane was narrow, and while she didn't expect to meet another car, there was always the possibility that a visitor to the cove and its thin strip of beach might barrel along, departing in a rush and assuming no one else would be out here in this kind of weather.

To her right rose a hillside where gorse and yellow wort made a tangled coverlet. To her left the Polcare valley spread out, an enormous green thumbprint of meadow bisected by a stream that flowed down from Stowe Wood, on higher ground. This place was different from traditional combes in Cornwall, which was why she'd chosen it. A twist of geology made the valley wide, as if glacially formed – although she knew this could not be the case – instead of canyonlike and constrained by river water wearing away aeons of unyielding stone. Thus, she never felt hemmed in in Polcare Cove. Her cottage was small, but the environment was large, and open space was crucial to her peace of mind.

Her first warning that things were not as they should have been occurred as she pulled off the lane onto the patch of gravel and grass that served as her driveway. The gate was open. It had no lock, but she knew that she'd left it securely closed for that very reason the last time she'd been here. Now it gaped the width of a body.

Daidre stared at this opening for a moment before she swore at herself for being timid. She got out of the car, swung the gate wide, then drove inside.

When she parked and went to shut the gate behind her, she saw the footprint. It pressed down the soft earth where she'd planted her primroses along the drive. A man-size print, it looked like something made from a boot. A hiking boot. That put her situation in an entirely new light.

She looked from the print to the cottage. The blue front door seemed unmolested, but when she quietly circled the building to check for other signs of intrusion, she found a windowpane broken. This was on a window next to the door that led outside to the stream, and the door itself was off the latch. Fresh mud formed a clump on the step.

Although she knew she should have been frightened, or at least cautious, Daidre was, instead, infuriated by that broken window. She pushed the door open in a state of high dudgeon and stalked through the kitchen to the sitting room. There she stopped. In the dim light of the tenebrous day outside, a form was coming out of her bedroom. He was tall, he was bearded, and he was so filthy that she could smell him from across the room.

She said, 'I don't know who the hell you are or what you're doing here, but you *are* going to leave directly. If you don't leave, I shall become violent with you, and I assure you, you do *not* want that to happen.'

Notice that buried within Daidre's approach to the cottage are dramatic questions. These are laid down in order – one hopes – to keep the reader intrigued about this woman. More on dramatic questions later. For now, the main element of a crime novel has been introduced along with two characters, the setting, the atmosphere and the mood. It has taken me eleven pictures, a good many hikes on the South-West Coast Path in Cornwall and a book on the geology of the area, but I'm feeling pretty good about the results.

Before we leave this exploration of research, I'd like to look at various options for learning about place if you can't afford to go there. At the time I was preparing *Careless in Red*, I'd probably been to England more than twenty times over the years. But as this sort of topographical gumshoeing isn't possible for everyone, what's a writer to do?

My first suggestion is to choose a location based not only on your interests but also on your ability to study the place. Many writers – probably most writers – use their own immediate environment as a jumping-off point. T. Jefferson Parker uses various locations in southern California for his novels, which makes getting to the specific setting easy for him, as that's where he lives. The same can be said for James Lee Burke (Louisiana), the late Tony Hillerman (the Southwest), Jane Hamilton (the Midwest), David Guterson (the Pacific Northwest) and countless other writers.

My second suggestion is to use the vast resources of the Internet. Put your potential location into a search engine and see what comes up. Follow the trails that the Internet leaves for you. Use Facebook as a possible source of people who live in your chosen location. Use Twitter to do the same. Use Google Earth to see the area. Use Amazon to find nonfiction books about it.

Finally, use the public library as well.

I like to go to locations in order to understand them. But this isn't the case for everyone, and some locations are too difficult or too expensive to get to.

## Optional Exercise 1

Image 12 is also one of the pictures I took along the South-West Coast Path. Soon into my walks I noticed that along the path various makeshift memorials stood, accompanied by a few impressive permanent markers as well as benches with metal plaques remembering someone. It's possible that the one depicted below had been placed at the spot where Nick died. Perhaps he was a surfer who made an error among the many reefs in the area, perhaps he was a suicide, perhaps he was a sea cliff climber who favoured the spot, perhaps he ventured too near the edge of the cliff and tumbled over. He could even have died elsewhere, his survivors choosing to remember him in the hours after his funeral by walking to the cliff and leaving a little memorial to him. We don't know, but the possibilities are there, and they all suggest story.

IMAGE 12

Using this photograph, develop an idea of what happened to Nick. Using this photograph, try to render a scene in which the setting is made clear as a character experiences it. Nick is someone. Who? What happened to him? Why?


## Optional Exercise 2

Choose a place where you can observe and take notes. This can be in your own house, or it can be a location with which you're familiar because you go there frequently: the local coffee house, the dog park, an antiques shop, the petrol station you use, a lunch spot where you meet your best friend, your place of employment, its cafeteria or car park. It can be wherever you spend a lot of your time. Take some notes on what you see, smell, taste, touch and hear when you are in this place. Take note of any particular detail that you've never really noticed before. In doing this, find something within that environment that suggests story to you. Create a paragraph-long explanation of who-where-what-why-how that uses what you saw and noted.

# CHAPTER 2

# Characters

*The Plot Kernel and What Follows It*

Long before I went to Cornwall, I had made my decision about using surfing as part of *Careless in Red* because of a conversation I'd had with someone from my UK publishing company about a small town called Bude. During this conversation, Bude's association with surfing had come up. I'd never before heard about surfing in the UK, and I assumed that most readers – other than those from the UK – wouldn't think of England as a surfing spot either. Because of this, I reasoned that they might find the idea of surfing in such an area interesting. So in the initial stages of my process, I intended the novel to be about the death of a surfer. Ultimately I went in a different direction, one that was based upon the part of my research that involves interviewing people.

When I do my preliminary reading, my location research and my interviewing, I'm attempting to come up with something that I call the plot kernel. For me, this is a general statement or a set of statements that will illuminate the through line (which is to say, the path that takes us to the conclusion) of the novel. It acts as a guide to illustrate for me what it is that I'm going to be writing about, and it also directs me towards a specific ending.

Because I write crime novels, the plot kernel expresses itself through the killer, the victim and the motive for the killing. In a YA novel, the kernel might be the heroine, the challenge she faces and the result. In women's fiction, it

might be the heroine, the issue at hand in her life or in her family, and the resolution. Every story begins somewhere for the writer, even if, upon reflection, the
writer isn't at all sure where she actually came up with the idea in the first place.

In my preliminary reading about Cornwall, I had discovered that in
addition to surfing, the sport of sea cliff climbing had many enthusiasts. As
part of my research into the various locations, then, I made arrangements
to interview two sea cliff climbers. It was during one of these interviews
that I arrived at my means of murder as well as my victim.

As I indicated in the Prologue, I find it extremely useful to let anyone I
interview know that I'm writing a crime novel for which I'm looking
for a means of murder. I've discovered over time that almost everyone gets

IMAGE 13

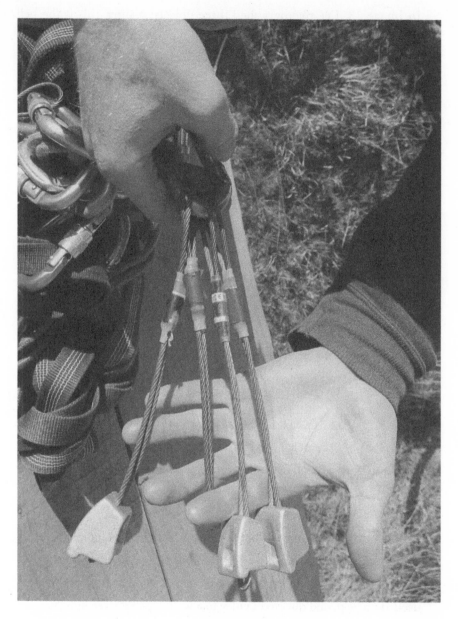

IMAGE 14

into the spirit of the deadly game called How-Would-I-Kill-Someone.
Images 13 and 14 illustrate this.

In Image 13, I've photographed three objects: a sling (this is the belt wrapped around the pole), a knotted rope and a carabiner joining the sling to the rope. In Image 14, I've photographed what are called chock stones. My interviewee, Rob Byron of Outdoor Adventures, had taken me outside after our interview in order to demonstrate how these objects were all used as well as to show me how they could be doctored in such a way as to cause a deadly fall.

At the end of the interview with Rob, I had part of my plot kernel in place. I'd decided that my victim was going to be a young man engaged in the dangerous sport of sea cliff climbing. The means of murder would be the damage done to a piece of climbing equipment.

That left me looking for the last two parts of the plot kernel. I would need these before I could go on: the killer and the killer's motive. The killer ended up emerging from a conversation I had with my husband, who suggested a revenge novel: someone out to avenge the death of his or her child. So now I had what I always need: the killer, the victim, the motive and the means. I could now engage in the next part of the process: the creation of characters.

Before I get into that, however, I'd like you to see how the interview with Rob Byron ultimately found its way into the novel. The *she* in question is Bea Hannaford, the officer in charge of the investigation into the death of the sea cliff climber.

*Over here* referred to a shop selling sporting goods: both equipment and clothing for outdoor activities. Hannaford did an admirably quick recce of the place, found what she wanted, told the shop assistant they needed no help, and directed Lynley to a wall. Upon it were hung various metallic devices, mostly of steel. It wasn't rocket science to sort out they were used for climbing.

She chose a package that held three devices constructed of lead, heavy steel cable and plastic sheathing. The lead was a thick wedge at the end of a cable perhaps one quarter inch thick. This looped through the wedge at one end and also formed another loop at the other end. In the middle was a tough plastic sheath, which wrapped tightly round the cable and thus held the two sides of it closely together. The result was a sturdy cord with a slug of lead at one end and a loop at the other.

'This,' Hannaford said to Lynley, 'is a chock stone. D'you know how it's used?'

Lynley shook his head. Obviously, it was meant for cliff climbing. Equally so, its loop end would be used to connect the chock stone to some other device. But that was as much as he could sort out.

DI Hannaford said, 'Hold up your hand, palm towards yourself. Keep your fingers tight. I'll show you.'

Lynley did as she asked. She slid the cable between his upright index and middle fingers, so that the slug of lead was snug against his palm and the loop at the other end of the cable was on her side of his hand.

She said, 'Your fingers are a crack in the cliff face. Or an aperture between two boulders. Your hand is the cliff itself. Or the boulders themselves. Got it?' She waited for his nod. 'The lead piece – that's the chock stone – gets shoved down the crack in the cliff or the aperture between the boulders as far as it can go, with the cable sticking out. In the loop end of the cable' – here she paused to scan the wall of climbing gear till she found what she wanted and scooped it up – 'you clip a carabiner. Like this.' She did so. 'And you fix your rope to the carabiner with whatever sort of knot you've been taught to use. If you're climbing up, you use chock stones on the way, every few feet or whatever you're comfortable with. If you're abseiling, you can use them at the top instead of a sling to fix your rope to whatever you've chosen to hold it in place while you descend.'

She took the chock stone from him and replaced it along with the carabiner on the wall of goods. She turned back and said, 'Climbers mark each part of their kit distinctly because they often climb together. Let's say you and I are climbing. I use six chock stones or sixteen chock stones; you use ten. We use my carabiners but your slings. How do we sort it all out quickly and without discussion in the end . . . ? By marking each piece with something that won't easily come off. Bright tape is just the ticket. Santo Kerne used black electrical tape.'

Lynley saw where she was heading with this. He said, 'So if someone wishes to play fast and loose with someone else's kit, he merely needs to get his hands on the same kind of tape—'

'And the equipment itself. Yes. That's right. You can damage the equipment, put identical tape over the damage, and no one is the wiser.'

What's important about putting one's own research into a novel is to make a natural part of an ongoing scene and a logical next step in the plot rather than just stop the story, produce your research like Athena emerging from the head of Zeus, and then start up the story again. Research needs to be buried, and the writer buries it by making it part of what's happening at a precise moment in the narrative. In what comes before this scene, Lynley and Hannaford leave the police station because Bea Hannaford knows that Santo Kerne's equipment has been damaged. She explains the use of the equipment to Lynley, which is logical since her next step will be to talk about what it means that more than one piece of equipment has been damaged.

If the plot kernel is a decent one – which merely means a workable one – it will prompt me to ask questions. The answers to these questions will enable me to people the world of the plot kernel in a generic fashion, which is all I want at this stage. If you consider the plot kernel of *Careless in Red*, I hope you can see that there are immediate questions offered, primarily:

Who is the sea cliff climber? (Answer: a nineteen-year-old boy who is
    something of a free spirit.)

Who is the killer? (Answer: a man out to avenge the death of his son,
     which took place more than twenty years earlier.)
If the climber is only nineteen, who is his father? (Answer: a forty-four-
     year-old man attempting to open a destination sports-oriented hotel.)
If the climber is only nineteen, who is his mother? (Answer: a forty-
     three-year-old woman with untreated bipolar disorder.)
Does the nineteen-year-old have a girlfriend? (Answer: yes, an eighteen-
     year-old with whom he has just ended a tumultuous relationship.)
Does she have siblings? (Answer: yes, a twenty-two-year-old ne'er-do-
     well brother.)
Who is their father? (Answer: a forty-eight-year-old surfboard shaper.)

And on and on I go, developing questions about characters not only
from the plot kernel but also from the answers to the primary questions
that came out of the plot kernel.

Only when I've asked sufficient questions to people the world of the plot
kernel do I move on to the next step of the process: giving my generic characters specific names.

At this point in my process, I've returned from my research trip. I've
printed all the photographs that I took in Cornwall (generally between two
hundred and three hundred pictures); I've written the precise location of
each picture on the back of it, and I've organised the pictures in a way that
I'll find useful for the novel (i.e., all beach pictures together, various villages
together, all surfboard-making pictures together, and on and on); I've
printed all of my interviews and digitally recorded location notes (which
I've typed into my laptop each evening while in Cornwall doing the research); I've chosen a few – but not all – locations from those I've seen; I've

given them names where necessary. For *Careless in Red*, Bude became Casvelyn, Morwenstow became Alsperyl, a cider farm was renamed, as were a surfboard making establishment, a pasty maker's shop, a town newspaper, and the location of Daidre Trahair's cottage. Other places would ultimately remain as named: Widemouth Bay and Zennor among them.

So at this point I know the world in which my characters are going to operate, and now I have to create them with enough clarity that I'll understand *how* they'll operate.

I begin with each character's name, and no name is chosen at random. It has to be a name that I can actually write about (not every name works for me), and it's even better if that name suggests something to the reader. To illustrate this latter point: Bill Johnson isn't going to suggest much to the reader while Mack the Knife is going to suggest plenty.

For *Careless in Red*, then, I would begin with the nineteen-year-old victim, and I would call him Santo Kerne. His father would be Benesek Kerne, called Ben. His mother would be Dellen Kerne. His girlfriend would be Madlyn Angarrack. Her brother would be Cadan Angarrack, and their father would be Lew Angarrack. These are mostly Cornish names, but they are also names that resonated for me. Additionally, I believed they were names that were different enough one from the other that the reader wouldn't confuse them, for nothing is worse than reading a novel only to discover that ten characters have surnames beginning with the letter *G*. At the end of the day, more than just their names must distinguish them, but at least the writer is giving herself a head start by assigning names than bear no resemblance to one another.

Names have power attached to them in that they can shortcut around needless explanations. Names can suggest ethnicity, background, personality, education, relationships, proclivities, etc. In the books I write – nearly all of which take place in Great Britain – names also suggest social class. There is a reason, after all, why there is not, nor will there ever be, a King Kevin or a King Keith (with my apologies to all the Kevins and Keiths in the world). Kevin and Keith are perfectly nice names, but everyone in the UK would be able to tell you at once what their social class probably is. The same goes for Sheila, Chantal, Jade, Linda and scores of other names that will never grace the person of a queen or princess.

Once I've peopled the world of my plot kernel, I move on to create these people. Doing this, I write what I call a character analysis, and I always do it in a particular fashion: I work in present tense because the character I'm creating is meant to be a real, living human being and when I get into the novel itself, I want the reader to be exposed to a life that has existed before the story begins and a life that will go on after the story ends. I write entirely in a stream-of-consciousness fashion. I don't worry if I misspell something, if the sentences run on and on, if I encounter a detail that I will have to embellish upon later. All along I'm not listening to the noise in my mind but rather I'm feeling my body's reaction to what I'm doing. I'm waiting for the moment when my body shouts 'Yes, yes, yes!' because that's the moment when I know I'm on the right track.

The important element in creating characters for my novels is this: the only character who is created *to do anything specific* is the killer. Every other character is created just to exist as a living, breathing human being who illustrates what William Faulkner said should be evident in every character: the human heart in conflict.

How is all this done without knowing the actual plot of the novel? It's done by using what I do know: the plot kernel, the world of the plot kernel, the questions and answers that have come from the plot kernel, what I have learned while doing my research (the actual means of the murder, the various locations), what I have developed so far (my choice of specific locations that will illuminate characters as they appear in them). Thus, in my novels, once I have the plot kernel and the various locations I've seen while on my journey through Cornwall, everything else rises from the characters: the subplots, conflicts, theme, motifs, agendas and the shape of the through line of the story. What this means is that when it comes to the real writing of the novel, character comes first for me and character counts most. What this also means is that my characters inform the plot of the book and not the reverse. This prevents my ending up with characters who are one-dimensional. This also prevents any feeling on my part that 'the characters aren't doing what I want them to do.' The reason I don't find myself in a situation in which my characters are 'misbehaving' is that prior to the activity of creating them, I have no preconceived notion at all about how they're going to behave or what their agendas are or what sets them off. The analysis of them tells me that.

I follow a prompt sheet when I create a character. I use it merely to make certain I've touched on as many elements of an individual as I can. I don't employ every item on the prompt sheet, for the prompt sheet is just a stimulus and what I write in stream-of-consciousness fashion is the response.

Below you can see the actual form my prompt sheet takes. I set this next to my computer, and from it I create a dossier about each character.

### Character Prompt Sheet

Name

Age

Height

Weight/Build

Birthplace

Colour hair/eyes

Physical peculiarities/unique details

Educational background

Best friend

Enemies

Family (mother, father, siblings, etc.)

Core need

Pathological manoeuvre

Ambition in life

Gestures when talking

Gait

Strongest character trait

Weakest character trait

Laughs at or jeers at

Life philosophy

Political leaning

Hobbies

What others first notice about him/her

What the character does alone

One-line characterisation

Will reader like/dislike character?

Does he/she change in the story? How?

Significant event that moulded the character

Significant event that illustrates who the character is now

This prompt sheet acts only as my guide, and from it emerges the character who rises up and tells me who he is, how he is going to act and to react, what his attitudes are, what his relationships to other people look like, etc. In his creation, as I indicated earlier, I've been the character's biographer, psychoanalyst, social worker, spiritual guide, mentor, religious counselor, physician, psychiatrist, etc.

What follows is an actual character analysis from *Careless in Red*. The character is Selevan Penrule, one of the older individuals in the novel. You'll note some sections are rendered in bold. The bold represents areas that I highlighted after writing all the character analyses for the novel. At that point, I reread each of them, and with yellow marking pen, I highlight the details that I most want to remember. This will be especially useful when I put all of the analyses together and need to find a useful item by flipping through all of the created characters.

---

**SELEVAN PENRULE:** Selevan Penrule is 65 years old and he owns the caravan park through which Santo trespasses to get to one of the sites where he surfs. Or maybe one of the sites where he climbs. He also has a granddaughter who has in the past been bitten by the Santo bug, and she lives there with Penrule and she's the real reason why Penrule won't allow Santo on his land.

**Penrule is a Cornishman born and bred.** He's a man who raised cattle on the land until he realised that he could turn the whole place into a caravan park for holiday makers and make, at least to his way of thinking, in one summer what it would take him two years to make as he worked the farm. So he sold off the cattle and used the money plus money he borrowed to turn the whole place into a caravan site. **Some people live there all year long but most people have units that remain there and they just come on weekends, holidays, and in the summer. It's a bare-bones holiday park and it's out in the open so the wind is fierce. But Penrule has big plans for it. Penrule always has big plans and he doesn't like people to get in the way of his making them happen.**

Penrule is a bitter man. He always was. He always wanted to be in a different life but he never knew how to get there. He was a dairy farmer because his father and his father's father and his father's father's father were dairy farmers on this same land. It was a family tradition and he couldn't see a way out of the family tradition although he didn't want any part of it.

Why did he end up as a dairy farmer then? Because **his father had a stroke** and he had to come home to help. He'd been in the Royal Navy but as he was the only son, he got compassionate leave and then a discharge when it became apparent that someone was going to have to take over the farm if his parents were to survive. His mother was less than useless running the dairy farm. She'd been a 'society catch' the way Penrule's father talked about her. But the truth of the matter was that she was just a minister's daughter from Casvelyn who had never been on a farm and was wooed and won by Penrule's father who went to church determined to find himself a wife the day he inherited the farm from his father.

So she was unequipped to be of significant help on the farm, especially where animals are concerned. She could do the house stuff and she learned to cook – albeit badly – and to can fruits. But that was the extent of it **aside from her needlepoint which she sold at Friday market when she was able to get organised enough to finish a project.** That's what Penrule always saw as a boy: unfinished projects.

Penrule was determined to have a career in the Royal Navy, but this was thwarted when his father had his stroke. Penrule's sister could not take over the farm as she was married to a sheep farmer in Shropshire and they weren't in a position to help. She came for a while until Penrule himself got home. But then she had to return to her own farm and her family. It was a no-brainer that Penrule would take over the farm as he couldn't sell it out from under his mother's substantial butt.

So he worked the farm and he stayed with it mostly out of habit. **He himself married to get a helpmate on the farm and not for love.** He picked someone he thought he could put up with: a local girl who had no ambition beyond husband and family. She was someone who did her duty on all fronts: cooked, cleaned, was available sexually, had kids. But theirs was an empty life and all the kids (there were five) got away as soon as they could and return rarely. None of them were willing to take over the farm. None of them were even interested. This enraged Penrule who did his duty by his own parents and expects his children to do their duty by him. He can't see that times have changed since he was a boy. He expects things to be the same.

The defection of his kids embitters him. He gets no pleasure from their various successes or from his grandchildren. **He won't travel to see them and when they come to Cornwall, he does not make them welcome.** He is a man of few words and what words he has are bitter ones. Being with him is a chore. It's no wonder his wife doesn't call out for help or seek help when she first has heart trouble.

When she dies without being under the care of a physician a post-mortem has to be performed. They discover she had a heart condition that she had to have known about but did not talk about. **Penrule realises that she was just waiting to die to escape him.** This sends him into a tailspin. His selling the cows and setting up the cara-van park is a way for him to recover.

His granddaughter comes to live with him because she's in trouble in her own environment. She's seventeen and she works in the pasty making place, perhaps. Or in Clean Barrel Surf Shop. She knows Santo (obviously), but she also knows Cade and Will. She drinks and smokes and perhaps she has had a relationship with Santo. Or maybe she wanted one and couldn't get one. Yes, this is more likely. She's not Santo's type. She's not into clean living. She's interested in him but she can't attract him, not like Madlyn and Aldara can. What's her name? I'd say it's Tammy Penrule. She's the daughter of Penrule's oldest son. She's fallen in with a bad crowd wherever she lives and this is the family's attempt to set her on the right path before she goes over the edge.

What does Penrule look like? He's bald and wears a peaked cap at all times – indoors and out – because he's embarrassed about being bald. **He has perfect false teeth – white and straight – that look very odd in his weathered face.** His face is round and deeply lined and has collapsed from the cheekbones down. He's got a beer belly but he claims to be solid as a rock. He's an endomorph. He dresses in jeans and boots and a black knit sweater and a waxed jacket all the time. It's his uniform. He puts it on in the morning when he rolls out of bed. He drinks **endless cups of Bovril.** He eats Vegemite on toast for breakfast and lunch. He occasionally adds an egg or bacon or sausage to this. Or beans. He loves Heinz beans. No he has toast, Vegemite and beans for breakfast and a bacon bap for lunch. Every day. If you open his cupboards what you find is cans and cans of baked beans, jars of Bovril and Vegemite, bottles of ketchup which he uses on his bacon bap, and boxes of PG Tips.

He completed school to the point that he was able to join the Royal Navy. He was an indifferent student, not because he was not intelligent but because he wanted to be out of this place that he lived in. He was aware of the contrast in Cornwall to the rest of the country: the amount of poverty, the end of the mining industry, the difficulty in climbing out of the conditions in which one lives . . . He sees this and he realises that the only way out is to get out, which was his plan. Out as soon as possible. But he didn't make it out and this is something that he's bitter about.

**Bitterness characterises most of his life.** He was never able to reframe a single experience. His idea is that you're supposed to work for what you want and God is supposed to give it to you. **He has the idea that if you don't get what you want it's because you've done something morally wrong along the line.** His understanding is the moral wrong he did was to his wife: marrying someone he didn't love and expecting her to be a workmate.

Is he religious now? He goes to church. But he is angry at God. So he has no peace.

What is his core need in life? Forgiveness, I would say. Or is it to have things his way? To make things happen? Or is it escape? It seems that he's wanted to escape from the very beginning and all his efforts to escape have been thwarted. **So it must be escape.** Escape the prison of his circumstances but also escape the body he has. Escape his baldness, even. He can't admit who he is. So what he's done is designed always to escape whatever circumstances he found himself in. The navy was to escape the farm. The marriage was to escape sole responsibility for his mother and the farm. What would he have done while he was a farmer to escape the marriage? Would he be a drinker? A gambler? A religious zealot? **Maybe he's a fixture at the Salthouse Inn. He definitely is that and he knows Jago from the Salthouse Inn.** They are of an age, so they're friends . . . as much as Jago can be a friend to anyone. Does Penrule know or learn something about Jago? Perhaps.

Since there is no escape, what's his pathological manoeuvre? **I would say anger.** He goes right to anger. He's angry about so many things in his life. No matter what kind of stress he faces, he takes things directly to irrational anger.

Why of all people does his son send Tammy to live with Penrule? It's a lesson that he hopes she will learn, I guess. Or maybe he just can't control her and he thinks his father can.

Why does Penrule take Tammy on? **Because she represents to him a form of escape as well.** If he can have her in his life and if he can make a success with her, he will have escaped. He will also have a form of forgiveness for what he did to his wife's life.

What moulded him: poverty and the need to escape it.

What illustrates who he is now? Once he learns about Santo's rejection of Tammy, he won't let Santo use his land although he's allowed him to use it before.

CHARACTERS

Just freewriting off the top of my head, I've developed information that will allow me to step into the skin of Selevan Penrule in an effort to *become* him should his point of view be used in the book. It will also allow me to step into his skin when he has to relate to other characters. If I'm going to use his POV in the novel, I also have a leg up on what his voice is going to sound like, for from the analysis comes his attitude and attitude is essential in developing a character's voice.

Once Selevan is developed, then, he can step onto the page of the novel as a fully realised human being. In the following scene, he's in conversation with his granddaughter, who has come to live with him because her parents are unable to dissuade her from the life path she's chosen and they're hoping her grandfather can make a dent in her determination. As you read, you'll notice that Tammy Penrule is very different from the girl described in Selevan's character analysis. I changed her because I realised the alteration in her character was going to encourage more dramatic questions. It also avoids stereotyping her.

Selevan Penrule thought it was rubbish, but he joined hands with his granddaughter anyway. Across the narrow table in the caravan, they closed their eyes and Tammy began to pray. Selevan didn't listen to the words although he caught the gist of them. Instead, he considered his grandchild's hands. They were dry and cool but so thin that they felt like something he could crush simply by closing his own fingers roughly over them.

'She's not been eating right, Father Penrule,' his daughter-in-law had told him. He hated what she called him – 'Father Penrule' made him feel like a renegade priest – but he'd said nothing to correct Sally Joy since speaking to him at all was something that she and her husband hadn't bothered with for ages. So, he'd grunted and said he'd fatten the girl up. It's being in Africa, woman, don't you know that? You cart the girl off to Rhodesia –

'Zimbabwe, Father Penrule. And we're actually in—'

'Whatever the hell they want it to be called. You cart her off to Rhodesia and expose her to God only knows what and that would kill anyone's appetite, let me tell you.'

Selevan realised he was taking things too far at that point, because Sally Joy said nothing for a moment. He imagined her there in Rhodesia or wherever she was, sitting on the porch in a rattan chair with her legs stretched out and a drink on the table next to her . . . lemonade, it would be, lemonade, with a dash of . . . what is it, Sally Joy? What's in the glass that would make Rhodesia go down a trick for you?

He harrumphed noisily and said, 'Well, never mind then. You send her along. I'll get her sorted.'

'You'll watch her food intake?'

'Like a peregrine.'

Which he had done. She'd taken thirty-nine bites tonight. Thirty-nine spoonfuls of a gruel that would have made Oliver Twist lead an armed rebellion. No milk, no raisins, no cinnamon, no sugar. Just watery porridge and a glass of water. Not even tempted by her grandfather's meal of chops and veg, she was.

'. . . for Your will is what we seek. Amen,' Tammy said, and he opened his eyes to find hers on him. Her expression was fond. He dropped her fingers in a rush.

He said roughly, 'Bloody stupid. You know that, eh?'

She smiled. 'So you've told me.' But she settled in so that he could tell her again, and she balanced her cheek on her palm.

'We pray before the bloody meal,' he groused. 'Why d'we got to bloody pray at the bloody end as well?'

She answered by rote, but with no indication that she was tiring of a discussion they'd had at least twice a week since she'd come to Cornwall. 'We say a prayer of thanks at the beginning. We thank God for the food we have. Then at the end we pray for those who don't have enough food to sustain them.'

'If they're bloody alive, they have enough bloody food to bloody sustain them, don't they?' he countered.

'Grandie, you know what I mean. There's a difference between just being alive and having enough to be sustained. Sustained means more than just living. It means having enough sustenance to *engage*. Take the Sudan, for example—'

'Now you hang on right there, missy-miss. And don't move either.' He slid out from the banquette. He carried his plate the short distance to the caravan's sink as a means of feigning other employment, but instead of beginning the washing up, he snatched her rucksack from the hook on the back of the door and said, 'Let's just have a look.'

She said, 'Grandie,' in a patient voice. 'You can't stop me, you know.'

He said, 'I know my duty to your parents is what I know, my girl.'

He brought the sack to the table and emptied its contents and there it was: on the cover a young black mother in tribal dress holding her child, one of them sorrowful and both of them hungry. Blurred in the background were countless others, waiting in a mixture of hope and confusion. The magazine was called *Crossroads*, and he scooped it up, rolled it up, and slapped it against his palm.

'Right,' he said. 'Another bowl of that mush for you, then. Either that or a chop. You can take your choice.' He shoved the magazine into the back pocket of his drooping trousers. He would dispose of it later, when she'd gone to bed.

'I've had enough,' she said. 'Truly. Grandie, I eat enough to stay alive and well, and that's what God intended. We're not meant to carry round excess flesh. Aside from being not good for us, it's also not right.'

'Oh, a sin, is it?'

'Well . . . it can be, yes.'

'So your grandie's a sinner? Going straight to hell on a plate of beans while you're playing harps with the angels, eh?'

She laughed outright. 'You know that's not what I think.'

'What you think is a cartload of bollocks. What I *know* is that this stage you're in—'

'A stage? And how do you know that when you and I have been together . . . what? Two months? Before that you didn't even *know* me, Grandie. Not really.'

'Makes no difference, that. I know women. And you're a woman despite what you're doing to make yourself look like a twelve-year-old girl.'

She nodded thoughtfully, and he could tell from the expression on her face that she was about to twist his words and use them against him as she seemed only too expert at doing. 'So let me see,' she said. 'You had four sons and one daughter, and the daughter – this would be Aunt Nan, of course – left home when she was sixteen and never returned except at Christmas and the odd bank holiday. So that leaves Gran and whatever wife or girlfriend your sons brought round, yes? So how is it that you know women in general from this limited exposure to them, Grandie?'

'Don't you get clever with me. I'd been married to your gran for forty-six years when the poor woman dropped dead, so I had plenty of time to know your sort.'

'My "sort"?'

'The female sort. And what I know is that women need men as much as men need women and anyone who thinks otherwise is doing their thinking straight through the arse.'

'What about men who need men and women who need women?'

'We'll not talk about that!' he declared in outrage. 'There'll be no perversion in *my* family and have no doubt about *that*.'

'Ah. That's what you think, then. It's per*ver*sion.'

'That's what I *know*.' He'd shoved her possessions back into the ruck-sack and replaced it on the hook before he saw how she'd diverted them from his chosen topic. The damn girl was like a freshly hooked fish when it came to conversation. She flipped and flopped and avoided the net. Well, that would *not* be the case tonight. He was a match for her wili-ness. The cleverness in *her* blood was diluted by having Sally Joy for a mother. The cleverness in his blood was not.

He said, 'A stage. Full stop. Girls your age, they all have stages. This one here, it might look different from another girl's, but a stage is a stage. And I know one when I'm looking it in the eyes, don't I.'

'Do you.'

'Oh aye. And there've been signs, by the way, in case you think I'm blowing smoke in the matter. I saw you with him, I did.'

She didn't reply. Instead, she carried her glass and bowl to the sink and began the washing up. She scraped the bone from his chop into the rubbish, and she stacked the cooking pots, the plates, the cutlery and the glasses on the work top in the order in which she intended to wash them. She filled the sink. Steam rose. He thought she was going to scald herself some night, but the heat never seemed to bother her.

When she began to wash but still said nothing, he picked up a tea towel for the drying and spoke again. 'You hear me, girl? I saw you with him, so do *not* be declaring to your granddad that you have no interest, eh? I know what I saw and I know what I know. When a woman looks at a man in the way you were looking at him . . . That tells me you don't know your own mind, no matter what you say.'

She said, 'And where did this seeing take place, Grandie?'

'What does it matter? There you were, heads together, arms locked . . . the way *lovers* do, by the way . . .'

'And did that worry you? That we might be lovers?'

'Don't try that with me. Don't you bloody try that again,

missy-miss. Once a night is enough and your granddad isn't fool enough to fall for it twice.' She'd done her water glass and his lager pint, and he snatched up the latter and pushed the tea towel into it. He screwed it around and gave it a polish. 'You were *interested*, you bloody were.'

She paused. She was looking out of the window towards the four lines of caravans below their own. They marched towards the edge of the cliff and the sea. Only one of them was occupied at this time of year – the one nearest the cliff – and its kitchen light was on. This winked in the night as the rain fell against it.

'Jago's home,' Tammy said. 'We should have him over for a meal soon. It's not good for elderly people to be on their own so much. And now he's going to be . . . He'll miss Santo badly, though I don't expect he'll ever admit it.'

Ah. There. The name had been said. Selevan could talk about the boy freely now. He said, 'You'll claim it was nothing, won't you. A . . . what d'you call it? A passing interest. A bit of flirting. But I saw and I know you were willing. If he'd made a move . . .'

She picked up a plate. She washed it thoroughly. Her movements were languid. There was no sense of urgency in anything that Tammy did. She said, 'Grandie, you misconstrued. Santo and I were friends. He talked to me. He *needed* someone to talk to, and I was the person he chose.'

'That's him, not you.'

'No. It was both. I was happy with that. Happy to be . . . well, to be someone he could turn to.'

'Bah. Don't lie to me.'

'Why would I lie? He talked, I listened. And if he wanted to know what I thought about something, I told him what I thought.'

'I saw you with your arms *linked*, girl.'

She cocked her head as she looked at him. She studied his face and then she smiled. She removed her hands from the water and, dripping as they were, she put her arms around him. She kissed him even as he stiffened and tried to resist her. She said, 'Dear Grandie. Linking arms doesn't mean what it might have meant once. It means friendship. And that's the honest truth.'

'Honest,' he said. 'Bah.'

'It is. I always try to be honest.'

'With yourself as well?'

'Especially with myself.' She went back to the washing up and cleaned her gruel bowl carefully, and then she began on the cutlery. She'd done it all before she spoke again. And then she spoke in a very low voice, which Selevan might have missed altogether had he not been straining to hear something quite different from what she next said.

'I told him to be honest as well,' she murmured. 'If I hadn't, Grandie . . . I'm rather worried about that.'

The deviations from Penrule's character analysis – when it comes to Tammy – are part of the joy and the fun of writing: the moment when a character decides she isn't *quite* as previously revealed during the analysis stage. But while there are details that change from the analysis, what doesn't change is Selevan's voice, his attitude, and the form that his dialogue takes. His dialogue, especially, is character-specific, and the specificity is illustrated through the choice of words which will reflect his attitude. Thus we have:

*'What's in the glass that would make Rhodesia go down a trick for you?'* and

*'We pray before the bloody meal. Why d'we got to bloody pray at the bloody end as well?'* and

*'So your grandie's a sinner? Going straight to hell on a plate of beans while you're playing harps with the angels, eh?'* and

*'What I know is that women need men as much as men need women and anyone who thinks otherwise is doing their thinking straight through the arse.'*

No other character in the novel speaks like this. That's what character-specific dialogue is meant to be.

I'd also like to point out the final two lines of the scene between Selevan and Tammy, for they constitute a dramatic question. Something has gone on between Tammy and the murder victim, and this is weighing on her mind. The reader doesn't know what this is, and there is only one way to learn, which is, of course, to continue reading.


## Optional Exercise 1

Take these three generic characters: a thirty-year-old man, a nineteen-year-old girl and a fifty-two-year-old woman. Name each of these characters in such a way that something is immediately suggested about them: their personality, their ethnicity, their background, how they are related to each other, their level of education, their birth order, anything. (My favourite example of this came from a seventh grader when I was speaking to his class: Fried Chicken Sally.) As you consider the possible names, can you sense a story out there with these three characters featured in it? If not, look at the following example and ask yourself if a story could come of how the characters have been named.

Man, thirty years old – Jeff 'the Hammer' Cribbs

Girl, nineteen years old – Fatima Binte Nur

Woman, fifty-two years old – Hester Silverman

Given these names, do you see any potential stories arising from them? Do you feel any relationship among them? What about conflict? If you feel the twinge of a tale growing inside you, that comes from the power of naming a character. You can take this one step further and actually name the relationships that exist among them. Once you've done that, you should be able to see more clearly how a story can emerge from who they are.

## Optional Exercise 2

Establish a relationship among the three characters from Exercise 1. Make this a relationship that has the potential for tension. For example: mother/ mother's much younger boyfriend/daughter, or teacher/former student/ principal, or stepmother/stepdaughter/stepdaughter's much older boy- friend, or kidnapper/victim/kidnapper's previous victim. Consider the various kinds of tension that could be present in this relationship. Jot a few down. Choose one and move that tension into an expression of open con- flict. Write it in a paragraph or two.

# Digging Deeper into Character

*The Core Need*

There are two ingredients in the analysis of a character that help me more than any other when it comes to understanding what sort of person I'll be dealing with when she first steps into a scene in the novel. The first of these two ingredients is something that I call the core need. I think of this as an essential need, seeking to be met, that's at the root of everything a character does. At the same time, however, the character does not necessarily know what her core need is because it remains within her psyche and only self-awareness or self-examination can illuminate it. Examples of core needs are:

The need for approval

The need for perfection or to be seen as perfect

The need to be seen as empathetic

The need to be right

The need to be competent

The need to control events and people

The need for nurturance

The need for excitement

The need to be seen as authentic

The need for admiration

The need for attention

The need to be of service

The need for connection

The need for an adrenaline rush

And on and on.

Core needs are emotional or physical or psychological. The meeting of a character's core need relieves her existing anxiety, avoids the mere occasion of anxiety, eases stress, or rests the troubled mind.

So how does a writer know what a character's core need is? It grows out of the character analysis, because it begins to emerge as you freewrite about the character. Knowing what need is actually driving a character's behaviour allows the writer to give depth and shading to a character, making the creation multidimensional.

Examine how her need emerges in this character analysis of Aldara Pappas.

**ALDARA (means winged gift) PAPPAS:** Aldara Pappas is forty-five years old, an extremely sexy Greek woman who emigrated to England with her family when she was a child. She grew up in London and **moved to Cornwall with her first husband when they bought an old mansion and turned it into a hotel/spa just outside St. Ives.** She is the woman that Santo has taken up with prior to his murder.

She was born in Greece, one of seven children. Her father went to London when she was five to take up a job washing dishes because he wanted to better their family circumstances. He sent money home and the mother saved most of it until they had enough for passage for the whole family. At that time the family was only five people: parents and three kids. Four more children were born in England after the mother's arrival there. The father went on to become an executive chef in one of London's grand hotels. He made a real success of his life despite the fact that he never mastered English as well as he wanted to. His lack of mastery of English, though, did not stand in the way of his getting ahead and this is the lesson that he taught his children: **nothing will stand in the way of your success except yourself.**

Aldara has no children. Her **first husband was sterile**, something that they did not know and something that he would not allow himself to be tested for, so much had he tied manhood into the ability to produce kids. What he did was lie, however. He lied about having been tested and having everything A-okay. Truth was, he was never tested because he was too scared and Aldara instead underwent fertility treatments in order to produce a child. Of course she couldn't produce a child no matter how many eggs she had and no matter the condition of her uterus. When she finally understood that her husband had lied to her about having his own status tested, she divorced him. **With her settlement from the divorce she bought the cider farm where Madlyn Angarrack works in the jam kitchen.**

What does Aldara look like? She's beautiful but not in the English sense. She's got short dark hair, rather severely cut. She has enormous dark eyes. She has sculpted eyebrows. She has a firm jaw that gets set quite easily when she wants her own way, which is most of the time. She is perfectly proportioned. She's five feet and eight inches with great legs and a wonderful butt. She knows how to dress to make the best of her colouring and her shape, and she dresses that way. **Even if she's wearing a boiler suit, it's a tailored boiler suit and it's done in red which looks great on her.** She wears gold: earrings, a chain with a cross on it, rings and bracelets. But like everything else about her, it is not overdone. She looks younger than 45 but in no way does she remotely look like a woman Santo's age. She may **look about 35** but that's the extent of it.

How does she come to get involved with Santo? Santo comes to pick up Madlyn and Aldara talks to him as he waits for Madlyn to get off her shift. Aldara says she will show him around and she takes him to the orchard on a tractor to show him the pyramid style they use in pruning the apple trees. **Does she proposition him? I would say she does.** She tells him that if he gets tired of his little girlfriend and if he wants to see what it's like to be with a woman, to phone her. She is quite direct. She says, 'I like the look of you. I like thinking what it would be like for us both to have you in my bed,' or words to that effect. She might even tell him she's tired of her own man (who works at the farm or is a newspaperman) because 'the brain, you know, habituates to the lover. After a time the lover becomes less a lover and more an inconvenience.' **She explains that Santo would not be a permanent lover or her only lover.** What he would do is make her able to continue having sex with her boyfriend by providing her the frisson of excitement she needs to keep the other relationship going. Secrecy, you see, she tells him. If you and I have a secret, it makes the other relationship more potent. She suggests he do the same with Madlyn. But Santo doesn't live like that. If he's to become Aldara's lover, then he can't be a lover of Madlyn also.

Aldara has to give him something to think of. A taste of her. What would it be? Perhaps the sexual tension in the suggestion. That's all. She permits nothing else. She is no dummy. She knows how to lead men by their dicks.

**What makes her irresistible to men is her self-confidence, intelligence and passion for what she's doing.** When she took up the cider farm she learned everything there was to know about making cider and she's made this place a rip-roaring success. She allows people in for tours and there's a tasting room, a shop and a café associated with it. She runs the entire enterprise, and she's involved in every aspect of it.

What's her background that she can do this? I would say that she is **university educated and her degree is in business.** She was the business mind behind the hotel/spa. She managed its day-to-day affairs and was in charge of the staff. She was a hard but fair taskmaster, and the entire staff respected her. They were devastated to see her go. The hotel/spa has sunk in its fortunes with her departure.

Aldara always worked, as did everyone in her family. They are people who are **not afraid of hard work.** While their father climbed the ladder as an executive chef, they ran a small restaurant in Highgate. All the children and the mother. It was a success. They never tried to outbuild what they were able to support with their own work. The kids all went to school and university in London so that they could work in the restaurant in their free time. None of them took gap years and none of them travelled on holidays with their mates. Their lives revolved around the family. 'In it together' was their motto.

This attitude on the part of the family – that family is everything – made Aldara's sense of betrayal even greater when her husband lied about his fertility. He, too, is Greek. She met him through community involvement with her orthodox church. It was a love match, and she married him full of hope. Their plans were for a big family since they both came from big families. The years they tried to conceive weighed on them both before his lie and his stupid machismo broke her.

Her own family would like her to move back to London but she decided to make it on her own with the settlement from her husband. **She always thought she had ten times his brains and she was always keeping silent to allow him to feel more intelligent and more competent than she.** She finished doing that when she discovered he was a liar.

She was never unfaithful to him and he was never unfaithful to her. It was the lie she couldn't stand. And the fact that the lie rose from his sense of manhood. **To her, this whole manhood thing is** ridiculous. **You do not determine a person's worth by what is or is not hanging between the person's legs, she would say.**

**She's friends with Daidre.** Perhaps she knows her from a woman's group? Perhaps they've met because Daidre has been at the farm? **If Daidre is a vet she could have seen Aldara's orchard pig for some malady . . .** Yes, that would be it. So when Daidre sees Santo, she not only knows who it is, but she also knows about his involvement with Aldara Pappas, her friend. These two women are not best friends, but they are the closest thing to that that either of them would be available for. They see each other, they talk frankly to each other, they're both well educated and both on their own and self-supporting. They are completely different with regard to their pasts but the fact that they are on equal footing otherwise gives them a bond. They don't see each other often but when they do, they are not superficial. They trust each other to keep quiet about confidences.

**Maybe Aldara also knows Ben Kerne and Lew Angarrack through some sort of small business owners' association.** She knows that Ben Kerne needs a good business model to follow and she knows he needs to get his wife out of the business which he would do if he were not so intent upon keeping an eye on her. Dellen Kerne is going to run that fledging business into the ground, is Aldara's attitude.

Aldara's core need is to **prove herself the equal to men.** Really, just to prove herself: she is in a constant quest to prove her competence, to prove her sexual allure, to prove her superiority, to prove her knowledge. She doesn't do this in an overbearing way and she doesn't seek to prove other people less than. **She works towards an inner bar that she herself keeps raising.** If other people are put off by this or hurt by this, that can't be helped and she certainly doesn't see it as her responsibility.

What then is her pathology? A form of paranoia, I would say. But this one is one that blames others when she herself is less than competent about something. She gets furious with them and she's quick, to fire them. She's arrogant and thinks she's always right and when she's frightened, she just digs in and holds firm to her belief. She will not hear arguments to the contrary.

Her ambition now: to make the cider farm a success. She has taken a derelict apple orchard and turned it into this farm through power of will. She is determined that nothing will stand in her way of making it successful and proving she is the equal of any man. One of the reasons she admires Daidre is because Daidre is a woman who is a success in a man's world.

Does Aldara have any sidelines? She certainly wouldn't engage in anything that might be seen as a womanly pursuit. And yet she is essentially all woman. Does she collect something, pursue something, have a special interest in something? Maybe she's really into politics? History? What about a particular period in Cornish history? Cornish mining? Is she a great walker of the South-West Coast Path? What sort of exercise does she get? She's not a beach person but she could be a walker. Let's make her a walker, I think. What if she plays classical guitar? I think I see her with classical guitar, but this is something she does in private. She would see it as a weakness to let anyone know of her interest in making music. She even takes lessons.

What would you notice about her first? Her eyes, which are amazing. What moulded her? Her family ties. And the betrayal by her husband. What shows who she is today? Her treatment of men.

Unlike Selevan Penrule, once Aldara Pappas appeared in *Careless in Red*, she remained throughout as she was created. Not everything about her was pulled out of the ether of my brain, however. This is because when I create my characters, I do so *after* I've completed my location research, and on my research trip I've seen things and learned things that will ultimately help me to know who the people are inside the book I hope to write.

In the case of *Careless in Red*, the location research ended up giving me the occupations of all the characters, the leisure activities engaged in by the characters, the housing of the characters, as well as their hobbies, collections and social class.

Images 15 and 16 illustrate this point.

Prior to setting off for Cornwall, I had read about a number of places that seemed to have story potential, and I wanted to see them. One was the cider farm I eventually gave to Aldara Pappas. This farm served the purpose of providing a contrast between the sultry Greek woman and the means through which she makes her living. Image 15 shows the main work buildings of the farm. Image 16 shows the pigs – including the enormous Gloucester Old Spot – whose job it is to eat what remains once the crops of apples have been pressed.

We first see the cider farm through the eyes of Daidre Trahair, the

IMAGE 15

IMAGE 16

woman who owns the cottage in Polcare Cove, where we've already been. Daidre's arrival allows the farm to be described for the reader.

> Daidre didn't return to the cottage when she left Thomas Lynley at the Salthouse Inn. Instead, she drove east. The route she took twisted like a discarded spool of ribbon through the misty countryside. It passed through several hamlets where lamps shone at windows in the dusk, then dipped through two woodlands. It divided one farmhouse from its outbuildings, and ultimately it came out on the A388. She took this road south and veered off on a secondary road that tracked east through pastureland where sheep and dairy cows grazed. She turned off where a sign pointed to Cornish Gold with Visitors Welcome printed beneath the name of the place.

Cornish Gold was half a mile down a very narrow lane, a farm comprising vast apple orchards circumscribed by stands of plum trees, these last planted years ago as a windbreak. The orchards began at the crest of a hill and spread down the other side in an impressive fan of acreage. Before them, in stair-step fashion, stood two old stone barns, and across from these, a cider factory formed one side of a cobbled courtyard. In the centre of this, an animal pen traced a perfect square and within that square snuffled and snorted the ostensible reason for Daidre's visit to this place, should anyone other than the farm's owner ask her. This reason was an orchard pig, a huge and decidedly un-friendly Gloucester Old Spot that had been instrumental in Daidre's meeting the owner of the cider farm soon after the woman's arrival in this part of the world, a journey she'd made over thirty years from Greece to London to St. Ives to the farm.

At the side of the pen, Daidre found the pig waiting. He was named Stamos, after his owner's former husband. The porcine Stamos, never a fool and always an optimist, had anticipated the reason for Daidre's visit and had lumbered to the rail fence cooperatively once Daidre came into the courtyard. She had nothing for him this time, however. Packing peeled oranges into her bag while still at her cottage had seemed a questionable activity while the police were hanging about, intent upon watching and noting everyone's movements.

She said, 'Sorry, Stamos. But let's have a look at the ear all the same. Yes, yes. It's all form. You're quite recovered, and you know it. You're too clever for your own good, aren't you?'

The pig was known to bite, so she took care. She also looked round the courtyard to see who might be watching because, if nothing else, one had to be diligent. But no one was there, and that was reasonable. For it was late in the day, and all employees of the farm would have long gone home.

She said, 'Looking perfect now,' to the pig and then she crossed the remainder of the courtyard where an arch led to a small rain-sodden vegetable garden. Here she followed a brick path – uneven, overgrown, and pooled with rainwater – to a neat white cottage from which the sound of classical guitar came in fits and starts. Aldara would be practising. That was good, as it likely meant she was alone.

The playing stopped instantly when Daidre knocked on the door. Steps hurriedly approached across the hardwood floor inside.

Daidre's interactions with Stamos the pig lay down a dramatic question in the form of *She also looked round the courtyard to see who might be watching because, if nothing else, one had to be diligent.* Thus, the reader knows something is on her mind besides the ear of the pig, and once again the reader stays in the story, one hopes, in order to learn what that something is.

It is when Daidre moves to the interior of the house that we meet Aldara Pappas for the first time, and a scene from Daidre's POV allows me to use the setting in addition to the description of character to begin to reveal Aldara.

'Daidre! What on earth . . . ?' Aldara Pappas was backlit from within the cottage, so Daidre couldn't see her face. But she knew the great dark eyes would hold speculation and not surprise, despite her tone of voice. Aldara stepped back from the door, saying, 'Come in. You are so very welcome. What a lovely surprise that you should come to break the tedium of my evening. Why didn't you phone me from Bristol? Are you down for long?'

'It was a sudden decision.'

Inside the cottage it was quite warm, the way Aldara liked it. Every wall was washed in white, and each one of them displayed highly coloured paintings of rugged landscapes, arid and possessing habitations of white – small buildings with tiles on their roofs and their window boxes bursting with flowers, with donkeys standing placidly against their walls and dark-haired children playing in the dirt before their front doors. Aldara's furniture was simple and sparse. The pieces were brightly upholstered in blue and yellow, however, and a red rug covered part of the floor. Only the geckos were missing, their little bodies curving against the surface of whatever their tiny suctioned feet could cling to.

A coffee table in front of the sofa held a bowl of fruit and a plate of roasted peppers, Greek olives and cheese: feta, undoubtedly. A bottle of red wine was still to be opened. Two wineglasses, two napkins, two plates and two forks were neatly positioned. These gave the lie to Aldara's words. Daidre looked at her. She raised an eyebrow.

'It was a small social lie only.' Aldara was, as ever, completely unembarrassed to have been caught out. 'Had you walked in and seen this, you would have felt less than welcome, no? And you are always welcome in my home.'

'As is someone else, apparently, tonight.'

'You are far more important than someone else.' As if to emphasise this, Aldara went to the fireplace, where a fire was laid and matches remained only to be used. She struck one on the underside of the mantel and put it to the crumpled paper beneath the wood. Apple wood, this was, dried and kept for burning when the orchard trees were pruned.

Aldara's movements were sensuous, but they were not studied. In the time Daidre had known the other woman, she'd come to realise that Aldara was sensual as a result of simply being Aldara. She would laugh and say, 'It's in my blood,' as if being Greek meant being seductive. But it was more than blood that made her compelling. It was confidence, intelligence and complete lack of fear. Daidre admired this final quality most in the other woman, aside from her beauty. For she was forty-five and looked ten years younger. Daidre was thirty-one and, without the olive skin of the other woman, knew she would not be so lucky in fourteen years' time.

Having lit the fire, Aldara went to the wine and uncorked it, as if underscoring her declaration that Daidre was as valued and important a guest as whomever Aldara was actually expecting. She poured, saying, 'It's going to have a bite. None of that smooth French business. As you know, I like wine that challenges the palate. So have some cheese with it, or it's likely to take the enamel from your teeth.'

She handed over a glass and scooped up a chunk of cheese, which she popped into her mouth. She licked her fingers slowly, then she winked at Daidre, mocking herself. 'Delicious,' she said. 'Mama sent it from London.'

'How is she?'

'Still looking for someone to kill Stamos, of course. Sixty-seven years old and *no* one holds a grudge like Mama. She says to me, "Figs. I shall send that devil figs. Will he eat them, Aldara? I'll stuff them with arsenic. What d'you think?" I tell her to dismiss him from her thoughts. I have, I tell her. "Do not waste energy on that man," I tell her. "It's been nine years, Mama, and that is sufficient time to wish someone ill." She says, as if I had not spoken, "I'll send your brothers to kill him." And then she curses him in Greek at some length, all of which I'm paying for, naturally, as I'm the one who makes the phone calls, four times a week, like the dutiful daughter I have always been. When she's finished, I tell her at least to send Nikko if she truly intends to kill Stamos because Nikko's the only one of my brothers who's actually good with a knife and a decent shot with a gun. And then she laughs. She launches into a story about one of Nikko's children and that is that.'

Daidre smiled. Aldara dropped onto the sofa, kicking off her shoes and tucking her legs beneath her. She was wearing a dress the colour of mahogany, its hem like a handkerchief, its neckline V-ing towards her breasts. It had no sleeves and was fashioned from material more suitable to summer on Crete than spring in Cornwall. Little wonder that the room was so warm.

Daidre took some cheese and wine as instructed. Aldara was right. The wine was rough.

'I think they aged it fifteen minutes,' Aldara told her. 'You know the Greeks.'

'You're the only Greek I do know,' Daidre said.

'This is sad. But Greek women are much more interesting than Greek men, so you have the best of the lot with me. You've not come about Stamos, have you? I mean Stamos the lowercase pig, of course. Not Stamos the uppercase Pig.'

'I stopped to look at him. His ears are clear.'

'They would be. I did follow your instructions. He's right as rain. He's asking for a girlfriend as well, although the last thing I want is a dozen orchard piglets round my ankles. You didn't answer me, by the way.'

'Did I not?'

'You did not. I'm delighted to see you, as always, but there's something in your face that tells me you've come for a reason.' She took another piece of cheese.

'Who're you expecting?' Daidre asked her.

Aldara's hand, lifting the cheese to her mouth, paused. She cocked her head and regarded Daidre. 'That sort of question is completely unlike you,' she pointed out.

'Sorry. But . . .'

'What?'

Daidre felt flustered, and she hated that feeling. Her life experience – not to mention her sexual and emotional experience – placed in opposition to Aldara's experience left her seriously wanting and even more seriously out of her depth. She shifted gears. She did it baldly, as baldness was the only weapon she possessed. 'Aldara, Santo Kerne's been killed.'

Aldara said, 'What did you say?'

'Are you asking that because you didn't hear me or because you want to think you didn't hear me?'

'What happened to him?' Aldara said, and Daidre was gratified to watch her replace her bit of cheese on the plate, uneaten.

'He was apparently climbing.'

'Where?'

'The cliff in Polcare Cove. He fell and was killed. A man out walking the coastal path was the one to find him. He came to the cottage.'

'You were there when this happened?'

'No. I drove down from Bristol this afternoon. When I got to the cottage, the man was inside. He was looking for a phone. I came in on him.'

'You came in on a man inside your cottage? My God. How frightening. How did he . . . ? Did he find the extra key?'

'He broke a window to get in. He told me there was a body on the rocks and I went down to it with him. I said I was a doctor—'

'Well, you *are* a doctor. You might have been able to—'

'No. It's not that. Well, it is in a way because I could have done something, I suppose.'

'You must more than *suppose*, Daidre. You've been educated well. You've qualified. You've managed to acquire a job of enormous responsibility and you cannot say—'

'Aldara. Yes. All right. I know. But it was more than wanting to help. I wanted to see. I had a feeling.'

Aldara said nothing. Sap crackled in one of the logs and the sound of it drew her attention to the fire. She looked at it long, as if checking to see that the logs remained where she had originally placed them. She finally said, 'You thought it might be Santo Kerne? Why?'

'It's obvious, isn't it?'

'Why is it obvious?'

'Aldara. You know.'

'I don't. You must tell me.'

'Must I?'

'Please.'

'You're being—'

'I'm being nothing. Tell me what you want to tell me about why things are so obvious to you, Daidre.'

'Because even when one thinks everything has been seen to, even when one thinks every *i* has been dotted, every *t* has been crossed, even when one thinks every sentence has a full stop at the end—'

'You're becoming tedious,' Aldara pointed out.

Daidre took a sharp breath. 'Someone is dead. How *can* you talk like that?'

'All right. *Tedious* was a poor choice of words. *Hysterical* would have been better.'

'This is a human being we're talking about. This is a teenage boy. Not nineteen years old. Dead on the rocks.'

'Now you *are* hysterical.'

'How can you be like this? Santo Kerne is *dead.*'

'And I'm sorry about that. I don't want to think of a boy that young falling from a cliff and—'

'*If* he fell, Aldara.'

Aldara reached for her wineglass. Daidre noted – as she sometimes did – that the Greek woman's hands were the only part of her that was not lovely. Aldara herself called them a peasant's hands, made for pounding clothes against rocks in a stream, for kneading bread, for working the soil. With strong, thick fingers and wide palms, they were not hands made for delicate employment. 'Why "if he fell"?' she asked.

'You know the answer to that.'

'But you said he was climbing. You can't think someone. . .'

'Not someone, Aldara. Santo Kerne? Polcare Cove? It's not difficult to work out who might have harmed him.'

'You're talking nonsense. You go to the cinema far too often. Films make one start believing that people act like they're playing parts devised in Hollywood. The fact that Santo fell while he was climbing—'

'And isn't that a bit odd? Whyever would he climb in this weather?'

'You ask the question as if you expect me to know the answer.'

'Oh, for heaven's sake, Aldara—'

'Enough.' Aldara firmly set her wineglass down. 'I am *not* you, Daidre. I've never had this . . . this . . . oh, what shall I call it . . . this awe of men that you have, this feeling that they are somehow more significant than they actually are, that they are necessary in life, essential to a woman's completion. I'm terribly sorry that the boy is dead, but it's nothing to do with me.'

'No? And this . . . ?' Daidre indicated the two wineglasses, the two plates, the two forks, the endless repetition of what should have been but never quite was the number two. And there was the additional matter of Aldara's clothing: the filmy dress that embraced and released her hips when she moved, the choice of shoes with toes too open and heels too high to be practical on a farm, the earrings that illustrated the length of her neck. There was little doubt in Daidre's mind that the sheets on Aldara's bed were fresh and scented with lavender and that there were candles ready to be lit in her bedroom.

A man was at this moment on his way to her. He was even now pondering the removal of her clothes. He was wondering how quickly upon his arrival he could get down to business with her. He was thinking of how he was going to take her – rough or tender, up against the wall, on the floor, in a bed – and in what position, of whether he'd be up for the job of doing it more than twice because he knew merely twice would not be enough, not for a woman like Aldara Pappas. Earthy, sensual, ready. He damn well *had* to give her what she was looking for because if he didn't, he'd be tossed aside and he didn't want that.

Daidre said, 'I think you're going to find otherwise, Aldara. I think you're going to see that this . . . what happened to Santo . . . whatever it is—'

'That's nonsense,' Aldara cut in.

'Is it?' Daidre put her palm on the table between them. She repeated her earlier question. 'Who're you expecting tonight?'

'That doesn't concern you.'

'Are you completely mad? I had the police in my cottage.'

'And that worries you. Why?'

'Because I feel *responsible*. Don't you?'

Aldara seemed to consider the question, because it was a moment before she replied. 'Not at all.'

'And that's that, then?'

'I suppose it is.'

'Because of this? The wine, the cheese, the lovely fire? The two of you? Whoever he is?'

Aldara rose. She said, 'You must leave. I've tried to explain myself to you time and again. But you see how I am as a moral question and not what it is, which is just a manifestation of the only way I can function. So yes, someone is on his way and, no, I'm not going to tell you who it is, and I'd vastly prefer it if you were not here when he arrives.'

'You refuse to be touched by anything, don't you?' Daidre asked her.

'My dear, that is definitely the pot and the kettle,' was Aldara's reply.


Inside the house of the cider farm's owner, we learn why Daidre Trahair has come to see Aldara Pappas at the same time as we learn something of Aldara's backstory, something of her relationship to the victim in the novel, and a good amount about her various attitudes. We also are exposed to another dramatic question in Aldara's words at the end, strengthening the reader's curiosity about this woman Daidre Trahair.

Aldara's core need plays out during the novel mainly through her relationships with various men. It largely colours her attitude towards them, and it's present in the manner in which she greets the news of Santo's death. She defends herself against anyone's perceiving this need by using her flippancy, that shrug of the shoulders in the face of another character's potential judgment of the way she's chosen to live her life. As created, she has a lot of potential for attitude, and it's attitude that allows characters to rise above what I call Wonder Bread people: bland and lacking in subtlety and texture.

The second ingredient of the analysis that builds my understanding of a character is that character's psychopathology, or what I call her pathological manoeuvre. I define the pathological manoeuvre as an aberrant behaviour, a conflicted or confused mental state, a self-created bodily oddity, an unusual but revealing reaction to something, or an erroneous belief. It's something that lies within an individual, generally (but not always) out of view of the public and covered over by whatever persona an individual projects. It is triggered in moments when anxiety, stress, fear, or the troubled mind can't be soothed or relieved or when situations occur in which the core need of that character cannot be met and the anxiety this creates produces a behaviour that temporarily reduces that anxiety. There are as many pathological manoeuvres as there are dangerous, crazy, neurotic, psychotic, criminal, harmful, evil, unkind, vicious, useless or inexplicable actions, beliefs, appearances or thoughts. Examples of pathological manoeuvres are self-mutilation, aggression against others, bullying, eating disorders, drug addictions, alcoholism, uncontrollable rages, physical ailments with no known cause (hysterical blindness, hysterical paralysis, etc.), obsessive thoughts, compulsive behaviors (like hand washing), obsessions, nymphomania, satyriasis, chronic lying, all manias, all phobias, reaction formation, etc.

We *see* a character's psychopathology in the action she engages in – acts that, all judgement aside, tell us something is wrong with that person, such as being in the shower for three hours, such as hoarding, such as klepto-mania, such as pyromania, such as bodily disfigurement or acts of self-harm. Think of Lady Macbeth. She verges on wearing her pathological manoeuvres like her clothes.

We *hear* the psychopathology in a character when her thoughts – spoken aloud – tell us something is wrong: such as object hatred, such as paranoid accusations, such as obsessions that are given voice, such as xenophobia, racism, misogyny, misanthropy, etc.

Attempting to meet a core need gives characters an agenda in each scene, creating an undercurrent that makes the character more real for the reader. When a pathological manoeuvre is at work in a scene, it adds crit-ical elements as well. It heightens tension and it either develops, increases, or illustrates conflict, which is the core of drama.

Consider the creation of Cadan Angarrack, one of the POV characters in the novel. In constructing the analysis of Cadan, I'm seeking to under-stand the circumstances from which he comes so that I'll know how Cadan will act when driven to meet his core need, and so that I also will know how he will react when stymied in this endeavour.

**CADAN ANGARRACK:** Cadan (Cade) Angarrack is twenty-two years old. He is the older brother of Madlyn, and he lives at home with his sister and his father. He works at Adventures Unlimited because he wasn't able to work successfully for his father. He tried and his father tried, but their personalities do not mesh and they never have. His father is a perfectionist and Cade is anything but a perfectionist. He's a good-time boy and he likes action. The precision work of surfboard shaping isn't something that he could do. He wasn't able to pay close enough attention to his work. He is an adrenaline junkie and his favour-ite thing to do is trick bicycle riding. This is something his father finds absurd in a kid his age because trick bike riding is done on a small bike and his dad thinks he looks ludicrous.

What does he look like: He's dark like his sister, with curly hair that he keeps cut short. He's about five feet and eight inches, not particularly tall, but he's built well because of all the physical activity he engages in. He has olive skin, so he tans well in the summer and his tan seems to linger most of the winter as well because as soon as he has enough money, he goes off for weekends where there is sun. He loves the sun and **his ambition is to live somewhere where there is perpetual sunshine** so that he can do the outdoor activities he loves 7 days a week.

What **activities** does he love: trick biking, free cliff climbing (no ropes), surfing, abseiling, hang gliding, trick skiing, snowboarding. He loves anything that will give him the high of adrenaline pumping through his veins. He hates anything that is heavy-duty work with little payoff of adrenaline: like hiking, for example. What a waste. Or trekking along the coastal path. What a bigger waste.

He **always looks beaten up** and this is something anyone notices about him when they see him. He's always got cuts and bruises somewhere on him, but this doesn't bother him. He has **a very high tolerance for pain**. Being beaten up is the price one pays for excitement. One of the things he loves to do is to be out in a storm. He figures that if he has to live in this place, he may as well get something exciting out of it.

He finished secondary school . . . just. He did not pass his GCSEs with good marks. He was too busy doing other things: like sports in school. He excelled in sports. He didn't like being on a team, but being on a team was a requirement that his father placed on him and he cooperated. **He played rugby. He liked the contact, the pushing and shoving.**

He's happy-go-lucky, and this has made him seem irresponsible. He's filled with ideas about what Ben Kerne should do with Adventures Unlimited. He himself is . . . what there? An instructor? An equipment maintenance man? A custodian? Abseiling instructor in the season and part of the skeleton maintenance staff in the off-season? Yes, that's it. So **in the off-season, he's repairing and maintaining the equipment, he's painting, he's replacing things, he's dealing with plumbing, he's making sure the windows and doors are operational, he's cleaning carpets, etc.**

What are his relationships like with his sister and his father? His relationship with his father is mostly good because Cade refuses to let his father push his buttons. **He fends his father off with humour.** 'Face it, man, I'm a walking death wish' would be something he would say with a laugh. He doesn't let his father in too close. **He doesn't let anyone in too close.** If he has any close relationship, it's with his macaw or **parrot**. Maybe a Mexican green parrot. The bird lives in his bedroom but goes to work with him. In fact he goes everywhere with him, even waiting for him while he engages in whatever activity he is engaging in. The parrot's wings are not clipped. He's merely perfectly loyal to Cade. What's the bird's name? Pooh. As in Winnie the? No, as in that's what he'll do on your shoulder if you aren't careful to give him bathroom breaks. Pooh's favourite food is what? Chips? No. Bacon Streakies, which are maize, rice, and soya snacks.

Why doesn't he let people in too close? Because of his mother. Because she left. He was close to her, he essentially adored her, and she left. He never really recovered from that, but he has never talked about it. **Once she left, he refused to be close to her again.** He would go on the visits to her that were required of him, but that's all he'd do. He hates his stepfather because his stepfather thinks he's a loser. His stepfather is a professional of some sort. Maybe a banker or insurance salesman.

His sister? What is his relationship with her like? He loves her and thinks she's got what it takes to make it as a pro surfer. She's dedicated where he is not. He's into a lot of things. The fact that she can focus on her surfing is something he admires and he can't figure it out that she would fall for and pursue Santo to the detriment of her surfing since he would never do that. When Santo breaks it off with Madlyn, how does Cade react? Well, he thinks she was stupid to get involved with Santo in the first place. He can see Santo's effect on women and he's been around Santo long enough to see how Santo gets hooked into any woman who indicates she wants him. He also thinks Madlyn is throwing away her future as a competitive surfer when she gets involved with Santo so when Santo breaks off with her, he thinks she should say good riddance and get back to surfing. He definitely doesn't understand her demons because he stalwartly refuses to face his own.

Does he have a girlfriend? No way. He isn't interested. He will have casual sex if it's available among girls in the town, but that's it. Better yet, he remains celibate during the off-season, claiming that he's saving his energy for the girls who holiday in town in the spring and summer. But the truth of the matter is that he doesn't want a relationship because he's seen how they end. What he wants is casual sex. This makes him look like the Casanova of the town. So he has casual sex at or after parties in town or he has sex with girls who are on holiday.

Is he a seducer? Yes. **Definitely.** He pursues them because he likes sex. Has he had a relationship with Kerra? I would say she tried, but it failed because no way is he ever going to be controlled by anyone.

What is his core need? **Action.** Action allows him to keep one step ahead of his feelings and he definitely wants to be one step ahead of his feelings because he's got a lot of pain associated with ways he believes he's let his father down and with ways he thinks he drove his mother off. Neither of these are true. But it's how Cade sees life.

Maybe Cade offered to beat Santo up or 'take care of Santo' when his sister was most upset. Of course he didn't intend to do anything to Santo, but maybe she doesn't know this. Did he climb with Santo? As he's interested only in free climbing, I would say that maybe they did climb, but one was doing solo climbing and the other was doing free climbing. Maybe they engaged in contests: who could get up the cliff face first?

What's his pathological manoeuvre? He becomes **the Party Boy**. Wild and crazy partying. At his worst, he's into **binge drinking** or whatever the Brits call that heavy drinking that goes on in city centres. He does not engage in this drinking in Casvelyn, however. **He goes to Truro to the centre of town.** In his earlier years, he has had parties at his father's house.

How does he feel about his father's girlfriend and her kids? The kids love him but he is bugged by them. That's how he describes it: bugged. Truth is he's afraid that they're going to become part of the family unit, and he doesn't know how he's going to handle it. **He sees that his father is a good dad to them, and he's jealous although he would never say it. Since his father has taken up with the girlfriend, Cade spends a lot of time away from home and at Adventures Unlimited.**

Does he have hobbies? It's his bird: teaching his bird to talk and do tricks. What he likes best about the parrot is that parrots live so long. This bird will be with him forever.

Does he have ambition? His ambition is to **get out of England** and into the sun. To this end, he would like to go to Spain, to Majorca, to Morocco, to South Africa. He has no interest at all in going to the US. He's seen enough American television to be totally put off by it. Does he have a savings account for this? Nope. He spends money like water. He also lends it without considering the person who is borrowing it. He does this not because he wants to buy friendship but because he wants to be liked.

What single event influenced Cade into being who he is? Probably their mother's departure. When she quickly remarried, it didn't take a rocket scientist for him to figure out that she'd had this guy on the side. And how did she meet him? She was a freelance journalist and she was interviewing him on background for something. Cade felt betrayed by all this, especially since I would say his mother used him once as an excuse to meet her boyfriend, taking Cade with her to do something in some town . . . wherever she lives . . . it's Bristol, right . . . and then supposedly running into the guy. Cade wasn't stupid. He put two and two together.

Event that illustrates his personality now? Perhaps his reaction to Santo's death. Santo kept messing around and it was bound to happen that he'd mess around with the wrong woman once too often and pay the price. He shrugs. If you're going to mess around with someone more than once, he thinks, you have to be prepared to pay for it.

If you examine this character analysis, you can see in the first paragraph that I am feeling my way towards his core need when I decide that Cadan is a party boy and that he is an adrenaline junkie. His activities as listed in the first and third paragraphs of the analysis support the adrenaline junkie aspect of his character. As I continue to write about him during his creation, I find that I'm heading towards a core need for *action*, this constant action being how he manages to stay one step ahead of his feelings. His pathological manoeuvre, then, encourages him to strike out at himself and others when he is under the stress of being denied a way to meet his need for action. He engages in binge drinking, which hurts him and can also – when done in public – hurt others.

Thus, when Cadan is introduced in the novel, I've given myself a lot to work with and there's nothing that I have to pull out of the ether.

Cadan Angarrack didn't mind the rain. Nor did he mind the spectacle that he knew he presented to the limited world of Casvelyn. He trundled along on his freestyle BMX, with his knees rising to the height of his waist and his elbows shooting out like bent arrows, intent only on getting home to make his announcement. Pooh bounced on his shoulder, squawking in protest and occasionally shrieking, 'Landlubber scum!' into Cadan's ear. This was decidedly better than applying his beak to Cadan's earlobe, which had happened in the past before the parrot learned the error of his ways, so Cadan didn't try to silence the bird. Instead he said, 'You tell 'em, Pooh,' to which the parrot cried, 'Blow holes in the attic!' an expression whose provenance was a mystery to his master.

Had he been out working with the bicycle instead of using it as a means of transport, Cadan wouldn't have had the parrot with him. In early days, he'd taken Pooh along, finding a perch for him near the side of the empty swimming pool while he ran through his routines and developed strategies for improving not only his tricks but the area in which he practised them. But some damn teacher from the infants' school next door to the leisure centre had raised the alarm about Pooh's vocabulary and what it was doing to the innocent ears of the seven-year-olds whose minds she was trying to mould, and Cadan had been given the word. Leave the bird at home if he couldn't keep him quiet and if he wanted to use the empty pool. So there had been no choice in the matter. Until today, he'd had to use the pool because so far he'd made not the slightest inroad with the town council about establishing trails for air jumping on Binner Down. Instead, they'd looked at him the way they would have looked at a psycho, and Cadan knew what they were thinking, which was just what his father not only thought but said: Twenty-two years old and you're playing with a *bicycle*? What the hell's the matter with you?

Nothing, Cadan thought. Not a sodding thing. You think this is *easy*? Tabletop? Tailwhip? Try it sometime.

But of course, they never would. Not the town councillors and not his dad. They'd just look at him and their expressions would say, Make something of your life. Get a job, for God's sake.

And that was what he had to tell his father: gainful employment was his. Pooh on his shoulder or not, he'd actually managed to acquire another job. Of course, his dad didn't need to know *how* he'd acquired it. He didn't need to know it was really all about Cadan asking if Adventures Unlimited had thought about the use to which its decrepit crazy golf course could be put and ending up with a brokered deal of maintenance work in the old hotel in exchange for utilising the crazy golf course's hills and dales – minus their windmills, barns, and other assorted structures, naturally – for perfecting air tricks. All Lew Angarrack had to know was that, sacked once again for his myriad failures in the family business – and who the *hell* wanted to shape surfboards anyway? – Cadan had gone out and replaced Job A with Job B within seventy-two hours. Which was something of a record, Cadan decided. He usually gave his dad an excuse to remain in a state of cheesed-off-at-him for five or six weeks at least.

He was jouncing along the unpaved lane behind Victoria Road and wiping the rain from his face when his father drove past him on the way to the house. Lew Angarrack didn't look at his son, although his expression of distaste told Cadan his father had clocked the sight he presented, not to mention been given a reminder of why his progeny was on a bicycle in the rain and no longer behind the wheel of his car.

Up ahead of him, Cadan saw his father get out of the RAV4 and open the garage door. He reversed the Toyota into the garage, and by the time Cadan wheeled his bicycle through the gate and into the back garden, Lew had already hosed off his surfboard. He was heaving his wet suit out of the four-by-four to wash it off as well, while the hosepipe burbled freshwater onto the patch of lawn.

Cadan watched him for a moment. He knew that he looked like his father, but their similarities ended with the physical. They had the same stocky bodies, with broad chests and shoulders, so they were built like wedges, and the same surfeit of dark hair, although his father was growing more and more of it over his body, so that he was starting to look like what Cadan's sister privately called him, which was Gorilla

Man. But that was it. As to the rest, they were chalk and cheese. His father's idea of a good time was making sure everything was permanently in its place with nothing changing one iota till the end of his days, while Cadan's was . . . well, decidedly different. His father's world was Casvelyn start to finish and if he ever made it to the north shore of Oahu – big dream, Dad, and you just keep dreaming – that would be the world's biggest all-time miracle. Cadan, on the other hand, had miles to go before he slept and the end of those miles was going to be his name in lights, the X Games, gold medals and his grinning mug on the cover of *Ride BMX*.

We see Cadan in action immediately, and through the use of his thoughts vis-à-vis being a spectacle, I can begin to give the reader a sense of what he looks like, following this with a fuller description from Cadan's POV as he compares himself to his father in the final paragraph. (Note: Since POV characters don't self-describe during a scene [unless a writer uses the hackneyed technique of having a character gaze into the mirror], the writer must figure out a way to describe them. Hence, Cadan's comparison of himself to his father.) Additionally, I have opportunities in this scene to give Cadan attitude and to begin developing his voice. This happens in the second paragraph not only through the choice of words that distinguish his POV from that of the other POV characters, but also his reactions to the teacher, the town councillors and to his father. The selection of action as his core need has allowed me to begin the scene in motion, and it has illuminated his relationship with his father and given the reader a sense of who he is.

As I've noted, a character's core need and her psychopathology add to the tension and the conflict in a scene. While the core need and psychopathology act to reveal who a character actually is, they also act to reveal who other characters are – through their reactions to the needs and the manoeuvres of those with whom they're interacting. Consider the creation of Dellen Kerne, the mother of the murder victim in the novel:

**DELLEN KERNE:** Dellen is the mother of the murder victim. At the time of the story she is 43 years old, one year younger than her husband, Ben. She's a woman who at one time was beautiful but whose looks have faded with what she's put her body through. She is **a little overweight** although not much, more **voluptuous-gone-to-seed** than anything else and **she's a smoker**. She no longer drinks – indeed, she belongs to AA although she doesn't work the programme well – and smoking is the last of her vices. She's shed the rest of them: sugar, alcohol and simple carbohydrates with the exception of chips. **She still eats chips although she has it down to once a week.** She has blonde hair which is no longer the blonde of her girlhood but now the blonde of the bottle. But it suits her because she grew up blonde. Blonde was one of the things she couldn't let go of. She has blue eyes. Her **skin is prematurely aged**, both from the sun and from the cigarettes. She wears makeup but she wears it well. She stays out of the sun now, although it's probably too late for that to do much good as the damage has been done. **She has the deep grooves of the smoker on her upper lip. She has the cough of the smoker, too.**

She was always curvy as a girl. She knew her body was her best feature. She knew it attracted men because it had attracted men from her childhood. She is the victim of **childhood molestation**, but she doesn't talk about this and most of the time she convinces herself it didn't happen anyway. The molester was . . . who? An uncle? A friend of the family? **A friend of the family** that she had been instructed to call Uncle Hugo? Yeah. It was **Uncle Hugo** and it went on for a number of years. **She never told anyone, and Uncle Hugo made it worth her while to keep her mouth shut:** toys, dresses, dolls, trips for ice cream, boat rides, etc. He never took her alone, so her parents were never suspicious. He took her brother as well. **Only what her parents never knew was that he gave her brother a little something to help him sleep so that he and Dellen could have their 'special time' together.**

So Dellen **associates her body with power** and she's used it that way her entire life. She's also mentally ill – **bipolar** – and when she's in a manic state, she becomes inappropriately sexual and she always has done. Marriage did not change that.

She lived in Pengelly Cove all of her life until she followed Ben to Truro. She is one of two children, and her father supported the family with **fishing**. He had two boats and a couple of crewmen, and they supplied hotels and restaurants with fish. He made a decent living from this, but they were not rich. Her mother also worked, alongside Ben's mother, in **a hotel in Pengelly Cove.** Ben's mother, however, worked in reception and in the office. Dellen's mother worked as a cleaner.

Dellen is **the firstborn child,** the apple of her father's eye because she is so pretty. She has sensuous, bee-stung lips, and as a child, she had perfect skin and gorgeous hair. She developed early: **by the time she was nine she needed to wear a bra,** and her period began when she was eleven. Her parents' greatest fear was that she would become pregnant, and she lived up to that fear by the time she was **fifteen, when she had her first abortion**. She had two abortions in the time she was with Ben and two abortions prior to Ben. You would think she would have done something to prevent this, but she always said she could not remember to take birth control pills. The reality is that she was not only acting out but also acting to be rescued.

This is Dellen's core need: **to be rescued**. She needed it as a little girl when Uncle Hugo was molesting her, but she didn't get it then and she continues to need it to this day. The fact that there is nothing she needs to be rescued from doesn't matter. The need is there, and it has gone unfulfilled since it wasn't fulfilled at the time she required. So no matter what, she has this sense that **she needs the knight to come along and take her away from all this.**

'All this' could be anything stressful. **When she is under stress, her behaviour is triggered, and her behaviour is to seduce men.** Most of her adult life she's had affairs and Ben understands that she's sick. He doesn't forgive her behaviour. But he understands it. Since they've been married, she's had more affairs than he wants to think about – during Santo's illness, as part of postpartum blues, when business wasn't going well and he (Ben) had to work extra hours, when he became a partner, when her mother developed ovarian cancer and died within three months – and **now with Santo's death it's likely she's going to go into an episode again. She's even had two abortions while she was married to Ben because she knows they're not his children.** He has agreed to these abortions, but he's walked the floors many nights because of them as well.

Rescue is her core need. Inappropriate sexuality is her pathological manoeuvre.

She is the marketing director at Adventures Unlimited. But there is a limit to what she can accomplish so she has an **assistant, a young man just out of technical college who's a whiz with computers.** He seems unlikely to be attractive to her, which is why Ben hires him although he would have preferred to hire a girl so that Dellen wouldn't have temptation. I would say that **Dellen has already come on to him,** an act that she calls 'testing the waters'. Think of her like Jessica Lange's character in *Blue Sky*. She's sick. She's not evil.

She left school at sixteen, as soon as she was able. She has always had one kind of job or another: shop assistant, waitress, house cleaner, child minder. **But she was always waiting for someone to come along and rescue her from these jobs.** Being sexual – getting a young man in her thrall – was a way that she saw herself as being rescued. The ultimate rescue, of course, was going to be to get some guy to marry her. Ben was the lucky one.

She has no girlfriends, not a single one. **She couldn't keep them** because she would go after their boyfriends or their husbands. She doesn't know how to be friends with other women. She only knows how to relate to men. And even then, it's purely sexual. On any other level as a human being, she's unable to connect.

How does she feel about her children? **She adores Santo.** He looks a great deal like her and as he is a sexual and sensual being, like her, she can relate. **But in her bad periods, both children have to be kept away from her** because they cause her undue stress and she cannot cope. So they are sent to their grandparents, Ben's parents. **They've sometimes been there for two months at a time.** Her relationship with her daughter has not been good since the daughter became an adolescent and became aware of her mother's sexual behaviour. **Her mother acted inappropriately around the boys who were interested in the daughter,** even with boys as young as twelve, and that was it. They have had no real relationship since although the daughter still lives at home and works in the family business. She does it for her father's sake because she feels sorry for him.

Her relationship with her own family is distant. Her parents washed their hands of her when she had her second abortion. They didn't know what was wrong with her and they didn't have the resources to find out. **For a time she lived with Uncle Hugo**, getting what she could off him in exchange for the occasional use of her body. By the time she met Ben, she was living with a flatmate above a café in Pengelly Cove. This flatmate was one in a long series. Dellen couldn't keep a flatmate any longer than she could keep a girlfriend.

She's a wild one, but she's not a hard one. In other words, **she didn't mix in with gangs**. She was a loner but because she flirted so successfully, she was also always **the life and soul of any party**.

Ben meets her during one of her manic episodes. She reels him in. They have sex the fifth time they see each other, because Dellen is able to sense that Ben is different from other boys and she might be able to reel him in. It's Ben's first experience with sex. He can hardly believe his luck.

Obviously, what moulded her was Uncle Hugo. Being handed over to him without anyone knowing what he was doing to her, having to dissociate to survive the molestation, going into mania because of the stress, crashing into depression. She has used other people to cope with this – people who have been willing to rescue her for a period of time – and these people have always been men.

How does she dress? Seductively when she is in mania mode. When she is in depressive mode, she has been known not to dress at all. **The death of Santo will put her into mania mode.** She wears red when she's manic. No. That doesn't make sense. It will put her into depression, I would think. Or maybe not. It will trigger an incident. Maybe she is **in the middle of a mania when he's killed** [I love this].

She blames her husband for Santo's death because Santo was out there climbing to please him, to get a better job with Adventures Unlimited.

Ben accepts this as his due. He blames himself. So she's in crisis and it's likely she is going to have the first available man, which looks like coming on to Lynley or getting it off with the kid who's helping her with the marketing. In either case, she's on the edge of doing something to relieve her stress, but something that will also cause the family even more grief and something that will cause her husband humiliation. But that's fine by her. **She thinks he deserves to be humiliated.** It's his fault that Santo is dead.

But who's the woman that Santo is having the affair with, then? I thought it was a friend of his mother? Maybe it's an acquaintance of his mother or an acquaintance of his father: the estate agent who sold him the property that they turned into Adventures Unlimited? The wife of the contractor who worked on the building? The life partner of the contractor who worked on the building? The interior designer who worked with the family to put the project together and figure out how to use the old hotel's space? Yes, it's probably that one. She's a space expert, let's say, not an interior designer. **[I changed this. See Aldara Pappas.]**

In creating Dellen, I wanted to explore the character of someone who has untreated bipolar disorder. Rather than jump into that topic, however, I began with an understanding of what she looks like and what her backstory is. The fact that her disorder has always gone untreated is going to be reflected in her backstory, in her present story, and in her relationships with everyone, most particularly her relationships with her family. Their reactions to her during the scenes they share with her will illustrate, I hope, something about their characters as well as a great deal about Dellen.

Her most troubled relationship is with her daughter, and when she's in a scene with Kerra, the reader is allowed not only to witness Dellen at her most manipulative but also to experience Kerra's reaction to her mother's manipulations. Thus we have a two-birds-with-one-stone situation as I attempt to use one character's core need – to be rescued – to reveal another character's attitude.

In the partial scene that follows, Kerra confronts her mother in the bedroom that she shares with Kerra's father. She's found a postcard among the belongings of her boyfriend, and she's jumped to a painful conclusion because of that card, which she takes with her to confront her mother.

When [Kerra] turned, she saw that her parents' bed was lumpy and the sheets were stained. A pile of her father's clothes lay on the floor, as if his body had dissolved and left this trace of him behind. Dellen herself was not immediately evident, until Kerra walked round the bed and found her lying on the floor, atop a considerable pile of her own clothing. Red, this was, and it seemed to be every article of crimson that she possessed.

For only an instant as she gazed down upon her, Kerra felt renewed: a bulb's single flower finally being released from both the soil and the stalk. But then her mother's lips worked and her tongue appeared between them, French kissing the air. Her hand opened and closed. Her hips moved then rested. Her eyelids twitched. She sighed.

Seeing this, Kerra wondered for the first time what it was actually like to *be* this woman. But she didn't want to entertain that thought, so she used her foot to flip her mother's right leg roughly off her left leg. 'Wake up,' she told her. 'It's time to talk.' She gazed at the postcard's picture to gain the strength she needed. *This is it* her mother's red writing said. Yes, Kerra thought. This was definitely it. 'Wake up,' she said again, more loudly. 'Get up from the floor.'

Dellen opened her eyes. For a moment she looked confused, until she saw Kerra. And then she pulled to her the garments nearest her right hand. She clutched these to her breasts and, in doing so, she uncovered a pair of shears and a carving knife. Kerra looked from these to her mother to the clothes. She saw that every item on the floor had been rendered useless through slashing, slicing, hacking and cutting.

'I should have used them on myself,' Dellen said dully. 'But I couldn't. Still, wouldn't you have been happy had I done it? You and your father? Happy? Oh God, I want to die. Why won't anyone help me die?' She began to weep tearlessly and as she did so, she drew more and more of the clothing to her until she'd formed an enormous pillow of ruined clothes.

Kerra knew what she was meant to feel: guilt. She also knew what she was meant to do: forgive. Forgive and forgive until you were the incarnation of forgiveness. Understand until there was nothing left of you except that effort to understand.

'Help me.' Dellen extended her hand. Then she dropped it to the floor. The gesture was useless, virtually noiseless.

Kerra shoved the damning postcard back into her pocket. She grabbed her mother's arm and hauled her upwards. She said, 'Get up. You need to bathe.'

'I can't,' Dellen said. 'I'm sinking. I'll be gone soon enough and long before I can. . .' And then a wily shift, perhaps reading from Kerra's face a brittleness of which she needed to be wary. She said, 'He threw out my pills. He had me this morning. Kerra, he . . . he as much as raped me. And then he . . . And then he . . . Then he threw out my pills.'

Kerra shut her eyes tight. She didn't want to think about her parents' marriage. She merely wanted to force the truth from her mother, but she needed to direct the course of that truth. 'Up,' she said. 'Come on. Come *on*. You've got to get up.'

'Why will no one listen to me? I can't go on like this. Inside my mind is a pit so deep . . . Why won't anyone help me? You? Your father? I want to die.'

Her mother was like a sack of sand and Kerra heaved her onto the bed. There Dellen lay. 'I've lost my *child*.' Her voice was broken. 'Why does no one begin to understand?'

'Everyone understands.' Kerra felt reduced inside, as if something were simultaneously squeezing her down and burning her up. Soon there would be nothing of her left. Only speaking would save her. 'Everyone knows you've lost a child, because *everyone* else has lost Santo, too.'

'But his mother . . . only his mother, Kerra—'

'Please.' Something snapped within Kerra. She reached for Dellen and pulled her upright, forcing her to sit on the edge of the bed. 'Stop the drama,' she said.

'Drama?' As so often had happened in the past, Dellen's mood shifted, like an unanticipated seismic event. 'You can call this drama?' she demanded. 'Is that how you react to your own brother's murder? What's the matter with you? Have you no feelings? My God, Kerra. Whose daughter *are* you?'

'Yes,' Kerra said. 'I expect you've asked yourself *that* question a number of times, haven't you. Counting back the weeks and the months and wondering . . . Who does she look like? Who does she belong to? Who can I say fathered her and – this would be critical, wouldn't it, Dellen? – will *he* believe me? Oh, p'rhaps if I look pathetic enough. Or pleased enough. Or happy enough. Or *whatever* it is that you look when you know you've got to explain some mess you've made.'

Dellen's eyes had grown dark. She'd shrunk away from Kerra. She said, 'How can you possibly say . . . ?' and her hands rose to cover her face in a gesture that Kerra assumed was meant to be read as horror.

It was time. Kerra pulled the postcard from her pocket. She said, 'Oh, stop it,' and she knocked her mother's hands to one side and held the postcard to Dellen's face. She put a hand on the back of her neck so Dellen could not remove herself from their conversation. She said, 'Have a look at what I found. "This is it," Mum? "This is *it*"? What, exactly? What is "it"?'

'What are you talking about? Kerra, I don't—'

'You don't *what*? You don't know what I've got in my hand? You don't recognise the picture on this card? You don't recognise your own bloody writing? Or is it this: You don't know where this card even came from and if you *do* know – because we both damn well know that you know, all right? – then you just can't imagine how it managed to get there. Which is it, Mum? Answer me. Which?'

'It's nothing. It's just a postcard, for heaven's sake. You're behaving like—'

'Like someone whose mother fucked the man she thought she was

going to marry,' Kerra cried. 'In this cave where you fucked the rest of
them.'

In this scene, I'm attempting to show the reader the nature of Dellen's
sickness – the colour red is the indication of a manic episode on its way – as
well as the sort of manipulations in which she engages. Additionally, I'm
hoping to show Kerra fast approaching the end of her rope when she will
have to confront what it is within her that prompts her to believe she's been
betrayed. With very good reason – indeed, with a lifetime of reasons – she
distrusts her mother. But her partner, Alan, has given her no reason to
distrust him, and it is her natural inclination to distrust that Kerra will
have to come to terms with during the course of the novel. Since the scene
is written through her eyes (i.e., in her POV), we are exposed to a description of Dellen as well as to Kerra's attitude towards her.

I hope you can see that core needs and pathological manoeuvres are not
merely assigned to characters. They grow from my understanding of the
being I'm creating as I freewrite, and they take into account the characters'
backstories, both how they are developed and how they are used.

At this point, it should be obvious where a character's backstory comes
from: the stream-of-consciousness writing that drives the character analysis forward. If I'm touching as many of the bases as I can while I freewrite
about the character (the bases being the list found on the character prompt
sheet), I'm in the act of *creating* backstory as I go along, because I'm writing
about the character's relationships, her family background, her education,
her sexuality, etc., and what comes from this is her backstory.

Being aware of each character's backstory allows me to understand and
to illustrate her attitude towards any situation she finds herself in. It allows
me to understand her attitude towards other characters as well. Backstory

will be part of what determines a character's actions and reactions. It will add to tension and to conflict, the core of drama. It will help to keep a character *in* character because knowing the backstory allows me to see at once if a character would actually act the way she's acting in a scene.

The tricky bit about backstory is this, though: very little of it will actually appear in the book, and it's essential not to create what I call the Dread Flashback in order to fit the backstory into the novel. The Dread Flashback rips the reader out of the overall story, which is the last thing you want to happen. Because a flashback is a fully realised scene or even a group of scenes – and not just a momentary memory, for example – it can end up stalling out the story you're attempting to tell. Worse, it can end up sending your story hurtling in another direction. It's generally not related thematically to the rest of the novel either. This gives the reader the sense of a novel that's clunking and groaning along instead of running smoothly. So I advise you to resist the siren call of the Dread Flashback. Even if you've created the most compelling backstory *ever* for a character, I advise that you use it for attitude and for shading and not because you think your character must be explained to the reader in some fashion. Indeed, the point is that a well-drawn character doesn't *have* to be explained to the reader at all.

If you think of your own personal backstory, you will probably see that while it influences a lot of what you do, how you react, and what you think, it's not something that you bring up in general conversation unless you are asked about it or find it relevant to what's happening in the moment you're living through.

In *Careless in Red*, the character with the backstory that was most compelling for me was the POV character Daidre Trahair. Her backstory begged to be told. Yet it was crucial that the reader not know what she is hiding until she's ready to tell Lynley, who has quickly realised that she's hiding *something*. The moment when I felt I could hint at her backstory came from the following picture, which I took inside one of the many churches I visited when I was in Cornwall doing my location research. I

didn't know at the time if I would use it since I didn't yet have the plot kernel, the generic list of characters or the specific list of characters.

Image 17 shows something called an 'honesty stall'. It was at the back

IMAGE 17

of a church, and it displayed quirky secondhand items, some of which are depicted in the picture. One could purchase them, the cost of an item being put into a little strongbox that would be occasionally emptied. I'd never seen an honesty stall in a church before (and I had been in hundreds of English country churches at that point, having something of a passion for them), so I photographed this one. Whether I would use it or not wasn't something that I thought about at the time.

However, in writing a scene in which Daidre and Lynley go to a place called Pengelly Cove, I found an opportunity to touch upon not only her backstory but also what she was hiding.

An exploration of Pengelly Cove didn't take a great deal of time. After the shop and the two main streets, there was either the cove itself, an old church sitting just outside town or the Curlew Inn to occupy one's time. Once she was left alone in the village, Daidre began with the church. She reckoned it might be locked up tight, as so many country churches were in these days of religious indifference and vandalism, but she was wrong. The place was called St. Sithy's, and it was open, sitting in the middle of a graveyard where the remains of this year's daffodils still lined the paths, giving way to columbine.

Within, the church smelled of stones and dust, and the air was cold. There was a switch for lights just inside the door, and Daidre used this to illuminate a single aisle, a nave, and a collection of multi-coloured ropes that looped down from the bell tower. A roughly hewn granite baptismal font stood to her left, while to her right, an un-evenly placed stone aisle led to pulpit and altar. It could have been any church in Cornwall save for one difference: an honesty stall. This comprised a table and shelves just beyond the baptismal font, and upon it used goods were for sale, with a locked wooden box serving as the till.

Daidre went to inspect all this and found no organisation to it but rather a quirky charm. Old lace mats mingled with the odd bit of porcelain; glass beads hung from the necks of well-used stuffed animals. Books eased away from their spines; cake plates and pie tins offered garden tools instead of sweets. There was even a shoe box of historic postcards, which she flipped through to see that most of them were already written upon, stamped and received long ago. Among them was a depiction of a gipsy caravan, of the sort she hadn't seen in years: rounded on the top and gaily painted, celebrating a peripatetic life. Unexpectedly, her vision blurred when she picked up this card. Unlike so many of the others, nothing had been written upon it.

She wouldn't have done so at another time, but she bought the card. Then she bought two others with messages on them: one from an Auntie Hazel and Uncle Dan that depicted fishing boats in Padstow Harbour and another from Binkie and Earl showing a line of surfers standing in front of long Malibu boards that were upright in the Newquay sand. *Fistral Beach* scrolled across their feet, and this was apparently the location where – according to either Binkie or Earl – *It happened here!!!! Wedding's next December!*

With these in her possession, Daidre left the church. But not before she looked at the prayer board, where members of the congregation posted their requests for collective appeals to their mutual deity. Most of these had to do with health, and it came to Daidre how seldom people seemed to consider their God unless physical illness descended upon them or upon someone they loved.

She was not religious, but here was an opportunity, she realised, to step up to the spiritual cricket pitch. The God of chance was bowling and she stood in front of the wicket with the bat in her hands. To swing or not and what did it matter? were the issues before her. She'd been searching the Internet for miracles, hadn't she? What was this but another arena in which a miracle might be found?

She picked up the biro provided and a slip of paper, which turned out to be part of the back of an old handout on which a bake sale was being advertised. She flipped this to the blank side and she started to write. She got as far as *Please pray for*, but she found that she could advance no further. She couldn't find the words to shape her request because she wasn't even sure it *was* her request. So to write it and then to post it on a board for prayers proved too monumental a task, one that was coloured by a hypocrisy that she could not bear to live with. She replaced the pen, balled up the slip of paper and shoved it into her pocket. She left the church.

I didn't use the actual items in the real honesty stall, and it was only when I was in the middle of the scene that I realised how the moment and the stall could be used to heighten the reader's interest in Daidre and touch upon her backstory. For me, this is part of what's crucial to my process: the serendipity of seeing something and being able to use it later in a flash of inspiration.

You might be wondering how many characters I create and analyse for my novels. The number depends upon how many generic characters I see inhabiting the world of the crime and its subsequent investigation. Generally, it's about fifteen characters. Often it's more. And not all of the characters that I create end up appearing in the novel. I don't force anyone to 'come onstage'. Sometimes after I've created a character and have moved on to the plotting of the book, I see that while that individual was interesting and while she might colour someone's attitude or past, that character really isn't necessary to do what I'm attempting to do in the novel.

There are also times when an unanticipated character shows up for a single appearance in a single scene, and I discover this when I'm writing the plot outline. Cilla Cormack is an example of this. The detectives have been to Falmouth to dig up some information applying to Daidre Trahair. Cilla is the motorcycling granddaughter of one of the Trahair family's neighbours. She's been sent by her grandmother to bring Daidre the message. That's her only purpose in her only scene in the book. An analysis of her isn't necessary. But giving her an attitude is. You'll see her in action in a subsequent chapter.

## Optional Exercise 1

Earlier, you named three characters. You established the relationships among them. Now choose one of those three characters and create that character through an analysis. Write in present tense. Try to freewrite or stream-of-consciousness write. Use the character prompt sheet as a guide. There are no incorrect ways to do this, so give yourself the freedom to write as you will, moulding a living and breathing human being out of nothing but your willingness to try out a process.

## Optional Exercise 2

Having created the character, now reveal something about her or him in a brief scene. Do this by putting that character into some kind of action with a household appliance like a refrigerator, a vacuum, a washing machine, etc.

# CHAPTER 4

# Landscape

*The Inner and Outer World of Characters*

I think of my characters as having a landscape into which they fit, so I create two kinds of landscape for them: the landscape of place and the landscape of person. This gives me yet another area I can use to illustrate who the characters are because both landscape of place and landscape of person involve decisions that the characters have made. Those decisions say much about who they are.

The landscape of place deals with all aspects of the various environments in which a character operates. This can include the dwelling where she lives as well as the environment in which she works and otherwise operates. Image 18 is an example of one part of a character's landscape of place.

It's called a vinery, and it's used to grow grapes in a climate where they otherwise wouldn't grow. In the novel, it became part of a property called Binner Down House, where one of the suspects lives. The reader is introduced to the property first and the vinery second as the landscape description moves from general to specific:

Will lived at Binner Down House with nine surfers, male and female. He was the odd man out. He didn't ride the waves because he didn't like sharks and he wasn't overly fond of weever fish either. Cadan found

IMAGE 18

him on the south side of the property, which was an ancient place in the sort of condition a property gets into when it's near the sea and no one takes proper care of it. So the land surrounding it was overgrown with gorse, bracken and a tangle of sea grasses. A single gnarled cypress in what went for a front garden needed trimming, and weeds took the place of a lawn that had too long fought the good fight against them. The building itself was in sore need of repair, especially with regard to roof tiles and the wood surrounds of windows and doors. But the oc-cupants had more important concerns than property maintenance, and a disreputable shed in which their surfboards lined up like colour-ful place markers in a book served as ample evidence of this. As did their wet suits, which generally hung to dry from the lower branches of the cypress.

The south side of the house faced Binner Down, from whose en-
virons floated the lowing of cows. Along the wall of the building, a triangular sort of greenhouse had been fashioned. Its glass roof tilted into
the house, with one side of it also glass and the other comprising the
existing granite of the old building, but painted white to reflect the sun.
This was a vinery, Cadan had learned, its purpose being to grow
grapes.

Cadan found Will inside. He was bent to accommodate the tilted
glass of the ceiling, digging round the base of an infant grapevine.
When Cadan entered, Will straightened and said, 'Fuck all, it's about
bloody time,' before he saw who it was coming through the door.
'Sorry,' he then said. 'I thought it was one of them.' He was, Cadan
knew, referring to his surfing housemates.

'Still not helping round here?'

You'll note that the reader experiences Binner Down House from the
POV of Cadan Angarrack. The scene is crafted to go from the general
description of the location to the specific spot on the property where most
of the scene will occur. After that, the depiction of place narrows even
more when Cadan enters the vinery to speak to Will Mendick, our suspect.
To create this particular setting, I pulled together details of various locations that I had visited during my research trip to Cornwall: ramshackle
houses I'd seen in various beach environments; homes overgrown with
weeds, seagrasses and bracken; a field of cows I'd seen behind one house;
and a vinery at a great house I'd come across, a greenhouse in which Vic-
torians grew their table grapes.

Will's choice of living environment – this tumbling-down building that
he shares with nine surfers – and his engagement with the environment
form an introduction to him that, I hope, will remain in the reader's memory so that upon his next appearance the reader won't need to flip back
pages to see who he is. He will be fixed in the reader's mind. Additionally,

it's my hope that the vinery adds a detail that will lift the environment from a generic ramshackle house to a specific place.

One of the things I enjoy about doing location research is experiencing the unexpected and realising it can be useful at some point in the book. Such was the case with the landscape of place that Lynley discovers when he interviews one Eddie Kerne, the grandfather of the dead boy.

In dressing one morning to go out and about in Cornwall, I had the television on, and whatever programme I was watching at the time did a special story on a gentleman somewhere in the countryside in England who was determined to live off the land in the fullest sense of the word, including generating electricity from a fast-moving stream on his property. The story and the man stuck with me, giving me not only some telling details about Eddie Kerne, but also introducing the particular landscape in which Ben Kerne – the father of the victim – grew up. Here's what it looked like:

> Lynley parked near a stand of old bicycles. Only one of them had inflated tyres, and all of them were rusting to the point of disintegration. There appeared to be no direct route to the front or back door of the house. A path meandered from the bicycles in the vague direction of the scaffolding, but once in its near presence, it transformed to the occasional brick or two lying together amidst trampled weeds. By stepping from one set of bricks to the other, Lynley finally reached what seemed to be the entrance to the house: a door so pitted by weather, rot and insect life that it seemed hardly credible to assume it was in working order.
>
> It was, however. A few knocks forcefully applied to wood brought him face-to-face with an old and badly shaven gentleman, one eye

clouded by a cataract. He was roughly and somewhat colourfully dressed in old khaki trousers and a lime green cardigan that was drooping round the elbows. He had sandals and orange-and-brown Argyll socks on his feet. Lynley decided he had to be Eddie Kerne. He produced his identification for the man as he introduced himself.

Kerne looked from it to him. He turned and walked away from the door, heading wordlessly back into the bowels of the house. The door hung open, so Lynley assumed he was meant to follow, which he did.

The interior of the house wasn't a great improvement over the exterior. It appeared to be a work long in progress, if the age of the exposed timbers was anything to go by. Walls along the central passage into the place had long ago been taken down to their framing, but there was no scent of freshly replaced wood here. Instead there was a fur of dust upon the timbers, suggesting that a job had been begun years in the past without ever reaching completion.

A workshop was Kerne's destination, and to get to it he led Lynley through a kitchen and a laundry room that featured a washing machine with an old-fashioned wringer and thick cords crisscrossing the ceiling where clothing was hung to dry in inclement weather. This room emanated the heavy scent of mildew, a sensory ambience only moderately improved upon when they got to the workshop beyond it. They reached this spot by means of a doorless opening in the far wall of the laundry room, separated from the rest of the house by a thick sheet of plastic that Kerne shoved to one side. This same sort of plastic covered what went for windows in the workshop, a room that had been fashioned more recently than the rest of the house: it was made of unadorned concrete blocks. It was frigid within, like an old-time larder without the marble shelves.

Lynley thought of the term *man-cave* when he stepped into the workshop. A workbench, haphazardly hung cupboards, one tall stool and myriad tools were crammed within, and the overall impression was one of sawdust, oil leakage, paint spills and general filth. It comprised a somewhat dubious spot for a bloke to escape the wife and children, with his excuse the crucial tinkering on this or that project.

There appeared to be plenty of them on Eddie Kerne's workbench: part of a hoover, two broken lamps, a hair dryer missing its flex, five teacups wanting handles, a small footstool belching its stuffing. Kerne seemed to be at work on the teacups, for an uncapped tube of glue was adding to the other scents in the room, most of which were associated with the damp. Tuberculosis seemed the likely outcome of an extended stay in such a place, and Kerne had a heavy cough that made Lynley think of poor Keats writing anguished letters to his beloved Fanny.

Placing Eddie Kerne in a detailed landscape allows the reader what I hope is a glimpse into the man's character. Instead of someone who exists in the novel merely to give information to the police, he becomes a real individual with quirky tastes and somewhat bizarre beliefs. He has existed before the novel began. He will continue to exist once the novel ends. That's part of what landscape does, adding to the verisimilitude of what the reader is reading.

Anything the writer pulls out of an individual setting can illuminate character. The point is to make the depiction of that object *specific* to that character. It would be unlikely that Lynley would be living in the same sort of environment that houses Eddie Kerne. Indeed, it would be unlikely that any other character in *Careless in Red* would be living in such a place.

## Optional Exercise 1

You have earlier created a character. Now put that character into a setting. Do this by creating a two-page narrative that reflects landscape of place. It should move from the general landscape to a specific spot in that landscape where the character is at the moment of your narrative. In this narrative, use details of the vehicle he or she drives. Enrich the scene by illustrating the character's attitude towards either the vehicle or the setting.

Just as I create a landscape of place, I also create a landscape of person. I further subdivide this into the outer landscape of person and the inner landscape of person.

The outer landscape of person encompasses all the details of a character's physical appearance. There are many possibilities from which the details can emerge: manner of dress, hair type or lack thereof, hairstyle, body type, face, scars, birthmarks, teeth, skin, deliberate external alterations (shaven head, tattoos, ear gauges, nose rings, various piercings, plastic surgeries, failed plastic surgeries), birth defects, chosen adornments (jewellery, glasses, sunglasses, political buttons, T-shirts with slogans), hats and shoes (stilettos, Doc Martens, Birkenstocks, Roman sandals, flip-flops, tennis shoes, designer trainers, hiking boots). Within the description of a person, though, it's the careful selection of detail that makes the character memorable while it also reveals something about her. I call this a *telling* detail.

Additionally, a character's hobbies, pursuits, activities, interests, collections, souvenirs, etc., can be part of her landscape of person. They, too, reveal something about who the character is without my having to spell it out.

An examination of Image 19 and Image 20 can give you telling outer details of person without much difficulty. We should be able to draw conclusions or to make speculations about the characters depicted, and those conclusions can go beyond the fact that in one picture a man is holding a guitar and in the other a woman is holding a cat. The point is that the details of these people in the pictures make them individuals who are specific and not merely generic.

IMAGE 19

IMAGE 20

. . .

The inner landscape of person comprises what is going on *inside* a character. While this interior landscape is generally revealed to the reader in one form or another, it is not necessarily known by the other characters in the novel.

Inner landscape comes from the writer's knowledge of the agenda of every character in every scene. It comes from the writer's establishing what will be the overall intention of each character in the course of the novel. This inner landscape appears whenever a character pauses to reflect, consider, speculate, or dwell upon a circumstance that has occurred in the book. As so much also does, it should reflect the character's attitude.

> Despite Jago's warning, Cadan couldn't help himself. It was complete insanity and he damn well knew it, but he engaged in it anyway: the soft silken feel of her thighs tightening round him; the sound of her moaning and then the heightened growing rapturous *yes* of her response, and this set against a backdrop of waves crashing against the nearby shore; the mixed scents of the sea, of her female smells, and of wood rot from the tiny beach hut; the eternal female salt of her where he licked as she shrieked and *yes yes* as her fingers dug into his hair; the dim light from the cracks round the door casting a nearly ethereal glow on skin that was slick but lithe and firm and willing God so eager and ever so willing. . .
>
> It *could* have been like that, Cadan thought, and despite the growing lateness of the day he wasn't all that far from establishing Pooh in the sitting room, hauling his bicycle out of the garage and pedalling frantically to Adventures Unlimited to take Dellen Kerne up on her offer to meet at the beach huts. He'd seen just enough films in the cinema to know that the older woman–younger man bit was never perfect – let

alone permanent – which was a plus as far as he was concerned. The very idea of having it on with Dellen Kerne was all so right in Cadan's mind that it had moved quite beyond rightness into another realm altogether: into the sublime, the mystical, the metaphysical. The only metaphorical monkey in the barrel was, alas, Dellen herself.

The woman was a nutter, no question about it. Despite his longing to press his lips to various parts of her body, Cadan knew barm when he saw barm, providing barm was actually a word, which he seriously doubted. But if it wasn't a word, it needed to be one, and she was barm in spades. She was the walking, talking, breathing, eating, sleeping personification of barm, and the one thing Cadan Angarrack was besides randy enough to take on a herd of sheep was clever enough to give barm a wide berth.

Here we see the inner landscape of Cadan Angarrack as he reflects upon an offer of sex made to him by Dellen Kerne. These paragraphs are entirely in Cadan's head, and as such, they must show his attitude, be written in his voice and demonstrate his pattern of thought. Sexual opportunity in the form of his employer's wife has come knocking on his door, and there's an ironic flavour to how he's looking upon this prospect.

## Optional Exercise 2

Using the same vehicle from the last exercise, create a scene with the same character as before. The difference this time will be to use the vehicle and the character to display that character's inner landscape through a reflection, speculation, consideration, inner argument, memory, etc. I might repeat here that a character's memory is not the same as the Dread Flashback. A flashback, remember, is a scene fully played out. A memory is swift and fleeting, usually triggered by a sensory experience such as the scent of incense used on occasion in religious rituals, the smell of diesel fumes on a rainy day, the sound of children singing a familiar song from one's own childhood, etc.

It's important not to confuse landscape of character with setting. Setting is also filled with details, but these aren't specific to a character. Rather they are specific to a place, and their presence in a novel heightens the book's setting and makes it different from all others.

I've always loved books that thrust me into settings because the experience allows me to be where the characters are at any given moment. The key to creating setting is to remember that we experience place through all our senses, not merely through sight.

No place is identical to another place, and this is especially true in the UK. It's my job to pull from a place I'm visiting the elements that will make it come alive for the reader: the old mining works in Cornwall, the peel towers in Cumbria, the thatched cottages of Hampshire, the drystone walls of the Lake District, the pargeting of Cambridgeshire, the pillboxes of Essex, the downs, the moors, the building materials, the flora, the fauna, the weather, the quality of the air. All of this becomes part of my research, and then it becomes part of the setting of the book, and *then* a specific detail or a specific building or tree or rock or *whatever* within that setting becomes part of the landscape.

When I think I have all the material I need, I try to remember that my job is to *render* the setting, not to relate it. By this I mean that setting doesn't exist absent of characters in a novel. Something big or something small is going on in the setting, and the sooner I can make that happen, the better. Thus, as *Careless in Red* opens, the reader is thrust simultaneously into setting and character. Neither exists without the other.

# CHAPTER 5

# Dialogue

*Revealing a Character Through Speech*

Early in the novel, as we've seen, Daidre Trahair arrives at her holiday cottage in Cornwall and sees that it has been broken into:

Although she knew she should have been frightened, or at least cautious, Daidre was, instead, infuriated by that broken window. She pushed the door open in a state of high dudgeon and stalked through the kitchen to the sitting room. There she stopped. In the dim light of the tenebrous day outside, a form was coming out of her bedroom. He was tall, he was bearded, and he was so filthy that she could smell him from across the room.

She said, 'I don't know who the hell you are or what you're doing here, but you *are* going to leave directly. If you don't leave, I shall become violent with you, and I assure you, you do *not* want that to happen.'

Then she reached behind her for the switch to the lights in the kitchen. She flipped it and illumination fell broadly across the sitting room to the man's feet. He took a step towards her, which brought him fully into the light, and she saw his face.

She said, 'My God. You're injured. I'm a doctor. May I help?'

He gestured towards the sea. From this distance, she could hear the waves, as always, but they seemed closer now, the sound of them driven inland by the wind. 'There's a body on the beach,' he said. 'It's up on the rocks. At the bottom of the cliff. It's . . . he's dead. I broke in. I'm sorry. I'll pay for the damage. I was looking for a phone to ring the police. What is this place?'

'A body? Take me to him.'

'He's dead. There's nothing—'

'Are you a doctor? No? I am. Take me to him. We're losing time when we could otherwise be saving a life.'

The man looked as if he would protest. She wondered if it was disbelief. You? A doctor? Far too young. But he apparently read her determination. He took off the cap he was wearing. He wiped the arm of his jacket along his forehead, inadvertently streaking mud on his face. His light hair, she saw, was overlong, and his colouring was identical to hers. Both trim, both fair, they might have been siblings, even to the eyes. His were brown. So were hers.

He said, 'Very well. Come with me,' and he came across the room and passed her, leaving behind the acrid scent of himself: sweat, unwashed clothing, unbrushed teeth, body oil, and something else, more profound and more disturbing. She backed away from him and kept her distance as they left the cottage and started down the lane.

The wind was fierce. They struggled against it and into the rain as they made their way swiftly towards the beach. They passed the point where the valley stream opened into a pool before tumbling across a natural breakwater and rushing down to the sea. This marked the beginning of Polcare Cove, a narrow strand at low water, just rocks and boulders when the tide was high.

The man called into the wind, 'Over here,' and he led her to the north side of the cove. From that point, she needed no further direction. She could see the body on an outcropping of slate: the bright red windcheater, the loose dark trousers for ease of movement, the thin and exceedingly flexible shoes. He wore a harness round his waist and from this dangled numerous metal devices and a lightweight bag from which a white substance spilled across the rock. Chalk for his hands, she thought. She moved to see his face.

She said, 'God. It's . . . He's a cliff climber. Look, there's his rope.'

Part of it lay nearby, an extended umbilical cord to which the body was still attached. The rest of it snaked from the body to the bottom of the cliff, where it formed a rough mound, knotted skilfully with a cara-biner protruding from the end.

She felt for a pulse although she knew there would be none. The cliff at this point was two hundred feet high. If he'd fallen from there – as he most certainly had – only a miracle could have preserved him.

There had been no miracle. She said to her companion, 'You're right. He's dead. And with the tide . . . Look, we're going to have to move him or—'

'No!' The stranger's voice was harsh.

Daidre felt a rush of caution. 'What?'

'The police have to see it. We must phone the police. Where's the nearest phone? Have you a mobile? There was nothing . . .' He indi-cated the direction from which they'd come. There was no phone in the cottage.

'I haven't a mobile,' she said. 'I don't bring one when I come here. What does it matter? He's dead. We can see how it happened. The tide's coming in, and if we don't move him the water will.'

'How long?' he asked.

'What?'

'The tide. How long have we got?'

'I don't know.' She looked at the water. 'Twenty minutes? Half an hour? No more than that.'

'Where's a phone? You've got a car.' And in a variation of her own words, 'We're wasting time. I can stay here with the . . . with him, if you prefer.'

She didn't prefer. She had the impression he would depart like a spirit if she left things up to him. He would know she'd gone to make the phone call he so wanted made, but he himself would vanish, leaving her to . . . what? She had a good idea and it wasn't a welcome one.

She said, 'Come with me.'

Daidre's first moment of dialogue in the book at once establishes an aspect of her character. In doing so, it fulfils one of dialogue's purposes, which is to illustrate to the reader something about the nature of the person speaking, for the way a person speaks reveals as much about her character as do her actions, while her choice of words adds subtext to a scene, often by laying down dramatic questions. When characters are speaking, their words reveal, admit, incite, accuse, lie, inform, manipulate, misdirect, hint, order, encourage, etc., and in doing these things, they also act as a compact way to advance the story.

Revealing character, adding subtext, laying down dramatic questions, advancing the story: These are the functions of dialogue, making it a fundamental element of craft. Dialogue that doesn't fulfil any of these functions is dialogue that can be and probably should be deleted from a scene upon revision.

The moment Daidre Trahair speaks, we get the idea that she's someone who doesn't back down. She's tough, and she's probably had to be tough. But an instant later when she gets a better look at the man who's broken into her home, we are introduced to another aspect of her character as she realises that something is very wrong with him. She announces herself as a doctor, and she offers to help. Through this, we have two glimpses into her character and what follows this is dialogue from the man, which immediately addresses the plot of the novel, moving the story forward.

Because the characters are English, they must speak like English people, not only using English vocabulary but also English and not American
syntax. And their dialogue can suggest something about their social class
and their level of education. For example, the man says 'Very well' to
Daidre and not what would be said by the masses: 'Right then.'

*'We must phone the police.'*

*'Have you a mobile?'*

*'I haven't a mobile.'*

*'I was looking for a phone to ring the police.'*

These are all English ways of speaking, sometimes using a different
vocabulary from that used in American English, sometimes using different
syntax.

Consider the following scene between Aldara Pappas and Daidre
Trahair. It contains dialogue that's moulded to reflect their different cultures, backgrounds and education. At the same time, it reflects their characters. Since there is a third character in the scene, his dialogue needs to
do the same.

In the rearview mirror, she saw them come out of the police station.
Had Lynley been alone, she might have approached him for the conversation they needed to have, but as he was with both Sergeant Havers
and Inspector Hannaford, Daidre used this as a sign that the time
wasn't right. She was parked some way up the street, and when the
three police officers paused in the station's car park for a few words
together, she started her car and pulled away from the kerb. Intent
upon their conversation, none of them looked in her direction. Daidre
took that as a sign as well. There were those, she knew, who would call
her a coward for running just then. There were others, however,
who would congratulate her on having sound instincts towards self-
preservation.

She drove out of Casvelyn. She headed inland, first towards

Stratton and then across the countryside. She got out of her car at long last at the cider farm in the fast-fading daylight.

Circumstances, she decided, were asking her to forgive. But forgiveness ran in both directions, in every direction if it came down to it. She needed to ask as well as to give, and both of these activities were going to require practice.

Stamos the orchard pig was snuffling round his pen in the centre of the courtyard. Daidre went past him and round the corner of the jam kitchen, where inside and under bright lights two of the jam cooks were cleaning their huge copper pots for the day. She opened the gate beneath the arbour and entered the private part of the grounds. As before, she could hear guitar music. But this time more than one guitar was playing.

She assumed a record and knocked on the door. The music ceased. When Aldara answered, Daidre saw the other woman was not alone. A swarthy man in the vicinity of thirty-five was placing a guitar onto a stand. Aldara had hers tucked under her arm. She and the man had been playing, obviously. He was very good and, of course, so was she.

'Daidre,' Aldara said, neutrally. 'What a surprise. Narno was giving me a lesson.' Narno Rojas, she added, from Launceston. She went on to complete the introduction as the Spaniard rose to his feet and bowed his head slightly in acknowledgement. Daidre said hello and asked should she come back? 'If you're in the middle of a lesson. . . ,' she added. What she thought was, Leave it to Aldara to have found a male teacher of delectable appearance. He had the large dark eyes and thick eyelashes of a Disney cartoon hero.

'No, no. We've finished,' Aldara said. 'We were at the point of merely entertaining ourselves. Did you hear? Don't you think we're very good together?'

'I thought it was a recording,' Daidre admitted.

'You see?' Aldara cried. 'Narno, we *should* play together. I'm much better with you than I am alone.' And to Daidre, 'He's been lovely about giving me lessons. I made him an offer he could not refuse, and here we are. Isn't that the case, Narno?'

'It is,' he said. 'But you've much more the gift. For me, it is practice continual. For you . . . you merely need encouragement.'

'That's flattery. But if you choose to believe it, I won't argue. Anyway, that's the part you play. You're my encouragement, and I adore how you encourage me.'

He chuckled, raised her hand, and kissed her fingers. He wore a wide gold wedding band.

He packed his guitar into its case and bade them both farewell. Aldara saw him to the door and stepped outside with him. They murmured together. She returned to Daidre.

She looked, Daidre thought, like a cat who'd come upon an endless supply of cream. Daidre said, 'I can guess what the offer was.'

Aldara returned her own guitar to its case. 'What offer do you mean, my dear?'

'The one he couldn't refuse.'

'Ah.' Aldara laughed. 'Well. What will be will be. I have a few things to do, Daidre. We can chat while I do them. Come along, if you like.'

She led the way to a narrow set of stairs whose handrail was a thick velvet cord. She climbed and took Daidre up to the bedroom, where she set about changing the sheets on a large bed that took up most of the space.

'You think the worst of me, don't you?' Aldara said.

'Does it matter what I think?'

'Of course, it does not. How wise you are. But sometimes what you think isn't what is.' She flung the duvet to the floor and whipped the sheets off the mattress, folding them neatly rather than balling them up as another person might have done. She went to an airing cupboard in the tiny landing at the top of the stairs and brought out crisp linens, expensive by the look of them and fragrant as well. 'Our arrangement isn't a sexual one, Daidre,' Aldara said.

'I wasn't thinking—'

'Of course you were. And who could blame you? You know me, after all. Here. Help me with this, won't you?'

Daidre went to assist her. Aldara's movements were deft. She smoothed the sheets with affection for them. 'Aren't they lovely?' she asked. 'Italian. I've found a very good private laundress in Morwenstow. It's a bit of a drive to take them to her, but she does wonders with them, and I wouldn't trust my sheets to just anyone. They're too important, if you know what I mean.'

She didn't want to. To Daidre sheets were sheets, although she could tell these likely cost more than she made in a month. Aldara was a woman who didn't deny herself life's little luxuries.

'He has a restaurant in Launceston. I was there for dinner. When he wasn't greeting guests, he was playing his guitar. I thought, How much I could learn from this man. So I spoke with him and we came to an agreement. Narno will not take money, but he has a need to place members of his family – and he has a very large family – in more employment than he can provide at his restaurant.'

'So they work for you here?'

'I have no need. But Stamos has a continual need for workers round the hotel in St. Ives, and I find a former husband's guilt is a useful tool.'

'I didn't know you still speak to Stamos.'

'Only when it is helpful to me. Otherwise, he could disappear off the face of the earth and, believe me, I wouldn't bother to wave good-bye. Could you tuck that in properly, darling? I can't abide rucked sheets.'

She moved to Daidre's position and demonstrated deftly how she wanted the sheets seen to. She said, 'Nice and fresh and ready,' when she was done. Then she looked at Daidre fondly. The light in the room was greatly subdued, and in it Aldara shed twenty years. She said, 'This isn't to say we won't, eventually. Narno will, I think, make a most energetic lover, which is how I like them.'

'I see.'

'I know you do. The police were here, Daidre.'

'That's why I've come.'

'So you were the one. I suspected as much.'

'I'm sorry, Aldara, but I had no choice. They assumed it was me. They thought Santo and I—'

'And you had to safeguard your reputation?'

'It isn't that. It *wasn't* that. They need to get to the bottom of what happened to him, and they aren't going to get there if people don't start telling the truth.'

'Yes. I do see what you mean. But how often the truth is . . . well, rather inconvenient. If one person's truth is an unbearable blow to another person and simultaneously unnecessary for him to know, need one speak it?'

'That's hardly the issue here.'

'But it does seem that no one is quite telling the police everything there is to tell, wouldn't you say? Certainly, if they came to you at first instead of to me, it would be because little Madlyn did not tell them everything.'

'Perhaps she was too humiliated, Aldara. Finding her boyfriend in bed with her employer . . . That might have been more than she wanted to say.'

'I suppose.' Aldara handed over a pillow and its accompanying case for Daidre to sort out while she herself did the same with another. 'It's of no account now, though. They know it all. I myself told them about Max. Well, I had to, hadn't I? They were going to uncover his name eventually. My relationship with Max was not a secret. So I can hardly be cross with you, can I, when I also named someone to the police?'

'Did Max know . . . ?' Daidre saw from Aldara's expression that he did. 'Madlyn?' she asked.

'Santo,' Aldara said. 'Stupid boy. He was wonderful in bed. Such energy he had. Between his legs, heaven. But between his ears . . .' Aldara gave an elaborate shrug. 'Some men – no matter their age – do not operate with the sense God gave them.' She placed the pillow on the bed, and straightened the edge of its case, which was lace. She took the other from Daidre and did the same, going on to turn down the rest of the linen in a welcoming fashion. On the bedside table, a votive candle was nestled in a crystal holder. She lit this and stood back to admire the effect. 'Lovely,' she said. 'Rather welcoming, wouldn't you say?'

Daidre felt as if cotton wool were stuffed into her head. The situation was so much *not* what she believed it should be. She said, 'You don't actually regret his death, do you? D'you know how that makes you look?'

'Don't be foolish. Of course, I regret it. I would not have had Santo Kerne die as he did. But as I wasn't the one to kill him—'

'You're very likely the reason he died, for God's sake.'

'I very seriously doubt that. Certainly Max has too much pride to kill an adolescent rival and anyway Santo *wasn't* his rival, a simple fact that I could not make Max see. Santo was just . . . Santo.'

'A boytoy.'

'A boy, yes. A toy, rather. But that makes it sound cold and calculating and believe me it was neither. We enjoyed each other and that's what it was between us, only. Enjoyment. Excitement. On both parts, not just on mine. Oh, you *know* all this, Daidre. You cannot plead ignorance. And you quite understand. You would not have lent your cottage had you not.'

'You feel no guilt.'

Aldara waved her hand towards the door, to indicate they were to leave the room and go below once more. As they descended the stairs, she said, 'Guilt implies I am somehow involved in this situation, which I am not. We were lovers, full stop. We were bodies meeting in a bed for a few hours. That's what it was, and if you really think that the mere act of intercourse led to—'

A knock came on the door. Aldara glanced at her watch. Then she looked at Daidre. Her expression was resigned, which told Daidre later that she should have anticipated what would come next. But, rather stupidly, she had not.

Aldara opened the door. A man stepped into the room. His eyes only for Aldara, he didn't see Daidre. He kissed Aldara with the familiarity of a lover: a greeting kiss that became a coaxing kiss, which Aldara did nothing to terminate prematurely. When it did end, she said against his mouth, 'You smell all of the sea.'

'I've been for a surf.' Then he saw Daidre. His hands dropped from Aldara's shoulders to his sides. 'I'd no idea you had company.'

'Daidre's just on her way,' Aldara said. 'D'you know Dr. Trahair, my dear? Daidre, this is Lewis.'

He looked vaguely familiar to Daidre, but she couldn't place him. She nodded hello. She'd left her bag on the edge of the sofa, and she went to fetch it. As she did so, Aldara added, 'Angarrack. Lewis Angarrack.'

I intend this scene to accomplish several things. First, dramatic questions are laid down in the form of the final two sentences of the first paragraph and everything in the third paragraph. Second, the story itself is advanced: We learn that Madlyn Angarrack has discovered her boyfriend – the murder victim Santo Kerne – in bed with Aldara, who was her employer at the time; we learn that the character Max – one of Aldara's lovers – knows that Aldara also took Santo Kerne as a lover; finally, we learn that Aldara is also the lover of Lew Angarrack, Madlyn's father.

In addition to this information, Aldara's character emerges more fully as we see her sexuality and her beliefs regarding her sexuality; we experience her sensual nature, her ethnicity, and her moral compass. She's also being deliberately provocative in what she reveals to Daidre. She knows Daidre disapproves of her lifestyle with regard to men, so her dialogue and her actions reflect her indifference to Daidre's disapproval.

Note that, throughout, Daidre doesn't speak like Aldara. Additionally, even in his brief appearance, Narno has a style of speaking that is different from both Daidre's and Aldara's. This is what I call *character-specific dialogue*. Reading the next selection, examine the ways in which Bea Hannaford's manner of speech differs from Thomas Lynley's.

'We'll sort out a car for you,' Bea Hannaford said to Lynley. 'You're going to need one.'

They stood outside the entrance to Royal Cornwall Hospital. Ray had gone on his way, after telling Bea that he couldn't promise her anything and after hearing her retort of 'how true,' which she knew was an unfair dig but which she used anyway because she'd long ago learned that when it came to murder, the end of charging someone with a homicide justified any means one employed to get there.

Lynley replied with what sounded to Bea like care. 'I don't believe you can ask this of me.'

'Because you outrank me? That's not going to count for much out here in the hinterlands, Superintendent.'

'Acting, only.'

'What?'

'Acting superintendent. I was never promoted permanently. I was just stepping in to fill a need.'

'How good of you. The very sort of bloke I'm looking for. You can step in to fill another rather burning need now.' She felt him glance her way as they proceeded towards her car, and she laughed outright. 'Not that need,' she said, 'though I expect you offer a decent shag when a woman puts a gun to your head. How old are you?'

'The Yard didn't tell you?'

'Humour me.'

'Thirty-eight.'

'Star sign?'

'What?'

'Gemini, Taurus, Virgo, what?'

'Is this somehow important?'

'As I said, humour me. Going along with the moment is so inexpensive, Thomas.'

He sighed. 'Pisces, as it happens.'

'Well, there you have it. It would never work between us. Besides, I'm twenty years older than you and while I fancy them younger than myself, I don't fancy them that young. So you're entirely safe in my company.'

'Somehow that's not a soothing thought.'

She laughed again and unlocked the car. They both climbed in, but she didn't insert the ignition key at once. Instead, she looked at him seriously. 'I need you to do this for me,' she told him. 'She wants to protect you.'

'Who?'

'You know who. Dr. Trahair.'

'She hardly wants that. I broke into her house. She wants me around to pay for the damage. And I owe her money for the clothing.'

'Don't be obtuse. She jumped to your defence earlier, and there's a reason for that. She's got a vulnerable spot. It may have to do with you. Or it may not. I don't know where it is or *why* it is, but you're going to find it.'

'Why?'

'Because you *can*. Because this is a murder investigation, and all the nice social rules fly out of the window when we start looking for a killer. And *that's* something you know as well as I do.'

Lynley shook his head, but it seemed to Bea Hannaford that this movement wasn't one of refusal so much as one that acknowledged a regretful understanding and acceptance of a single immutable fact: She had him by the short and curlies. If he did a runner, she'd fetch him back and he knew it.

What I hope the reader will intuit is the class difference between them, indicated through the formality of Lynley's speech and the informality of Bea's speech. Lynley's first sentence underscores this when he says, *'I don't believe you can ask this of me,'* instead of 'You can't tell me what to do' or 'Don't give me orders' or anything of that ilk. Bea's response immediately establishes the tone between them when she replies, *'Because you outrank me? That's not going to count for much out here in the hinterlands, Superintendent.'* Beyond that, her choice of words and linguistic expressions throughout are altogether different from Lynley's.

*'I expect you offer a decent shag when a woman puts a gun to your head.'*

*'. . . while I fancy them younger than myself, I don't fancy them that young.'*

And then in the narrative within her POV: *She had him by the short and curlies. If he did a runner, she'd fetch him back and he knew it.*

Both characters in the scene employ a different tone as well. Bea's is brusque and direct. Lynley's is polite yet wry. In each case I'm trying to keep their words a reflection of who they are.

The character analysis is what determines *how* a person is going to speak. The analysis gives me a good idea of what their style of speech will be, which words they will choose, the length and complexity of their sentences, and the subtext of their words or the lack of subtext. Once a character has been created I know what will affect how she speaks: not only her class and education but also her core need and her pathological man-oeuvre. Her agenda for the scene will lead me to provide subtext to her conversation. It will also be useful in laying down dramatic questions.

In the following selection, the characteristics of the two men – Ben Kerne and his father, Eddie – are revealed almost entirely through what they say to each other and how they say it.

Before [Ben] could avoid any longer, he picked up the phone on his desk. He punched in the numbers. He had little doubt his father would still be up and about the ramshackle house. Like Ben, Eddie Kerne was an insomniac. He'd be awake for hours yet, doing whatever it was one did at night when committed to a green lifestyle, as his father long had been. Eddie Kerne and his family had had electricity only if he could produce it from the wind or from water; they had water only if he could divert it from a stream or bring it up in a well. They had heat when solar panels produced it, they grew or raised what they needed for their food, and their house had been a derelict farm building, bought for a bargain and rescued from destruction by Eddie Kerne and his sons: granite stone by granite stone, whitewashed, roofed, and windowed so inexpertly that the winter wind hissed through the spaces between the frames and the walls. His father answered in his usual way, with the barked greeting, 'Speaking.' When Ben didn't say anything at once, his father went on with, 'If you're there, start yapping. If not, get off the line.'

'It's Ben,' Ben said.

'Ben who?'

'Benesek. I didn't wake you, did I?'

After a brief pause, 'And what if you did? You caring for anyone 'sides yourself these days?'

Like father, like son, Ben wanted to reply. I had a very good teacher. Instead he said, 'Santo's been killed. It happened yesterday. I thought you'd want to know, as he was fond of you and I thought perhaps the feeling was mutual.'

Another pause. This one was longer. And then, 'Bastard,' his father said. His voice was so tight that Ben thought it might break. '*Bastard*. You don't effing change, do you?'

'Do you want to know what happened to Santo?'

'What'd you let him get up to?'

'What did I do this time, you mean?'

'What happened, damn you? What God damn happened?'

Ben told him as briefly as possible. In the end he added the fact of murder. He didn't call it murder. He used *homicide* instead. 'Someone damaged his climbing kit,' he told his father.

'God damn.' Eddie Kerne's voice had altered, from anger to shock. But he shifted back to anger quickly. 'And what the hell were you doing while he was climbing some bloody cliff? Watching him? Egging him on? Or having it off with *her*?'

'He was climbing alone. I didn't know he'd gone. I don't know why he went.' The last was a lie, but he couldn't bear to give his father any additional ammunition. 'They thought at first it was an accident. But when they looked at his equipment, they saw it had been tampered with.'

'By who?'

'Well, they don't know that, Dad. If they knew, they'd make an arrest and matters would be settled.'

'*Settled?* That's how you talk about the death of your son? Of your flesh and blood? Of the means of carrying on your name? *Settled?* Matters get settled and you just go on? That it, Benesek? You and whatsername just stroll into the future and put the past behind you? But then, you're good at doing that, aren't you? So is she. She's bleeding *brilliant* at doing that, 'f I recall right. How's she taking all this? Getting in the way of her *lifestyle*, is it?'

Ben had forgotten the nasty emphases in his father's speech, loaded words and pointed questions, all designed to carve away one's fragile sense of self. No one was meant to be an individual in Eddie Kerne's world. *Family* meant adherence to a single belief and a single way of life. Like father, like son, he thought abruptly. What a cock-up he'd made of the rough form of paternity he'd actually been granted.

We see, hear and know based on this telephone call. At once we see the personality of Eddie Kerne and the nature of his relationship with his son. We see a demonstration of his attitude towards Ben's marriage to Dellen. We see how Eddie Kerne feels about Dellen. Between the men, we hear anger, bitterness, grief and dislike. At the end of it all, we know that something significant happened in Ben's past, that the police will be coming to talk to Eddie Kerne, and that Eddie possesses information about Ben that could hurt him should Eddie choose to reveal it. All of this has come from the dialogue, making it quite a powerful tool in storytelling.

Eddie Kerne's dialogue is rich with his attitude towards his son, and when dialogue is being used to reveal a character's attitude, what counts is the word choice within the dialogue. Attitude isn't revealed through the use of adverbs describing *how* something is spoken. Nor is it revealed through the use of tag lines offering verbs that, like adverbs, characterise the manner in which something is said, such as 'He sneered,' or snarled or snapped, etc.

The expression of attitude needs to be as specific to a character as everything else about her, using her particular syntax, vocabulary and slang. Sergeant Havers might say, for example, 'That's bollocks on a plate' as a reply, indicating her scorn towards whatever is being discussed. In contrast, Lynley might say 'That's utter nonsense,' while someone else might say 'Absolute rubbish.' In each case, the attitude expressed is the same but the choice of words expressing the attitude alters depending upon who is speaking.

In any scene, the writer is looking for moments in which a character's attitude can be demonstrated. Generally, these moments are present when one character is reacting to another, when a situation arises that calls for a reaction, when one character witnesses another character's behaviour, when life itself requires commentary. Within these moments, there are opportunities for subtext and agenda as well. There are also opportunities to lay down dramatic questions and to answer other dramatic questions previously laid down in other scenes.

Consider the various functions of dialogue that are being ticked off in the following scene:

The sound of an unmuffled engine came to her not long after she reached the top of the cliff. She'd been sitting upon an outcrop of limestone, watching the kittiwakes, and following the majestic arcs the birds made in the air as they sought shelter in niches in the cliff. But now she stood and walked back to the path. A motorcycle, she saw, was coming down the lane. It reached her cottage and veered into the pebbly driveway, where it stopped. The rider removed his helmet and approached the front door.

Daidre thought of couriers and messengers when she saw him: someone carrying a package for her, perhaps a message from Bristol? But she was expecting nothing and from what she could tell, the rider had nothing with him. He went round her cottage to seek another door or to look into a window. Or worse, she thought.

She made for the path and began to descend. There was no point to shouting because she couldn't have been heard from this distance. Indeed, there was also little point in hurrying. The cottage was some way from the sea and she was some way above the lane. Likely by the time she got back, the rider would have left.

But the thought that someone might be breaking into her cottage spurred her downward. She kept her glances going between her foot-work and her cottage as she went, and the fact that the motorcycle remained in place in her driveway kept her speed up and her curiosity piqued.

She arrived breathless and dashed in through the gate. Instead of a housebreaker half in and half out of a window, though, she found a girl clad in leathers lounging on her front step. She was sitting with her back against the bright blue door and her legs stretched out in front of her. She had a hideous silver ring through her septum and a turquoise-coloured choker tattooed brightly round her neck.

Daidre recognised her. Cilla Cormack, the bane of her own mother's life. Her gran lived next door to Daidre's family in Falmouth. What on *earth*, Daidre thought, was the girl doing here?

Cilla looked up as Daidre approached. The dull sun glinted off her septum ring, giving it the unappealing look of those rings once used on cows to urge their cooperation when they were attached to a lead. She said, 'Hey,' and gave Daidre a nod. She rose and stamped her feet as if with the need to get the circulation going.

'This is a surprise,' Daidre said. 'How are you, Cilla? How's your mum?'

'Cow,' Cilla said, by which Daidre assumed she meant her mother, Cilla's disputes with that woman being something of a neighbourhood legend. 'C'n I use your toilet or summick?'

'Of course.' Daidre unlocked the front door. She ushered the girl inside. Cilla clomped across the entry and into the sitting room. 'Through there,' Daidre said. She waited to see what would happen next because surely Cilla hadn't come all the way from Falmouth just to use the loo.

Some minutes later – during which time water ran enthusiastically and Daidre began to wonder if the girl had decided to have a bath – Cilla returned. Her hair was wet and slicked back and she smelled as if she'd decided to help herself to Daidre's scent as well. 'Better, that,' she said. 'Felt like bloody hell, I did. Roads're bad this time of year.'

'Ah,' Daidre said. 'Would you like . . . something? Tea? Coffee?'

'Fag?'

'I don't smoke. I'm sorry.'

'Figgers, that.' Cilla looked round and nodded. 'This's nice, innit. But you don't live here reg'lar, right?'

'No. Cilla, is there something . . . ?' Daidre felt stymied by her up-bringing. One didn't come out and ask a visitor what on earth she was doing visiting. On the other hand, it was impossible that the girl had just been passing by. Daidre smiled and tried to look encouraging.

Cilla wasn't the brightest bulb in the chandelier, but she did man-age to get the point. She said, 'My gran aksed me would I come. Said you di'n't have a mobile.'

Daidre felt alarmed. 'Has something happened? What's going on? Is someone ill?'

'Gran says Scotland Yard came by. She says you'd best know straightaway cos they were aksing about you. She says they went to your house first but when no one was home, they started banging doors up an' down the street. She phoned up Bristol to tell you. You wa'n't there, so she reckoned you might be here and she aksed would I come here to let you know. Whyn't you get yourself a mobile, eh? Or even a phone here? That'd make sense, you know. I mean, just like in a emer-gency. Cos it's one hell of a way to get here from Falmouth. And petrol . . . D'you know how much petrol costs these days?'

The girl sounded aggrieved. Daidre went to the sideboard in the dining room and fetched twenty pounds. She handed it over. She said, 'Thank you for coming. It can't have been easy, all this way.'

Cilla relented. She said, 'Well, Gran aksed. And she's a good old girl, innit. She always lets me stop there when Mum throws me out, which's about once a week, eh? So when she aksed me and said it was important . . .' She shrugged. 'Anyways. Here I am. She said you should know. She also said . . .' Here Cilla frowned, as if trying to remember the rest of the message. Daidre wondered that the girl's grandmother had not written it down. But then, it had probably occurred to the elderly woman that Cilla was likely to lose a note while a brief message of one or two sentences was not beyond her ability to pass along. 'Oh. Yeah. She also said not to worry because she di'n't tell them nuffink.' Cilla touched her septum ring, as if to make sure it was still in place. 'So why's Scotland Yard nosing round you?' she asked. Grinning, she added, 'What you done? You got bodies buried in the garden or summick?'

Daidre smiled faintly. 'Six or seven,' she said.

'Thought as much.' Cilla cocked her head. 'You've gone dead white. You best sit down. Put your head . . .' She seemed to lose the thread of where one's head was supposed to go. 'You want a glass of water, eh?'

'No, no. I'm fine. Haven't eaten much today . . . Are you sure you don't want something?'

'Gotta get back,' she said. 'I've a date tonight. M'boyfriend's taking me dancing.'

'Is he?'

'Yeah. We're taking lessons. Bit daft, that, but it's summick to do, innit. We're at that one where the girl gets thrown around a bit and you got to keep your back real stiff otherwise. Stick your nose in the air. That sorta thing. I got to wear high heels for it, which I don't like much, but the teacher says we're getting quite good. She wants us to be in a competition, she says. Bruce – that's m' boyfriend – he's dead chuffed 'bout it and he says we got to practise every day. So that's why we're going dancing tonight. Mostly we practise in his mum's sitting room, but *he* says we're ready to go out in public.'

'How lovely,' Daidre said. She waited for more. More, she hoped, would consist of Cilla's leaving the premises so that Daidre could come to terms with the message the girl had brought. Scotland Yard in Falmouth. Asking questions. She felt anxiety climbing up her arms.

'Anyway, got to dash,' Cilla said, as if reading Daidre's mind. 'Lookit, you best think about having a phone put in, eh? You could keep it in a cupboard or summick. Plug it in when you want it. That sort of thing.'

'Yes. Yes, I will,' Daidre told her. 'Thanks so much, Cilla, for coming all this way.'

The girl left her then, and Daidre stood on the front step, watching her expertly kick-start the motorcycle – no electronic ignition for *this* rider – and turn it in the driveway. In a few more moments and with a wave, the girl was gone. She zoomed up the narrow lane, curved out of sight, and left Daidre to deal with the aftermath of her visit.

Scotland Yard, she thought. Questions being asked. There could be only one reason – only one person – behind this.

As I pointed out earlier, this is Cilla Cormack's only appearance in the novel, but she still must emerge as a real human being, so her actions and her dialogue are going to be as different from Daidre's as possible. They're also going to say something about her class, her level of education, her background, and her relationships. And the conversation between Cilla and Daidre is going to move the story forward as well.

Cilla's word choice and her pronunciation of words define her first: *Summick, fag, figgers, innit, aksed, cos, anyways, nuffink, dead chuffed* and *lookit* mark her as part of the working class – or at least posing as a member of the working class – as well as they indicate her level of education. Her attitude of grievance towards the job she's been given emerges during the conversation. Her agenda in the scene – not only delivering the message but also getting money from Daidre – is expressed along with her sense of grievance. And all along, the story is moved forward in the form of the message she's brought: that Scotland Yard has been nosing around the neighbourhood where Daidre once lived as an adolescent.

Giving a character with a onetime appearance both an attitude and an agenda makes a scene not only real for the reader but also memorable. It also illustrates a real life that has existed before this scene occurs and that will continue to exist once Cilla hops back on her motorcycle to return to Falmouth for her dancing date with her boyfriend. The style of dance is *'that one where the girl gets thrown around a bit and you got to keep your back real stiff otherwise. Stick your nose in the air. That sorta thing.'*

What else might the reader notice about this scene?

Even Cilla's actions define her, as she stamps her feet, clomps across the entry, helps herself to Daidre's perfume.

Her appearance contains the telling details of the septum ring and the turquoise choker tattooed around her neck.

Daidre's attitude towards Cilla comes within her POV: *Cilla wasn't the brightest bulb in the chandelier, but she did manage to get the point.*

Cilla's words are used to reveal Daidre's reaction to the news about Scotland Yard: *'You've gone dead white. You best sit down. Put your head . . .'* She *seemed to lose the thread of where one's head was supposed to go.*

Further dramatic questions arise in the narrative with *Scotland Yard in Falmouth. Asking questions. [Daidre] felt anxiety climbing up her arms.*

Successful dialogue, then, serves several crucial functions in storytelling.

It adds to the revelation of character through what is said and through how it is said. As many details of character as possible float to the surface while a character is speaking. Consider Aldara Pappas's dialogue with Daidre as we've seen it earlier. We end up knowing a great deal about her without an information dump being used.

It displays a character's attitudes, beliefs, intentions and agendas towards the subject of the dialogue or towards the listener.

It acts as an efficient means of moving the story forward, adding tension, providing conflict and giving a scene subtext.

It distinguishes between characters and defines their relationships.

It conveys necessary information to the reader among which can be (in a crime novel, mystery, tea cosy or police procedural) clues and red herrings.

All of the fundamentals of fiction writing we've covered so far are at work in the scene that follows. Images 21 and 22, coming out of my location research in Cornwall, depict a decommissioned Royal Air Force station. It looks like what the British would call a rubbish tip and what Americans

IMAGE 21

IMAGE 22

would call a dump, but in reality some of its buildings were actually in use as places of business.

I decided to make the decommissioned station the spot where my surf-board shaper would do his work. LiquidEarth is the name of his enterprise, and when Bea Hannaford and Constable Mick McNulty go to speak with him, this is Bea's first look at the area. Because the scene is in her POV, we see the decommissioned air station through her eyes and we experience her reaction to it:

> LiquidEarth stood on Binner Down, among a collection of other small-manufacturing businesses on the grounds of a long-decommissioned Royal Air Force station. This was a relic of World War II, reduced all these decades later to a combination of crumbling buildings, rutted

lanes and masses of brambles. Between the abandoned buildings and along the lanes, the area resembled nothing so much as a rubbish tip. Disused lobster traps and fishing nets formed piles next to lumps of broken concrete; discarded tyres and moulding furniture languished against propane tanks; stained toilets and chipped basins became contrasting elements that fought with wild ivy. There were mattresses, black rubbish sacks stuffed with who-knew-what, three-legged chairs, splintered doors, ruined casings from windows. It was a perfect spot to toss a body, Bea Hannaford concluded. No one would find it for a generation.

Even from inside the car, she could smell the place. The damp air offered fires and cow manure from a working dairy farm at the edge of the down. Added to the general unpleasantness of the environment, pooled rainwater that was skimmed by oil slicks sat in craters along the tarmac.

She'd brought Constable McNulty with her, both as navigator and note taker. Based on his comments in Santo Kerne's bedroom on the previous day, she decided he might prove useful with matters related to surfing, and as a longtime resident of Casvelyn, at least he knew the town.

They'd come at LiquidEarth on a circuitous route that had taken them by the town wharf, which formed the northeast edge of the disused Casvelyn Canal. They gained Binner Down from a street called Arundel, off which a lumpy track led past a grime-streaked farmhouse. Behind this, the decommissioned air station lay, and far beyond it in the distance a tumbledown house stood, a mess of a place taken over by a succession of surfers and brought to wrack as a result of their habitation. McNulty seemed philosophical about this. What else could one expect? he seemed to say.

Bea saw soon enough that she was lucky to have him with her, for the businesses on the erstwhile airfield had no addresses affixed to them. They were nearly windowless cinder-block buildings with roofs of galvanised metal overhung with ivy. Cracked concrete ramps led up to heavy steel vehicle doors at the front of each, and the occasional passageway door had been cut into these.

McNulty directed Bea along a track on the far north edge of the airfield. After a spine-damaging jounce for some three hundred yards, he mercifully said, 'Here you go, Guv,' and indicated one hut of three that he claimed had once been housing for Wrens. She found that difficult enough to believe, but times had been tough. Compared to eking out an existence on a bomb site in London or Coventry, this had probably seemed like paradise.

When they alighted and did a little chiropractic manoeuvring of their spinal cords, McNulty pointed out how much closer they were at this point to the habitation of the surfers. He called it Binner Down House, and it stood in the distance directly across the down from them. Convenient for the surfers when you thought about it, he noted. If their boards needed repairing, they could just nip across the down and leave them here with Lew Angarrack.

They entered LiquidEarth by means of a door fortified with no less than four locks. Immediately, they were within a small showroom where in racks along two walls long boards and short boards leaned nose up and finless. On a third wall surfing posters hung, featuring waves the size of ocean liners, while along the fourth wall stood a business counter. Within and behind this a display of surfing accoutrements were laid out: board bags, leashes, fins. There were no wet suits. Nor were there any T-shirts designed by Santo Kerne.

The place had an eye-stinging smell about it. This turned out to be coming from a dusty room beyond the showroom where a boiler-suited man with a long grey ponytail and large-framed spectacles was carefully pouring a substance from a plastic bucket onto the top of a surfboard. This lay across two sawhorses.

The gent was slow about what he was doing, perhaps because of the nature of the work, perhaps because of the nature of his disability, his habits, or his age. He was a shaker, Bea saw. Parkinson's, the drink, whatever.

She said, 'Excuse me. Mr. Angarrack?' just as the sound of an electrical tool powered up from behind a closed door to the side.

'Not him,' McNulty said *sotto voce* behind her. 'That'll be Lew shaping a board in the other room.'

By this, Bea took it to mean that Angarrack was operating whatever tool was making the noise. As she reached her conclusion, the older gentleman turned. He had an antique face, and his specs were held together with wire.

He said, 'Sorry. Can't stop just now,' with a nod at what he was doing. 'Come in, though. You the cops?'

That was obvious enough, as McNulty was in uniform. But Bea stepped forward, leaving tracks along a floor powdered with polystyrene dust, and offered her identification. He gave it a cursory glance and a nod and said he was Jago Reeth. The glasser, he added. He was putting the final coat of resin on a board, and he had to smooth it before it began to set or he'd have a sanding problem on his hands. But he'd be free to talk to them when he was finished if they wanted him. If they wanted Lew, he was doing the initial shaping of the rails on a board and he wouldn't want to be disturbed, as he liked to do it in one go.

'We'll be sure to make our apologies,' Bea told Jago Reeth. 'Can you fetch him for us. Or shall we . . . ?' She indicated the door behind which the shrieking of a tool told the tale of some serious rail shaping.

'Hang on, then,' Jago said. 'Let me get this on. Won't take five minutes and it's got to be done all at once.'

They watched as he finished with the plastic bucket. The resin formed a shallow pool defined by the curve of the surfboard, and he used a paintbrush to spread it evenly. Once again Bea noted the degree to which his hand shook as he wielded the paintbrush. He seemed to read her mind in her glance.

He said, 'Not too many good years left. Should have taken on the big waves when I had the chance.'

'You surf yourself?' Bea asked Jago Reeth.

'Not these days. Not if I want to see tomorrow.' He peered up at her from his position bent over the board. His eyes behind his spectacles – the glass of which was flecked with white residue – were clear and sharp despite his age. 'You're here about Santo Kerne, I expect. Was a murder, eh?'

'You know that, do you?' Bea asked Jago Reeth.

'Didn't know,' he said. 'Just reckoned.'

'Why?'

'You're here. Why else if not a murder? Or are you lot going round offering condolences to everyone who knew the lad?'

'You're among those?'

'Am,' he said. 'Not long, but I knew him. Six months or so, since I worked for Lew.'

'So you're not an old-timer here in town?'

He made a long sweep with his paintbrush, the length of the board. 'Me? No. I come up from Australia this time round. Been following the season long as I can tell you.'

'Summer or surfing?'

'Same thing in some places. Others, it's winter. They always need blokes who can do boards. I'm their man.'

'Isn't it a bit early for the season here?'

'Not hardly, eh? Just a few more weeks. And now's when I'm needed most cos before the season starts is when the orders come in. Then *in* the season boards get dinged and repairs are needed. Newquay, North

Shore, Queensland, California. I'm there to do them. Use to work first and surf later. Sometimes the reverse.'

'But not now.'

'Hell no. It'd kill me for sure. His dad thought it'd kill Santo, you know. Idjit, he was. Safer than crossing the street. *And* it gets a lad out in the air and sunlight.'

'So does sea cliff climbing,' Bea pointed out.

Jago eyed her. 'And look what happened there.'

'D'you know the Kernes, then?'

'Santo. Like I said. And the rest of them from what Santo said. And that would be the limit of what I know.' He set his paintbrush in the bucket, which he'd put on the floor beneath the board, and he scrutinised his work, squatting at the end of the board to study it from tail to nose. Then he rose and went to the door behind which the rails of a board were being shaped. He closed it behind him. In a moment, the tool was shut off.

Constable McNulty, Bea saw, was looking about, a line forming between his eyebrows, as if he was considering what he was observing. She knew nothing about the making of surfboards, so she said, 'What?' and he roused himself from his thoughts.

'Something,' he said. 'Don't quite know yet.'

'About the place? About Reeth? About Santo? His family? What?'

'Not sure.'

She blew out a breath. The man would probably need a bloody Ouija board.

In examining the scene, we begin with a place description to establish the setting. More than one sensory impression is documented as Bea not only sees the place but also smells it. She reacts. Then we back off a bit in the fourth paragraph as we review exactly where they are in relation to the town of Casvelyn. The description of the route they took to get to the air station comprises various aspects of the real town that I used: Bude. Hence the town wharf, the 'Casvelyn Canal' and 'Binner Down,' to which I added the tumbledown house that we've already seen when Cadan goes to speak to Will.

As we approach LiquidEarth, I begin to take from my notes and photographs actual details that I found and photographed at Fluid Juice Surfboards, which was the model for LiquidEarth. The exterior of the cinder-block building is described as I actually found it, and all interiors of the place come from my visit there.

With Bea and Mick McNulty's encounter with the older man who is working at LiquidEarth, other fundamentals of fiction writing start to appear: his physical description, the telling detail of his 'specs' being held together with wire, the activity in which he's engaged (which also came directly from my visit to Fluid Juice) and his style of speaking: *'Not hardly, eh? Just a few more weeks. And now's when I'm needed most cos before the season starts is when the orders come in,'* and *'Hell no. It'd kill me for sure. His dad thought it'd kill Santo, you know. Idjit, he was. Safer than crossing the street.'*

Additionally, the scene contains two fundamentals we haven't covered yet: the THAD and foreshadowing. I'll be addressing the THAD in the next chapter, but for now suffice it to say that we see the THAD in Jago's activity while he's speaking to Bea and Mick. We see the foreshadowing in the final moments of the reading in which Constable McNulty – already established earlier in the novel as a surfer – sees something that's not quite right but isn't able to put his finger on what it is . . . yet.

So far, we've looked at how word choice and pronunciation can display a character's attitude and agenda. It's also crucial that dialogue differentiate between characters. This is done by giving each character a different pattern of speaking. The use of idioms helps in forming that pattern, as all patterns should be character-specific. Consider the various ways we have to signal affirmation or agreement: *yes, yep, yeah, sure, I think you're right, right on* and *Yes, indeed*. There are probably more, but I hope you see the point. It's unlikely that the character who says 'Yep' will also at some point say 'Yes, indeed.'

Character-specific phrases can be coined to differentiate among the speakers. For example, 'Bob's your uncle' and 'Don't get your knickers in a twist' are both British expressions. But in the voice of Barbara Havers, they become 'Bob's your grandmother's second son' and 'Let's untwist them, Inspector.' She puts her own spin on each expression, making it her own.

Note the differences, then, in how Lynley and Havers speak. Specifically, note the word choice within the dialogue.

He returned to his humming as he towelled himself off. He was still humming, towel wrapped round his waist, when he opened the door.

And came face-to-face with DS Barbara Havers.

He said, 'My God.'

Havers said, 'I've been called worse.' She scratched her mop of badly cut and currently uncombed hair. 'Are you always so chipper before breakfast, sir? Because if you are, this is the last time I'm sharing a bathroom with you.'

He could, for the moment, do nothing but stare, so unprepared was he for the sight of his former partner. She was wearing floppy sky blue socks in lieu of slippers and she had on pink flannel pyjamas printed everywhere with the image of vinyl records, musical notes and the phrase 'Love like yours is sure to come my way.' She seemed to realise he was examining her getup because she said, 'Oh. A gift from Winston,' in apparent reference to it.

'Would that be the socks or the rest of it?'

'The rest. He saw this in a catalogue. He said he couldn't resist.'

'I'll need to speak to Sergeant Nkata about his impulse control.'

She chuckled. 'I knew you'd love them if you ever saw them.'

'Havers, the word *love* does not do justice to my feelings.'

She nodded at the bathroom. 'You finished your morning what-evers in there?'

He stepped aside. 'It's all yours.'

She passed him but paused before closing the door. 'Tea?' she said. 'Coffee?'

'Come to my room.'

He was ready for her when she arrived, dressed for her day. He himself was clothed and he'd made tea – he wasn't desperate enough to face the provided coffee granules – when she knocked on his door and said unnecessarily, 'It's me.'

He opened it to her. She looked round and said, 'You demanded the more elegant accommodation, I see. I've got something that used to be the garret. I feel like Cinderella before the glass boot.'

He held up the tin teapot. She nodded and plopped herself onto his bed, which he'd made. She lifted the old chenille counterpane and inspected the job he'd done. 'Hospital corners,' she noted. 'Very nice, sir. Is that from Eton or somewhere else in your chequered past?'

'My mother,' he said. 'Proper bed making and the correct use of table linens were at the heart of her child rearing. Should I add milk and sugar or do you want to do your own honours?'

'You can do it,' she said. 'I like the idea of you waiting on me. This is a first, and it may be a last, so I think I'll enjoy it.'

He handed her the doctored tea, poured his own, and joined her on the bed as there was no chair. He said, 'What are you doing here, Havers?'

She gestured at the room with her teacup. 'You invited me, didn't you?'

'You know what I mean.'

She took a sip of tea. 'You wanted information about Daidre Trahair.'

'Which you could easily have provided me on the phone.' He thought about this and recalled their conversation. 'You were in your car when I phoned you on your mobile. Were you on your way down here?'

'I was.'

'Barbara. . .' He spoke in a fashion to warn her off: Stay out of my life.

She said, 'Don't flatter yourself, Superintendent.'

'Tommy. Or Thomas. Or whatever. But not superintendent.'

'"Tommy"? "Thomas"? Not bloody likely. Are we fine with "sir"?' And when he shrugged, 'Good. DI Hannaford has no MCIT blokes working the case for her. When she phoned the Met for your identification, she explained the situation. I got sent as a loan.'

'And that's it?'

'That's it.'

Lynley looked at her evenly. Her face was a blank, an admirable poker face that might have duped someone who knew her less well than he did. 'Am I actually meant to believe that, Barbara?'

'Sir, there's nothing else *to* believe.'

They engaged in a stare down. But ultimately there was nothing to be gained. She'd worked with him too long to be intimidated by any implications that might hang upon silence. She said, 'By the way, no one ever put your resignation through channels. As far as anyone's concerned, you're on compassionate leave. Indefinitely, if that's what it takes.' She sipped her tea again. '*Is* that what it takes?'

Lynley looked away from her. Outside, a grey day was framed by the window, and a sprig of the ivy that climbed on this side of the building was blowing against the glass. 'I don't know,' he said. 'I think I'm finished with it, Barbara.'

'They've posted the job. Not your old one but the one you were in when . . . You know. Webberly's job: the detective superintendent's position. John Stewart's applying. Others as well. Some from outside and some from within. Stewart's obviously got the inside track on it, and between you and me, that would be a disaster for everyone if he gets it.'

'It could be worse.'

'No, it couldn't.' She put her hand on his arm. So rare a gesture it was that he had to look at her. 'Come back, sir.'

'I don't think I can.' He rose then, to distance himself not from her but from the idea of returning to New Scotland Yard. He said, 'But why here, in the middle of nowhere? You could be staying in town, which makes far more sense if you're working with Bea Hannaford.'

'I could ask the same of you, sir.'

'I was brought here the first night. It seemed easiest to stay. It was the closest place.'

'To what?'

'To where the body was found. And why are we turning this into an examination of me? What's going on?'

'I've told you.'

'Not everything.' He studied her evenly. If she'd come to keep a watch over him, which was likely the case, Havers being Havers, there could be only one reason. 'What did you learn about Daidre Trahair?' he asked her.

She nodded. 'You see? You haven't lost your touch.' She downed the rest of her tea and held out her cup. He poured her another and put in a packet of sugar and two of the thimbles of milk. She said nothing else until he'd handed the cup back and she'd taken a swig. 'A family called Trahair are longtime residents of Falmouth, so that part of her story's on the up-and-up. The dad sells tyres; he's got his own company. The mum does mortgages for homes. No primary school records for a kid called Daidre, though. You were right about that. In some cases that might suggest she was sent off to school in the old way: booted out the door when she was five or whatever, home for half terms and the holidays but otherwise unseen and unheard till emerging from the great machine of proper' – she rolled the *r* to indicate her scorn – 'education at eighteen or whatever.'

'Spare me the social commentary,' Lynley said.

'I speak purely from jealous rage, of course,' Havers said. 'Nothing I would have liked better than to be packed off to boarding school directly after I learned to blow my nose.'

'Havers . . .'

'You haven't lost that tone of martyred patience,' she noted. 'C'n I smoke in here, by the way?'

'Are you out of your mind?'

'Just enquiring, sir.' She curved her palm around her teacup. 'So while I reckon she could have gone off to primary school, it doesn't seem likely to me because there she is in the local secondary comprehensive from the time she's thirteen. Playing field hockey. Excelling at fencing. Singing in the school choir. Mezzo-soprano if that's of interest.'

'And you're rejecting the idea of earlier boarding school for what reason?'

'First of all, because it doesn't make sense. I can see it done the reverse way: primary day school and *then* boarding school when she was twelve or thirteen. But boarding out through primary school and then returning home for secondary? This is a middle-class family. What middle-class family sends its kids off at that age and then has them back home when they're thirteen?'

'It's been known to happen. What's the second of all?'

'The second of . . . ? Oh. Second of all, there's no record of her birth. Not a cracker, not a hint. Not in Falmouth, that is.'

Lynley considered the implications of this. He said, 'She told me she was born at home.'

'The birth would still have to be registered within forty-two days. And if she *was* born at home, the midwife would have been there, yes?'

'If her father delivered her. . . ?'

'Did she tell you that? If you and she were exchanging intimate details—'

He glanced at her sharply, but her face betrayed nothing.

' – then wouldn't that have been an intriguing one to share? Mum doesn't make it to the hospital for some reason: like it's a dark and stormy night. Or the car breaks down. The electricity goes out. There's a maniac loose in the streets. There's been a military coup that history failed to record. There's a curfew due to racial rioting. The Vikings, having missed the east coast entirely because you know how Vikings are when it comes to having a decent sense of direction, have emerged from a time warp to invade the south coast of England. Or maybe aliens. They might have landed. But whatever the reason, there they are at home with Mum in labour and Dad boiling water without knowing what he's supposed to do with it but nature takes its course anyway and out pops a baby girl they call Daidre.' She placed her teacup on the narrow nightstand next to the bed. 'Which still doesn't explain why they wouldn't have registered the birth.'

He said nothing.

'So there's something she's not telling you, sir. I'm wondering why.'

'Her story about the zoo checks out,' Lynley told her. 'She *is* a large animal veterinarian. She does work for the Bristol Zoo.'

'I'll give you that,' Havers said. 'I went to the Trahairs' house once I had a look through the birth registry. No one was at home, so I spoke to a neighbour. There's a Daidre Trahair, definitely. She lives in Bristol and works at the zoo. But when I pressed a bit further for more information, the woman dummied up. It was just, "Dr. Trahair is a credit to her parents and a credit to herself and you write that down in that notebook of yours. *And* if you want to know more, I'll need to speak to

my solicitor first," before the door was shut in my face. Too many sodding cop dramas on telly,' she concluded darkly. 'It's killing our ability
to intimidate.'

Even in their banter, the two have completely different speech patterns
and word selections. Lynley maintains an ironic formality with her: *'I'll
need to speak to Sergeant Nkata about his impulse control'* is his reaction to the information that Barbara's crazy pyjamas were a gift from Winston Nkata,
while *'Havers, the word love does not do justice to my feelings'* is his reply to her *'I
knew you'd love them if you ever saw them.'*

For her part, Barbara Havers' dialogue maintains her irreverence until
the moment that Lynley drops his formality, when he uses her first name
and says to her, *'I don't know . . . I think I'm finished with it, Barbara,'* in reference to the fact that he's submitted his resignation to his superior at New
Scotland Yard but it has not been sent through channels yet. That alteration serves as a changing of gears, leading them to discuss the case in
hand, which at this point happens to be about what Havers has learned
about Daidre Trahair in her visit to Falmouth.

Yet even in their discussion of the case, they each maintain a specific
style of speaking, Havers' style being especially rich in attitude. And we
end up with a dramatic question as well, with *'When I pressed a bit further for
more information, the woman dummied up. It was just, "Dr. Trahair is a credit to her
parents and a credit to herself and you write that down in that notebook of yours. And if
you want to know more, I'll need to speak to my solicitor first," before the door was shut
in my face.'*

What about dialect, then? What does a writer do when the differences in
speech patterns come from dialect? All countries have regional dialects.
All countries have ethnic dialects. As far as the UK is concerned, it is not

for nothing that George Bernard Shaw pointed out that all one English-man has to do to be despised by another Englishman is to open his mouth and speak.

When I'm attempting to work out what a dialect is going to look like on the page, I begin by listening to how people pronounce words in the area where I've set my story. I take note of phrases that are unlike those in other areas, and I try to pick up on slang used by individuals who represent different levels of society, different professions, different ethnic groups, different cultures. Then I select which words or phrases I'm going to use to indicate that a character is from a particular region or socioeconomic group or culture or ethnicity.

It helps that I watch a great deal of British television, everything from costume dramas to modern crime dramas, from the news to talk shows featuring ordinary people venting their frustrations, casting aspersions upon friends, throwing around accusations, or telling their intimate personal stories to a studio audience. When I'm in England, I try to be as spongelike as possible, since language – hence dialect – is occurring everywhere around me all the time.

I try to remember that the English language is fluid, too. It frequently changes, and with the creation of social media, it's far less isolated and country-specific than it used to be. Certain phrases will always be indicative of a particular area or level of education or background, but others will not, having been subsumed into another culture through constant exposure to it.

For me, dialect works best when it's *suggested* rather than *depicted*. So I try to give merely the flavour of dialect. To do this, I look at *how* people say what they say, and I make a decision about what words I'll use to signal to the reader that a dialect is being spoken. Examples of this are:

Saying *summick* or *summat* for *something*
Saying *figgers* for *figures*
Saying *aksing* instead of *asking*

Saying *cos* instead of *because*

Dropping *t*'s or *g*'s at the end of a word

Arbitrarily placing *innit* at the end of a sentence. (It means *isn't it*, by the way, but it's used in a variety of creative ways that can't be translated into anything, really. In this, it's rather like Americans putting *you know* at the beginning or the end of a sentence when it's not required.)

Another way I try to suggest dialect is through the creative use of syntax, such as when Cilla says *'My gran aksed me would I come'* and *'They started banging doors up an' down the street.'*

However you address the issue of dialect, I think it's important to remember that deliberately misspelled words call attention to themselves (so do misspell if you want the attention) and that the use of full dialect often requires the reader to read aloud in order to understand what's being said. If that occurs, the reader has been pulled out of the story, which is the last place you want the reader to be.

## Optional Exercise 1

Try your hand at two pages of character-specific dialogue. First determine a situation that needs to be discussed and the two characters who need to discuss it. They might be two of the three characters you named earlier. Then establish a location and attempt to create dialogue that reflects each character's attitude and agenda while simultaneously moving a story forward. Consider adding tension or direct conflict in this scene. Remember as you go along that for dialogue to fulfil its purpose, it needs to:

Reveal character (think of Aldara and Daidre in conversation)

Convey action going on during the dialogue (think of Jago and the surfboard)

Foretell events (think of Daidre seeing that Aldara is expecting someone)

Crystallise or clarify relationships (think of Aldara speaking about Santo)

Move the plot forward (think of Scotland Yard checking up on Daidre)

Add interest or force to the narrative (think of Lynley and Havers in conversation in Lynley's hotel room)

Precipitate revelation, climax, or crisis (think of Dellen and Kerra)

Demonstrate conflict (think of Eddie and Ben)

If at least one of these purposes is not being served by the dialogue you're writing, remove it. My pet peeve is the silly response to a telephone ringing:

*She picked up the receiver. 'Hello?' she said.*

Argh! *Everyone* knows how a phone is answered. Everyone knows that the English-speaking recipient of the call generally says 'Hello' when answering the phone. Better expressed would be:

*I went for the phone. It was my brother. 'Listen up, kid,' were his first words. I knew when I heard them that trouble was on the other end of the line.*

Now you try it.

## Optional Exercise 2

Put two characters into a conversation, discussion, or argument that extends over two pages. Use *no* attribution, no taglines, no adverbs and no description of any kind. Make it obvious who is speaking to whom and what the subject is merely through creating a different style of speaking for each character. If you've never read 'Hills Like White Elephants' by Ernest Hemingway, you might want to give it a look to see how a master does it.

---

# CHAPTER 6

# The THAD

*Foundation of Good Storytelling*

THAD sounds like an odd little item. It's an unlikely term to be found in any book on writing, save my book on craft called *Write Away*. My writing students and I coined it years ago, as an acronym for Talking Heads Avoidance Device. By definition, it's an action that accompanies dialogue. Its simplest purpose is to avoid writing a scene that comprises only dialogue and taglines. However, there are more important and complicated purposes that attend it.

First, the THAD gives the writer an opportunity to reveal something about the *non-viewpoint* character in the scene, since generally the THAD is being engaged in by that character. While the character is engaging in it, the POV character observes what's going on and possibly offers attitude or judgment towards it. If you've created your characters in advance, you'll find that there are THADs buried within the analyses you've done because, among other areas you've explored in your creation of character, you've taken a look at the character's hobbies, collections, pursuits, interests, activities and beliefs. A THAD can come from any of these, and its ability to depict and illuminate character shouldn't be overlooked. No doubt you've heard the prescription to 'show, not tell' in your writing. Showing is exactly what a THAD can do. Imagine everything you can reveal about a character in the way he guts a fish, in the way she eats a soft-boiled egg, in the way he cleans a bicycle chain or polishes a shoe.

Second, the THAD can add texture to the viewpoint character if she is the one engaged in activity. The careful choice of the viewpoint character's THAD can reveal or illustrate the POV character's emotional state, psychological state or physical state. For example, if your viewpoint character is performing surgery, an artery might be just barely in sight, waiting to be 'accidentally' nicked. Or your alcoholic character might be cooking breakfast after an inebriated night, only to discover what the sight of an egg she's just cracked into a frying pan does to her digestive system and thus to her ability to believe the story she's been telling herself about how much she can handle when it comes to booze.

Third, the THAD can add details to the setting of the scene. If a character is going to be engaged in an activity, the activity is going to occur somewhere. The more that the character engages in the activity, the more we can see aspects of his personality while getting a fuller sense of place. When Barbara Havers and Bea Hannaford interview Will Mendick, he's living out his freegan beliefs by excavating for food in a wheelie bin behind a supermarket. This allows me both to make the scene more real and to reveal the attitudes of all three of the characters.

Fourth, the THAD can increase the tension or the conflict between the viewpoint and non-viewpoint characters. This works especially well if the THAD is something that makes the reader's skin crawl and allows her to project her reaction onto the character performing the THAD. Gutting a majestic but newly killed animal is an example of this, especially when the details are intimate and brutally given, such as pulling out the intestines, throwing them to the floor, stepping in them, and laughing about it all. Done in the presence of a character who's there to seek a donation for PETA, or a child who's supposed to be learning how to be a 'real man', or detectives who are there to ask about the animal-gutter's missing wife? Tension is built into the scene; conflict is inevitable.

A THAD's power lies in all the things it says without saying anything at all. It enriches the experience for the reader. Done well, it fixes the character in a reader's mind, which is crucial to a book in which there are many characters interacting with one another.

At the same time, a THAD can address other elements of storytelling. It can foreshadow events to come, it can alter the tone of a scene, it can set a mood, and it can underscore the theme.

Thus, the THAD is another of the tools of fiction writing available to you. Here it is at work in a scene told from Bea Hannaford's POV.

Bea pulled into a space that was near a large timber barn, which opened into the car park. Within, two tractors – hardly in use, considering their pristine condition – were serving as perches for three stately looking peacocks, their sumptuous tail feathers cascading in a colourful effluence across the tops of cabs and down the sides of engines. Beyond the barn, another structure – this one combining both granite and timber – displayed huge oaken barrels, presumably ageing the farm's product. Rising behind this building the apple orchard grew, and it climbed the slope of a hill, row after row of trees pruned to grow like inverted pyramids, a proud display of delicate blossoms. A furrowed lane bisected the orchard. In the distance, some sort of tour seemed to be bumping along it: an open wagon pulled by a plodding draught horse.

Across the lane, a gate gave entrance into the attractions of the cider farm. These comprised a gift shop and café along with yet another gate that appeared to lead to the cider-production area, the perusal of which demanded a ticket.

Or police identification, as things turned out. Bea showed hers to a young woman behind the till in the gift shop and asked to speak to Aldara Pappas on a matter of some urgency. The girl's silver lip ring quivered as she directed Bea to the inner workings of the farm. She said, 'Watching over the mill,' by which Bea took it that the woman they were looking for could be found at . . . perhaps a grinding mill? What did one do with apples, anyway? And was this the time of year to be doing it?

The answers turned out to be sorting, washing, chopping, slicing, pressing, and no. The mill in question was a piece of machinery – constructed of steel and painted bright blue – attached to an enormous wooden bin by means of a trough. The machinery of the mill itself consisted of this trough, a barrel-like bath, a water source, a rather sinister-looking press not dissimilar to an enormous vise, a wide pipe and a mysterious chamber at the top of this pipe, which at the moment was open and being seen to by two individuals. One was a man wielding various tools against the machinery that appeared to operate a series of very sharp blades. The other was a woman who seemed to be monitoring his every move. He was wearing a knitted cap that came down to his eyebrows, as well as grease-stained jeans and a blue flannel shirt. She was garbed in jeans, boots and a thick but cosy-looking chenille sweater. She was saying, 'Take *care*, Rod. I don't want you bleeding all over my blades,' to which he replied, 'No worries, luv. I been looking after clobber lots more difficult 'n this lot since you was in nappies.'

'Aldara Pappas?' Bea said.

The woman turned. She was quite exotic for this part of the world, not exactly pretty but striking, with large dark eyes, hair that was thick and shiny and black and dramatic red lipstick emphasising a sensual mouth. The rest of her was sensual as well. Curves in all the right places, as Bea knew her former husband might have said. She looked to be somewhere in her forties, if the fine lines round her eyes were anything to go by.

The woman said, 'Yes,' and gave one of those woman-evaluating-the-competition sort of looks both to Bea and to DS Havers. She seemed to linger particularly on the sergeant's hair. The colour of this was sandy, the style not so much a style as an eloquent statement about impatience: *Hacked over the bathroom sink* seemed to be the best description. 'What can I do for you?' Aldara Pappas's tone suggested the task was hopeless.

'A bit of conversation will do.' Bea showed her identification. She nodded to Havers to show hers as well. The sergeant didn't look happy about doing so since this required her to conduct an archaeological excavation through her shoulder bag, seeking the leather lump that went for her wallet.

'New Scotland Yard,' Havers told Aldara Pappas. Bea watched for a reaction.

The woman's face was still although Rod gave an appreciative whistle. 'What you get up to now, luv?' he asked Aldara. 'You been poisoning the customers again?'

Aldara smiled faintly and told him to carry on. 'I'll be at the house if you need me,' she said.

She told Bea and Havers to follow her, and she took them through the cobbled courtyard of which the mill formed one edge. The other edges consisted of a jam kitchen, a cider museum and an empty stall, presumably for the draught horse. In the middle of the yard, a pen housed a pig the approximate size of a Volkswagen Beetle. He snorted suspiciously and charged the fence.

'I could do with less drama, Stamos,' Aldara told the animal. Understanding or not, he retreated to a pile of what looked like rotting vegetation. He stuck his snout into this and flipped a portion of it into the air. 'Clever boy,' Aldara said. 'Do eat up.'

He was an orchard pig, she told them as she ducked through an arched gate that was partially concealed by a heavy vine, to the far side of the jam kitchen. PRIVATE was fixed onto a sign that swung from the gate's handle. 'His job used to be to eat the unusable apples after the harvest: let him loose in the orchard and stand aside. Now he's supposed to add an air of authenticity to the place, for visitors. The problem is that he wishes more to attack them than to fascinate them. Now. What can I do for you?'

Had they thought Aldara Pappas meant to make them welcome by leading them towards her house and offering them a nice steaming cuppa, they were soon corrected in that notion. The house was a farm cottage with a vegetable garden in front of it, odoriferous piles of manure sitting at the end of raised beds neatly defined by wooden rails. At one side of the garden was a small stone shed. She took them to this and dislodged a shovel and a rake from its interior, along with a pair of gloves. She brought a head scarf from the pocket of her jeans and used it to cover and hold back her hair in the fashion of a peasant woman or, for that matter, certain members of the royal family. Thus ready for labour, she began to shovel the manure and the compost into the vegetable beds. Nothing had been planted there yet.

She said, 'I'll continue with my chores while we talk, if you don't mind. How might I help you?'

'We came to talk about Santo Kerne,' Bea informed her. She jerked her head at Havers to indicate that the sergeant's usual brand of ostentatious note taking was to begin. Havers obliged. She was watching Aldara steadily, and Bea liked the fact that Havers didn't seem the least bit cowed by another – and decidedly more attractive – woman.

Aldara said, 'Santo Kerne. What about him?'

'We'd like to talk to you about your relationship with him.'

'My relationship with him. What about it?'

'I hope this isn't going to be your style of answering,' Bea said.

'My style of answering. What do you mean?'

'The Little Miss Echo bit, Miss Pappas. Or is it Missus?'

'Aldara will do.'

'Aldara, then. If it *is* your style – the echoing bit – we're likely to be with you most of the day, and something tells me you'd not appreciate that. We'd be happy enough to oblige, however.'

'I'm not sure I understand your meaning.'

'The gaff's been blown,' Sergeant Havers told her. Her tone was impatient. 'The chicken's flown the coop. The orchard pig's in the laundry. Whatever works.'

'What the sergeant means,' Bea added, 'is that your relationship with Santo Kerne has come to light, Aldara. That's why we're here: to sort through it.'

'You were bonking him till he was blue in the face,' Sergeant Havers put in.

'Not to put too fine a point on it,' Bea added.

Aldara thrust her shovel into the pile of manure and hefted a load of it onto one of the beds. She looked as if she would have preferred hefting it at Havers. 'This is your surmise,' she pointed out.

'This is what we were told by someone who knows,' Bea said. 'She, evidently, was the one to wash the sheets when you didn't get round to it. Now, since you had to meet at Polcare Cottage, may we assume there's a middle-aged Mr. Pappas somewhere who wouldn't be too pleased to know his wife was having it off with an eighteen-year-old boy?'

Aldara went for another shovelful of manure. She was working rapidly but barely took a deep breath, and she didn't come close to breaking a sweat. 'You may not assume. I've been divorced for years, Inspector. There's a Mr. Pappas, but he's in St. Ives, and we see virtually nothing of each other. We quite like it that way.'

'Have you children here, then? A daughter Santo's age, perhaps? Or an adolescent son you'd prefer didn't see his mummy dropping her knickers for another teenager?'

Aldara's jaw hardened. Bea wondered which of her comments had hit the mark.

'I met Santo for sex in Polcare Cottage for one reason only: because both of us preferred it that way,' Aldara said. 'It was a private matter, and that's what each of us wanted.'

'Privacy? Or secrecy?'

'Both.'

'Why? Embarrassed to be doing a kid?'

'Hardly.' Aldara drove her shovel into the earth, and just as Bea thought she intended to take a rest, she went for the rake. She climbed into the nearest planting bed and began energetically working the manure into the soil. She said, 'I have no embarrassment about sex. Sex is what it is, Inspector. Sex. And we both wanted sex, Santo and I. With each other, as it happens. But as this is something difficult for some people to understand – because of his age and my own – we sought a private place to . . .' She appeared to be looking for a euphemism, which seemed completely out of character in the woman.

'To service each other?' Havers offered. She managed to look bored, an I've-heard-it-all-before-now expression on her face.

'To be together,' Aldara said firmly. 'For an hour. For two or three early on, when we were new together and . . . still discovering, I would call it.'

'Discovering what?' Bea said.

'What pleased the other. It *is* a process of discovery, isn't it, Inspector? Discovery leading to pleasure. Or did you not know sex is about giving one's partner pleasure?'

Bea let that one pass. 'So this wasn't a love-and-heartbreak situation for you.'

Aldara cast her a look. It spoke of both incredulity and long experience. 'Only a fool equates sex with love, and I'm not a fool.'

'Was he?'

'Did he love me? Was this love-and-heartbreak, as you put it, for him? I have no idea. We didn't speak of that. When it comes to it, we spoke very little at all after the initial arrangement. As I've said, this was about sex. The physical only. Santo knew that.'

'Initial arrangement?' Bea asked.

'Are you echoing me, Inspector?' Aldara smiled, but she directed the expression to the earth that she was busily raking.

Briefly, Bea understood the impulse investigators often had to smack a suspect. She said, 'Why don't you explain this "initial arrangement" to us, Aldara? And while you're doing it, perhaps you can touch upon your apparent lack of feeling regarding the murder of your lover, which, as you might surmise, certainly looks as if it can be linked rather more directly to you than you otherwise might appreciate.'

'I had nothing to do with Santo Kerne's death. I regret it, of course. And if I'm not prostrate with grief over it, that would be because—'

'It wasn't a love-and-heartbreak situation for you, either,' Bea said. 'That's certainly clear as Swiss air. So what was it? What was it *exactly*, please?'

'I've told you. It was an arrangement he and I had for sex.'

'Did you know he was getting it elsewhere at the same time he was getting it from – or doing it to or *whatever* the hell it was – to you?'

'Of course I knew it.' Aldara sounded placid. 'That was part of it.'

'It? What? The arrangement? What was "it"? A threesome?'

'Hardly. Part of it was the secrecy of it all, the aspect of having an affair, the fact that he had someone else. I *wanted* someone with someone else. That's how I like it.'

Bea saw Havers blink, as if to clear her vision, like Alice finding herself down a rabbit hole with a randy bunny when prior experience had led her to expect only the Mad Hatter, the March Hare and a cup of tea. Bea herself didn't feel dissimilar.

She said, 'So you knew about Madlyn Angarrack, that she was involved with Santo Kerne.'

'Yes. That's how I met Santo in the first place. Madlyn worked for me here, in the jam kitchen. Santo fetched her at the end of the day several times, and I saw him then. Everyone saw him. It was most difficult not to see Santo. He was a highly attractive boy.'

'And Madlyn's a rather attractive girl.'

'She is. Well, of course, she would be. And so am I, if it comes to that. An attractive woman. I find that attractive people are drawn to each other, don't you?' Another glance in the direction of the police made it obvious that Aldara Pappas didn't consider this question to be one that either of them could answer from personal experience. She said, 'We took note of each other, Santo and I. I was at the point of needing someone very like him—'

'Someone with attachments?'

' – and I thought he might do, as there was a directness to his gaze that spoke of a certain maturity, a frame of mind that suggested he and I might speak the same language. We exchanged looks, smiles. It was a form of communication in which like-minded individuals say precisely what needs to be said and nothing more. He arrived early one day to fetch Madlyn, and I took him on a tour of the farm. We rode the tractor into the orchards, and it was there—'

'Just like Eve beneath the apple tree?' Havers said. 'Or were you the snake?'

Aldara refused to be drawn out. She said, 'This had nothing to do with temptation. Temptation depends on innuendo and there was no innuendo involved. I was forthright with him. I said the look of him appealed to me and I had been thinking what it would be like to have him in bed. How pleasant it might be for us both, if he was interested. I told him that if he wanted more than only his little girlfriend as a sexual partner, he was to phone me. At no time did I suggest he end his relationship with her. That would actually have been the last thing I wanted, as it might have made him rather too fond of me. It might have led to expectations of there being something more than was possible between us. On his part, these expectations, that is. On mine there were none.'

'I can see it might well have put you in a ludicrous light had he expected more and had you been forced to give it to him in order to keep him,' Bea noted. 'A woman your age going public – as it were – with a teenage boy. Trotting down the aisle in church on Sunday morning, nodding to your neighbours and all of them thinking how . . . well, how *lacking* in something you must be to have to settle for an eighteen-year-old lover.'

Aldara moved to another pile of manure. She fetched the shovel and began to repeat the process she'd followed for the first vegetable bed. The earth within became rich and dark. Whatever she intended to plant within the borders of the bed, it was going to flourish.

She said, 'First of all, Inspector, I don't concern myself with what other people think, as what other people think about me – or anyone else or any *thing* for that matter – does not rob me of a single eyelash. This was a private matter between Santo and me. I kept it private. So did he.'

'Not exactly,' Havers noted. 'Madlyn found out.'

'That was unfortunate. He wasn't careful enough, and she followed him. There was one of those dreadful scenes between them – the accosting, the accusing, the denial, the admission, the explaining, the pleading – and she ended their involvement on the spot. That put me in the very last position I wished to be in: as Santo's sole lover.'

'Did she know you were the woman inside the cottage when she turned up there?'

'Of course she knew. There was such a scene between them that I thought she might do violence. I had to emerge from the bedroom and do something about it.'

'Which was?'

'To separate them. To keep her from destroying the cottage or attacking him.' She leaned on her shovel and looked north, in the direction of the orchards, as if reliving her initial proposal to Santo Kerne and what that proposal had ultimately brought about. She said, as if she'd only just thought of the matter, 'It was not supposed to be such a drama. When it became one, I had to rethink my own involvement with Santo.'

'Did you give him the old heave-ho as well?' Havers asked. 'Not wanting big drama in your life.'

'I intended to, but—'

'I doubt he would have liked that much,' Havers said. 'What bloke would? Finding himself out of two dolly birds in one fell swoop instead of just one. Being reduced to what . . . wanking in the shower? . . . when before he was getting it on all sides. I'll wager he would've fought you on that one. Maybe even told you he could make things a bit tough on you, a bit embarrassing, if you tried to break it off.'

What I've given you is only part of a lengthy scene, but if we examine how it's constructed, you'll note that first Aldara's environment – the landscape in which she operates – is described. A return to the cider farm – this time in the point of view of Bea Hannaford, who has never been there – allows for an expansion in the previous description of the place and includes another character's reaction to Aldara Pappas and her life philosophy as it relates to her sexuality and its expression. As you read the partial scene, I hope you noticed that all three women have a different style of speaking, with Barbara Havers's style the most casual and colloquial. There are two THADs, the first one being the repair of the apple crushing machinery and the second being the shovelling and distributing of manure in the vegetable beds. Aldara's actions allow the reader to see her unspoken responses to what Bea and Barbara are saying. The full scene goes on to show an oddity to her actions as well: Aldara hasn't bothered to remove her good boots and put something else on her feet, such as Wellingtons. This strikes the wrong note as far as Bea is concerned. Aldara Pappas isn't as casual about her lovers as she would like everyone to think.

This is what a THAD looks like in action. It is added to make the scene more realistic, to avoid talking heads, and to allow more details about characters to be revealed. Also, during the scene, more information is offered to the reader, so the story is moved along.

## Optional Exercise 1

Previously, you created two pages of dialogue, the dialogue intended to differentiate between two characters. Now broaden that dialogue into the beginning of a scene. Use the following format:

Set the scene first, moving from the general landscape to the specific setting.
Choose a THAD that will illuminate the non-viewpoint character.
Include the attitude of the POV character towards whatever the THAD is.

## Optional Exercise 2

Create a list of THADs. Deliberately include ones that have big potential to reveal character while evoking a response in the POV character and in the reader. This is actually one of the most useful tools that you can create for yourself. To do it, use the present participle of the verb and just complete the 'picture'. Examples are:

Eating a soft-boiled egg _____

Burying _____

Creating _____

Painting _____

Cooking _____

Killing _____

Eradicating _____

Punching _____

Repairing _____

And on and on. Use verbs that offer you the most bang for the buck through what they can suggest about a character.

---

# CHAPTER 7

# Viewpoint and Voice

## *Who Can Tell the Story Best?*

Point of view is quite easy to understand in that it refers to the character or characters through whose eyes the story or an individual scene in the story is going to be seen or be told. In brief, there are six viewpoints from which a writer can choose:

**Objective viewpoint:** in which the narration stays outside the characters at all times and the story is told objectively and without attitude, as if by a reporter.

**Omniscient viewpoint:** in which an all-knowing narrator who is not the author but who exists outside and beyond the author tells the story. The omniscient narrator is a powerful being who can telescope scenes, collapse scenes, summarise narratives, make comments about characters and have opinions.

**First person:** in which a single character tells the story from her sole point of view and with her sole attitude.

**First person shifting:** in which the viewpoint character who's telling the story alters as the story progresses. The alteration is generally indicated by new chapters or new sections of the book, but this – like everything else in novel writing – is not a hard-and-fast rule.

**Third person:** in which the story is seen and told through the eyes
and with the attitude of a single character.

**Third person shifting:** in which the story is seen and told through
the eyes and with the attitudes of multiple characters.

To choose a viewpoint, then, the writer must answer two self-imposed
questions: Among the characters that I've created, who can tell the story
best? and Whose individual story – as revealed in the character analysis –
appears to be compelling enough to sustain a POV throughout the entire
novel?

You'll no doubt notice that first person POV and third person POV
sound very similar, and they are. As I see it, the main difference is that with
first person you have a narrator who is in a position to relate directly the
action in a scene as well as her thoughts, feelings, and reactions to what's
going on. With a third person narrative, however, action is normally rendered, rather than related. We're seeing it as it happens, not hearing about
it later or merely being told it's happening. Narrative reactions to what's
going on tend to be rendered as well.

What I mean by this is that the third person narrator isn't simply 'angry'
as a first person narrator is. Instead, the third person narrator experiences
the physiology of anger, relating for the reader what anger is doing to her
body, without using the word *anger* at all: her stomach tightens, heat suf-
fuses her face, her head begins to pound, her teeth clench so hard that they
ache. While a first person narrator would experience all this, it wouldn't
make sense to render it when the first person narrator could simply say 'I
was so angry I wanted to bite off his ear, just to taste his blood.'

You'll also note that I haven't mentioned second person as a point of
view. This is because it's rarely used, and even when it *is* used, its success
is limited. For me, additionally, the reading of a second person narrative is
both tiresome and exhausting. Because of its showboat nature, it draws attention to itself and, as a result, draws attention away from the story with

its constant repetition of *you*. I see it working well in a short story or even in a few pages of narrative in the body of a novel. But I personally doubt my ability to sustain interest with it, so I don't use it.

Once the writer makes the POV decision, the POV character or characters each must have a distinct *voice*. The POV character's voice is not the voice of the author. Instead, it's a voice that reflects who the character is, how the character thinks, what the character's attitudes are, what the character's agenda is.

Voice, then, is yet another tool the writer has to engage with the reader. Without it, a scene can lose a lot – if not all – of its punch. With it, the reader has a chance to connect in some way with the POV character. Engagement and connection are what lead to page turning in a character-driven novel. And any kind of novel can be character-driven: literary, commercial, genre-specific, young adult, children's chapter books and so on.

The following example is from Lynley's POV. Hence, it should reflect who he is, how he thinks, what he feels, what he imagines, etc. And the voice of the narration is his voice.

Because there was no point in putting it off, he went to the phone and punched in the numbers. He was hoping that there would be no answer, just a machine picking up so that he could leave a brief message without the human contact. But after five double rings, he heard her voice. There was nothing for it but to speak.

He said, 'Mother. Hullo.'

At first she said nothing and he knew what she was doing: standing next to the phone in the drawing room or perhaps her morning room or elsewhere in the grand sprawling house that was his birthright and even more his curse, raising one hand to her lips, looking towards whoever else was in the room and that would likely be his younger brother or perhaps the manager of the estate or even his sister in the unlikely event that she was still down from Yorkshire. And her eyes – his mother's eyes – would communicate the information before she said his name. It's Tommy. He's phoned. Thank God. He's all right.

She said, 'Darling. Where are you? *How* are you?'

He said, 'I've run into something . . . It's a situation up in Casvelyn.'

'My God, Tommy. Have you walked that far? Do you know how—' But she didn't say the rest. She meant to ask whether he knew how worried they were. But she loved him and she wouldn't burden him further.

As he loved her, he answered her anyway. 'I know. I do. Please understand that. It's just that I can't seem to find my way.'

She knew, of course, that he wasn't referring to his sense of direction. 'My dear, if I could do anything to remove this from your shoulders . . .'

He could hardly bear the warmth of her voice, her unending compassion, especially when she herself had borne so many of her own tragedies throughout the years. He said to her, 'Yes. Well,' and he cleared his throat roughly.

'People have phoned,' she told him. 'I've kept a list. And they've not stopped phoning, the way you think people might. You know what I mean: one phone call and there, I've done my duty. It hasn't been like that. There has been such concern for you. You are so deeply loved, my dear.'

He didn't want to hear it, and he had to make her understand that. It wasn't that he didn't value the concern of his friends and associates. It was that their concern – and what was worse, their *expression* of it – rubbed a place in him already so raw that having it touched by anything was akin to torture. He'd left his home because of this, because on the coast path there was no one in March and few enough people in April and even if he ran across someone in his walk, that person would know nothing of him, of what he was doing trudging steadily forward day after day, or of what had led up to his decision to do so.

He said, 'Mother . . .'

She heard it in his voice, as she would do. She said, 'Dearest, I'm sorry. No more of it.' Her voice altered, becoming more businesslike, for which he was grateful. 'What's happened? You're all right, aren't you? You've not been injured?'

No, he told her. He wasn't injured. But he'd come upon someone who *had* been. He was the first to come upon him, it seemed. A boy. He'd been killed in a fall from one of the cliffs. Now the police were involved. As he'd left at home everything that would identify him . . . Could she send him his wallet? 'It's form, I daresay. They're just in the process of sorting everything out. It looks like an accident but, obviously, until they know, they won't want me going off. And they do want me to prove I am who I say I am.'

'Do they know you're a policeman, Tommy?'

'One of them, apparently. Otherwise, I've told them only my name.'

'Nothing else?'

'No.' It would have turned things into a Victorian melodrama: My good man – or in this case woman – do you *know* who you're talking to? He'd go for the police rank first and if that didn't impress, he'd try the title next. *That* should produce some serious forelock pulling, if nothing else. Only, DI Hannaford didn't appear to be the sort who pulled on forelocks, at least not her own. He said, 'So they're not willing to take me at my word and who can blame them. I wouldn't take me at my word. Will you send the wallet?'

'Of course. At once. Shall I have Peter drive it up to you in the morning?'

He didn't think he could bear his brother's anxious concern. He said, 'Don't trouble him with that. Just put it in the post.'

He told her where he was and she asked – as she would – if the inn was pleasant, at least, if his room was comfortable, if the bed would suit him. He told her everything was fine. He said that he was, in fact, looking forward to bathing.

His mother was reassured by that, if not entirely satisfied. While the desire for a bath did not necessarily indicate a desire to continue living, it at least declared a willingness to muddle forward for a while. That would do. She rang off after telling him to have a good, long, luxurious soak and hearing him say that a good, long, luxurious soak was exactly his intention.

Here we have a scene in which two people of the same social class – Lynley and his mother – are speaking to each other on the phone. Because the narrative is in Lynley's POV, some scene setting can be done, which I handle through his imagination: his mother is somewhere in *the grand sprawling house that was his birthright and even more his curse*; she's standing, her hand to her lips as she hears his voice for the first time in several months; she glances at whoever else might be in the room with her when she takes the call. Then comes a speculation about his mother from Lynley's mind: *It's Tommy. He's phoned. Thank God. He's all right.*

Their dialogue needs to be specific to each of them, illustrating not only who they are as individuals but also what they are to each other. They have a chequered past that includes a sixteen-year estrangement. But tragedies have touched both of their lives, giving them a bond that I want the reader to see.

There's a formality to their patterns of speech. This grows out of their social class as well as the nature of their relationship and the circumstances of Lynley's departure from the family home to engage in the long trek on the South-West Coast Path. We see this formality in lines like *'My dear, if I could do anything to remove this from your shoulders . . .'* and *'There has been such concern for you. You are so deeply loved, my dear'* and *'So they're not willing to take me at my word and who can blame them. I wouldn't take me at my word. Will you send the wallet?'*

Lynley calls the dowager countess the formal *Mother*. He doesn't use *Mum* or *Mummy*, and throughout the scene he keeps himself under a deter-mined kind of control so that he can get through the conversation and state what he needs: his wallet, which contains his police identification. We know what he's enduring in the scene because it's told from his POV, and we see the excruciating nature of his suffering in his brief reflection: *He didn't want to hear it, and he had to make her understand that. It wasn't that he didn't value the concern of his friends and associates. It was that their concern – and what was worse, their* expression *of it – rubbed a place in him already so raw that having it touched by anything was akin to torture.*

So throughout, the reader is presented with Lynley's attitude and his emotional state, and both his reflections in the narrative and his dialogue indicate this. At the same time, the reader sees his mother's dialogue, dem-onstrating her voice, which is one of love and understanding and a desire to support her son. There's an exposure to their restrained emotions, and throughout his mother's dialogue we also see her attitude: She will indeed do anything for her son whose anguish touches her so deeply.

If you think about the character Barbara Havers and how her voice and her dialogue have been depicted in the readings so far, you can, I hope, conclude that she would not have approached a conversation with Lynley in the manner in which his mother approached it. As members of com-pletely different classes, everything about the way they speak is crafted to show who they are.

The development of a character's voice comes from the writer's know-ledge of the character. The more the writer knows about a character, the more easily the writer can develop the character's voice. Daidre Trahair, for example, like all the other characters, was created in advance of any writing of the novel. Among other things, I knew that she is the oldest child of a tin streamer (someone who tries to make a living by extracting tin from river stones) and that she was removed from her home at thirteen years of age along with a brother and a sister. At the time of their removal the children were unkempt, uneducated and badly taken care of. I knew that they were taken into care, and I knew that while Daidre ended up with a good family who saw to her needs and her education and who thought of her as their own child, her brother and sister were not so lucky. I also knew that until recently she had been estranged from her birth parents and her siblings. During the time of the novel, her mother is dying but persisting in the belief that a miracle can occur.

This is what Daidre sounds like in her own POV, her background allowing her some knowledge of mining that other characters might not share:

> This part of Cornwall was completely unlike the vicinity of Casvelyn. Here, Daidre parked her Vauxhall in the triangle of pebble-strewn weeds that served as a meeting point of the two roads, and she sat with her chin on her hands and her hands on the top of the steering wheel. She looked out at a landscape green with spring, rippling into the distance towards the sea, penetrated periodically by derelict towers similar to those one found in the Irish countryside, the domiciles of poets, hermits and mystics. Here, however, the old towers represented what remained of Cornwall's great mining industry: each of them an enormous engine house that sat atop a network of tunnels, pits and caverns beneath the earth. These were the mines that once had produced tin and silver, copper and lead, arsenic and wolfram. Their engine houses had contained the machinery that kept the mine operational:

pumping engines that rid the mines of water, and whims that hauled both the ore and the waste rock in bucketlike kibbles up to the surface.

Like gipsy caravans, the engine houses were the stuff of picture postcards now. But once they'd been the mainstay of people's lives, as well as the symbol of so many people's destruction. They stood all over the western part of Cornwall, and they existed in inordinate numbers particularly along much of the coast. Generally, they came in pairs: the tower of the mighty stone engine house rising three or four floors and roofless now, with narrow arched windows as small as possible to avoid weakening the overall structure, and next to it – often soaring above it – the smokestack, which had once belched grim clouds into the sky. Now both the engine house and the smokestack provided a nesting place for birds above and a hiding place for dormice below and, in the crannies and crevices of the structures, a growing place for herb Robert's pert magenta flowers that tangled with yellow bursts of ragwort as red valerian rose above them.

Daidre saw all this at the same time as she did not see it. She found herself thinking of another place entirely, on the coast opposite the one towards which she now gazed.

It was near Lamorna Cove, he'd said. The house and the estate upon which the house sat were together called Howenstow. He'd said – with some evident embarrassment – that he had no idea where the name of the place had come from, and from this admission she'd concluded – incorrectly or not – his ease with the life into which he'd been born. For over two hundred and fifty years his family had occupied both the house and the land, and apparently there had never been a need for them to know anything more than the fact of its being theirs: a sprawling Jacobean structure into which some long-ago ancestor had married, the youngest son of a baron making a match with the only child – the daughter – of an earl.

'My mother could probably tell you everything about the old pile,'
he'd said. 'My sister as well. My brother and I . . . I'm afraid we've both
rather let down the side when it comes to family history. Without Judith
– that's my sister – I'd likely not know the names of my own great-
grandparents. And you?'

'I suppose I did have great-grandparents somewhere along the
line,' she'd replied. 'Unless, of course, I came like Venus via the half
shell. But that's not very likely, is it? I think I'd have remembered such
a spectacular entry.'

So what was it like? she wondered. What *was* it like? She pictured
his mother in a great gilded bed, servants on either side of her gently
dabbing her face with handkerchiefs soaked in rose water as she la-
boured to bring forth a beloved son. Fireworks upon the announcement of an heir and tenant farmers tugging their forelocks and hoisting
jugs of homebrew as the news went round. She knew the image was
completely absurd, like Thomas Hardy meeting Monty Python, but
stupidly, foolishly she could not let it go. So she finally cursed herself,
and she scooped up the postcard she'd brought from her cottage. She
got out of the car into the chilly breeze.

She found a suitable stone just on the verge of the B3297. The rock
was light enough and not half buried, which made its removal easy. She
carried it back to the triangular juncture of the road and the lane, and
at the apex of this triangle she set the stone down. Then she tilted it and
placed the postcard of the gipsy wagon beneath it. That done, she was
ready to resume her journey.

The first two paragraphs fix Daidre in place. We see what she sees and
we learn what she knows about the mines in Cornwall and what they produced. We touch on her attitude with *the smokestack, which had once belched
grim clouds into the sky,* and then we suddenly step away from the countryside
with its ruined mine machinery as Daidre finds herself thinking about a

conversation she had with Lynley in which she learns a bit about where he is from. She finds this intimidating, and her imagination presents her with an image of Thomas Lynley's birth. She knows the image is ridiculous – *like Thomas Hardy meeting Monty Python* – but her own background makes it impossible for her to let that image go.

The end of the scene puts a stop to her mental wandering, but it also adds another layer to the mystery of Daidre while laying down dramatic questions about why Daidre does what she does, about who she is, and about how she feels.

To illustrate how a POV character needs to have a voice dissimilar to other POV characters, consider the following introduction to a scene with Cadan Angarrack.

> The rain stopped in Casvelyn not long after midday, and for this Cadan Angarrack was grateful. He'd been painting radiators in the guest rooms of Adventures Unlimited since his arrival that morning, and the fumes were causing his head to pound. He couldn't sort out why they had him painting radiators anyway. Who was going to notice them? Who *ever* noticed whether radiators were painted when they were in a hotel? No one except perhaps a hotel inspector and what did it amount to if a hotel inspector noticed a bit of rust in the ironwork? Nothing. Abso-bloody-lutely nothing. And anyway, it wasn't like the decrepit Promontory King George Hotel was being taken back to its former glory, was it? It was merely being made habitable for the hordes inter-ested in a holiday package on the sea that consisted of fun, frolic, food and some kind of instruction in an outdoor activity. And *that* lot didn't care where they stayed at night, as long as it was clean, served chips and stayed within the budget.
>
> So when the skies cleared, Cadan decided that a bit of fresh air was just the ticket. He would have a look at the crazy golf course, future location of the BMX trails, future site of the BMX lessons that Cadan

was certain would be requested of him once he had a chance to show his stuff to . . . That was the problem of the moment. He wasn't quite sure to whom he would be showing anything.

Indeed, he hadn't been certain he was even supposed to come into work on this day, as he wasn't sure that he had a job after what had happened to Santo. At first, he'd thought he simply wouldn't show up. He thought he'd let a few days roll by and then he'd phone and express whatever condolences he could come up with and ask did they still want him to do maintenance work. But then he reckoned a phone call like that would give them a chance to sack him before he'd even had a chance to demonstrate how valuable he could be. So he'd decided to put in an appearance at the place and to look as doleful as possible round any Kerne he might run into.

Cadan's voice needs to reflect his age and his attitude, and through a selection of details from his working life at Adventures Unlimited, we have a demonstration of both, supplemented by character-specific word choice. He's been taxed with painting all the radiators in the *decrepit Promontory King George Hotel,* and he asks himself the pertinent question, *What did it amount to if a hotel inspector noticed a bit of rust in the ironwork? Nothing. Abso-bloody-lutely nothing.* We learn that the hotel was *merely being made habitable for the hordes interested in a holiday package on the sea* and that these hordes *didn't care where they stayed at night, as long as it was clean, served chips and stayed within the budget.* Cadan isn't certain how he is supposed to be acting now that Santo Kerne is dead. *At first, he'd thought he simply wouldn't show up. He thought he'd let a few days roll by and then he'd phone and express whatever condolences he could come up with . . .* But he goes to work instead and intends *to look as doleful as possible round any Kerne he might run into.* The selection of words and the arrangement of thoughts make it clear that Cadan is no mourner of Santo Kerne's death. They also show his agenda – *future site of the BMX lessons that Cadan was certain would be requested of him* – and the frustration with which he daily greets the tedious work he's been doing since being dismissed from employment at his father's surfboard enterprise.

Compare Cadan's POV voice to Ben Kerne's POV voice in this scene with his wife, Dellen, in extremis over the death of their son:

> He finally entered their bedroom at midmorning. Dellen lay diagonally across the bed. She breathed a heavy, drug-induced sleep, and the bottle of pills that had sent her there was uncapped on the bedside table, where the light still burned, as it had likely done all night, Dellen too incapacitated to turn it off.
>
> He sat on the edge of the bed. She did not awaken. She hadn't changed out of her clothing on the previous night, and her red scarf formed a pool beneath her head, its fringe fanning out like petals with Dellen its centre, the heart of the flower.
>
> His curse was that he still could love her. His curse was that he could look at her now and, despite everything and especially despite Santo's murder, he could still want to claim her because she possessed and, he feared, would forever possess the ability to wipe from his heart and his mind everything else that was not Dellen. And he did not understand how this could be or what terrible twist of his psyche made it so.
>
> Her eyes opened. In them and just for an instant, before awareness came to her completely, he saw the truth in the dullness of her expression: that what he needed from his wife she could not give him, though he would continue to try to take it from her again and again.
>
> She turned her head away.
>
> 'Leave me,' she said. 'Or kill me. Because I can't—'
>
> 'I saw his body,' Ben told her. 'Or rather, his face. They'd dissected him – that's what they do except they use a different word for it – so they kept him covered up to his chin. I could have seen the rest but I didn't want to. It was enough to see his face.'

'Oh God.'

'It was just a formality. They knew it was Santo. They have his car. They have his driving licence. So they didn't need me to look at him. I expect I could have closed my eyes at the last moment and just said yes, that's Santo, and not have looked at all.'

She raised her arm and pressed her fist against her mouth. He didn't want to evaluate all the reasons why he was compelled to speak at this point. All he accepted about himself was that he felt it necessary to do more than relay antiseptic information to his wife. He felt it necessary to move her out of herself and into the core of her motherhood, even if that meant she would blame him as he deserved to be blamed. It would be better, he thought, than watching her go elsewhere.

*She can't help it.* He'd reminded himself of that fact endlessly throughout the years. *She is not responsible. She needs me to help her.* He didn't know if this was the truth any longer. But to believe something else at this late hour would make more than a quarter century of his life a lie.

'I bear the fault for everything that happened,' he went on. 'I couldn't cope. I needed more than anyone could ever give me and when they couldn't give it, I tried to wring it from them. That's how it was with you and me. That's how it was with Santo.'

'You should have divorced me. Why in God's name did you never divorce me?' She began to weep. She turned to lie on her side, facing the bedside table where her bottle of pills stood. She reached for them as if intending another dose. He took up the bottle and said, 'Not now.'

'I need—'

'You need to stay here.'

'I can't. Give them to me. Don't leave me like this.'

It was the cause, the very root of the tree. *Don't leave me like this. I love you, I love you . . . I don't know why . . . My head feels like something about to blow up, and I can't help . . . Come here, my darling. Come here, come here.*

Ben's choice of the powerful word *dissected* in reference to Santo's post-mortem acts as a means of shocking Dellen *to move her out of herself and into the core of her motherhood, even if that meant she would blame him as he deserved to be blamed.* Through this means, our storehouse of knowledge about these two people increases as the reason for his commitment to her becomes clearer to the reader. At the same time, the reader comes across that reference to blame, which prompts another dramatic question.

Once again, we see Dellen in manipulative mode as she asks why he never divorced her, as she weeps and turns from him, as she reaches for the pills she takes to relieve her of having to live with her mental illness and dysfunction. And with her words, *'Don't leave me like this,'* we see the history of her marriage to Ben. His excruciating sense of responsibility has tied them together for more than twenty-five years, and she's managed to keep that sense of responsibility strong in him, both immobilising and imprisoning him.

Ben Kerne's POV voice is nothing like Cadan Angarrack's. His vocabulary is different, as is his attitude. Cadan's use of idioms is absent in Ben's speech, and the tone that grows from their two points of view is – or should be – completely different.

## Optional Exercise 1

You've previously created an analysis of a character. Now create a scene, an opening for a scene, or a partial scene told from that character's POV and using a minimum of dialogue. Your effort should demonstrate your character's voice and should rise from your analysis of her or him. It should contain the character's attitude and tone. Subtext will enrich the scene as will dramatic questions.

What you're attempting to do is to show more about your character and your character's attitudes through your choice of words. Word choice is always going to be an essential key to giving a character a narrative voice. Carefully selected adjectives (I call these attitudinal adjectives), adverbs, verbs and nouns are critical here. So is the turn of phrase (*like Thomas Hardy meeting Monty Python*) that declares more about how a character is thinking and feeling than would full paragraphs of explanation.

A character's POV voice adds colour to the narrative. Getting to a character's voice requires you to get inside that character's skin and, as Atticus Finch would say, walk around in it for a while.

## Optional Exercise 2

Using the list below, alter the words into attitudinal words or attitudinal phrases, all of which should reveal something about a character whose POV we're in.

### ADJECTIVES

Pretty . . . as scum on a pond.
Overweight
Ignorant
Bucktoothed
Ramshackle
Smelly

### ADVERBS

Quickly
Fastidiously
Slowly

Awkwardly

Simply

Foolishly

## VERBS

Break

Enter

Speak

Run

Burn

Cook

## NOUNS

Mother

Dog

House

Boat

Teacher

Girlfriend

# CHAPTER 8

# Development

*Process, Decisions and the Plot*

M uch about my writing process involves tricking the brain, and I have a brain that desperately needs to be tricked when it comes to being creative. My modus operandi can best be described using only three words: *planning and organising.* I live off lists and I think in outlines. You name it, I can figure out an organised way to accomplish it. I do this merely because my brain is wired to do this, which means I am programmed by fate to love stationery stores, office supply stores, container stores and magazines that show me how to organise my linen closet.

But my affinity for lists, outlines, and organisation isn't particularly helpful in writing a novel other than to organise myself *for* the writing of a novel. So when it comes to the actual writing and to the use of language, I need to trigger the right side of my brain, the creative side. To do this, I trick my brain by working with both sides of it. First, I appease the left side of my brain, which begs for organisation, by imposing upon my work a form of organisation which consists of addressing myself to all the elements of craft I've mentioned so far in this book. Thus, I've created a 'system' for novel writing: location research, followed by a plot kernel, followed by generic characters to people the world of the plot kernel, followed by specific characters, etc. This system allows me to think I'm completely in control.

Oddly enough, thinking I'm in control liberates the creative side of me so that it can start working during the steps of my process that call for free-writing. This creative side of my brain shows itself in those *aha!* moments I come across as I stream-of-consciousness write about my characters. It will also show itself when I get to the running plot outline. There will also be 'Oh my gosh!' moments as I freewrite during all the stages of my process. Those 'Oh my gosh!' moments will illuminate character or delineate plot for me because the left brain is happy that I've ostensibly 'imposed order' upon what could otherwise be a chaotic endeavour.

It's my belief that we all have some sort of creative artist within us, but much of that artist is held too easily at bay by our fears. These are numerous: the fear of failure, the fear of success, the fear of completing something and having to say 'Now what?,' the fear of looking foolish in the eyes of our friends, the fear of being criticised or judged. Some of us have a fear of even beginning at all. John Steinbeck wrote about the fear of the blank page. Gabriel García Márquez wrote about having to stand in the shower for two hours to get up his courage to get to work. Others of us fear the committee in our heads, which comprises everyone in our lives who has ever felt the need to weigh in critically on something about us: our hair, our dress sense, our weight, our occupation, our choice of life partner, our decorating sense, our handwriting, our anything-at-all. What we're trying to do is get rid of all of that in order to create a piece of art without the mind throwing obstructions in our paths.

Thus, everything I do that's part of my process exists to help me let go of my fears, dismiss my committee, and beguile the right side of my brain. Because my process imposes upon the creative act a form of structure, I end up with documents, notes and photographs that I can refer to whenever I feel anxious about what will happen next in a story.

So far I've explained the initial part of my process: some kind of idea comes first. In the case of the novel we've been looking at as an example of my process, the idea that came first was, as I've indicated, 'I think I'll write a novel about surfing in Cornwall, since most people don't associate surfing with England.' That, however, would have never been enough to get me into a story, so the second part of the process for this novel was asking myself questions about both surfing and murder and discussing these questions with someone else (in this case, with my husband). The result of the discussion we had about who was going to die and why turned into the plot kernel: this novel was going to be about a killing that was done to avenge the accidental death of a young surfer that occurred more than twenty years earlier. The killer would be that young surfer's father, who has waited patiently to take his revenge on the man he has been told is responsible.

When it comes to novel planning, the point about plot kernels that I'd like to stress is that they're everywhere. Your job is to school yourself to see them and to be willing to let go of what you thought you were going to write about if that clearly is *not* where you're being led or if that clearly isn't working for you.

Consider the following two headlines from actual newspaper stories:

**DOWRY: GIRL GOES THROUGH HELL**

and

**WHY DID SYLVIA DIE?**
**WOMAN AND BOY FACE HEARING TOMORROW**
**IN GIRL'S TORTURE DEATH**

I can see immediate plot kernels for several different kinds of novels when I look at those headlines. From them, it seems to me, one can create crime, adventure, suspense, thriller, women's fiction, science fiction, fantasy, or literary novels. Why is this the case? It's the case because both of the headlines prompt questions. Each headline suggests a world that can be filled with generic and then specific characters. Each offers potential directions and a destination for the story.

The location research that I did in Cornwall added to the plot kernel I'd come up with. It also added to the basic story, to the depth of the characters' lives, to the atmosphere, to my understanding of the various settings, and to the plot. Hence, my walking on the South-West Coast Path gave me the sea cliffs, which gave me the location of the murder. My exploration of various beaches gave me the sea caves, the site of the long-ago death that's being avenged. Stumbling upon a Cornish mining museum gave me Daidre Trahair's background. The towns of Bude and Zennor and the hamlet of Morwenstow gave me numerous settings for scenes.

Once you have the kernel of a plot, you know it's workable if you can expand it by asking and answering the logical questions that grow from the kernel's existence. In a crime novel, for example, the questions have to do with *who* (Who died? Who committed the killing? Who else is involved? Who is the detective?), *where* (Where did the killing occur? Where was the body found? Where does the story take place?), *why* (Why did the killer kill the victim?), *when* (When did the killing occur? When was the body discovered? When did the police become involved?) and *how* (How was the crime committed?). This gives you the story in its most general terms.

From those general terms come the characters, individuals who would most likely be part of the world of the story. As you create them, you discover the conflicts among them, the subplots you'll be uncovering for the reader, and the theme that will unify your writing. Also from the general terms of the story will come the main location and possibly any secondary locations you'll use. This will tell you whether you need to go out and about to research your setting and what kind of additional information you may have to glean from the Internet, from the library, from interviews with experts, or from conversations with members of your writing group, with your spouse or partner, or with your friends.

Ultimately, should you find that you must do some location research, you will also find that this enables you to establish atmosphere (such as the gloominess of the South-West Coast Path in bad weather) and the mood (which, in *Careless in Red*, is sombre).

All of this is going to help you when you get to the rough draft. Additionally, this work helps develop what I call a *fallback position*: something to look at, something to read, something to consider as you craft the story. Everything you've done in advance of sitting down to write the actual novel is foundation work, and upon it you will be able to build – successfully – the structure that is the novel itself.

Developing the plot is, more than anything, a process of making decisions. Early on, you're making all sorts of decisions, many of which get tossed out as you reflect upon them and deem them unreasonable, unworkable, ill-conceived, hackneyed, etc. I try to avoid making any firm decisions until my research seems complete. Note that I've said when it *seems* complete because there's no way to know how much more information I'm going to need until I get into the body of the novel. Suffice it to say that I've taken the research as far as I can and from it I've been able to expand the plot kernel into a brief statement of story. I've found over the years that even when I'm finished with the location research and the research that may deal with the means of murder and the opportunity to murder, there is unanticipated research that needs to be done simply because it's impossible to know everything about a story in advance. And really, who would want to know everything about a story in advance anyway?

We've already looked at the fact that, once your preliminary work is done, the first decision that you need to make has to do with point of view: choosing the character or characters through whose eyes the story is going to be seen and told. What lies before you next is a second decision: the status quo. This is the personal situation or the condition of all the characters *prior* to whatever is going to launch the story. As an example, the status quo of Susie Creamcheese is that she is a marginally happy married woman with two young children and a third on the way. Nothing other than regular life has happened in her world yet. As far as she is concerned, all is well. The revelation of her status quo might include her backstory. It might not. But in any case, it's who and what and how she is before anything has occurred to ripple the surface of her life.

The third decision is one that determines what constitutes the primary event (sometimes called the inciting incident), which is something that disrupts the status quo and gets your story rolling. For the aforementioned Susie Creamcheese it can be that her husband arrives home to announce that: he wants a divorce, he has made a fifteen-year-old girl pregnant, he has run over a woman with a child in a pushchair and has fled the scene, he has been offered a job in Nigeria, he is going to run for political office, he has just been featured on *America's Most Wanted* for a crime he committed twenty years earlier, he has just lost their house and their life savings in a poker game. It can be anything, obviously. The sole requirement of the primary event is that it disrupts the status quo of the characters in the novel.

For *Careless in Red*, the primary event is the death of Santo Kerne. It upends nearly everyone's life, sets Lynley on a path he does not wish to travel, and makes all the other characters come to terms with something about themselves and the situation in which they've been living.

• • •

Your final decision deals with where your novel is going to begin. You have three choices.

You can begin before the beginning, which means that you're beginning *before* the primary event occurs. In doing this, the status quo of either your main character or one of the characters or a group of characters is made clear first. The advantage to this choice is that you have the opportunity to lay the groundwork for the story. But the disadvantage is that you must lay the groundwork in a compelling fashion so as to hold the reader's interest. In order to do this, you will have to be confident about your use of dramatic questions, tension and conflict. You will also have to establish a strong and interesting voice.

Or you can begin directly at the beginning. To do this, you are creating a scene in which the primary event occurs. The advantage here is that you're thrusting the reader immediately into an unfolding drama, so you have an opportunity to engage the reader at once. The disadvantage is that you must creatively play catchup in order to clarify the status quo of everyone in the novel: who they are, what they were doing, what their situation was *before* the primary event supervened in their lives.

Or you can begin after the beginning. The primary event, using this approach, has happened days, weeks, months, or years in the past. The status quo has, thus, already been disrupted. The advantage with this approach is that when the novel opens, people are already in conflict because something has occurred to create tension among the characters. Using this approach to beginning a novel, the opening scene acts as a large dramatic question that should keep the reader reading. The disadvantage here is that the writer must play catchup in several areas at the same time. She must be able to illustrate what the status quo was, and she must also be able to illustrate what the primary event was. While the writer has the advantage associated with having an array of topics from which scenes can be drawn, the writer has the disadvantage of not being able to create those scenes through flashback, always the bane of the neophyte writer.

When planning out *Careless in Red*, my decision was to begin moments before the primary event. The status quo of a single character is established: the man walking on the South-West Coast Path who turns out to be my central character, Thomas Lynley. Although the character isn't named, the reader learns the following in advance of the primary event:

He's been walking for forty-three days.

He is avoiding thoughts of both the future and the past (dramatic question).

He carries few items with him.

He is on a path above the ocean.

His family is deeply concerned about him (dramatic question).

He is determined to keep walking.

The reader witnesses the primary event along with the unnamed character: a flash of red as someone falls from a sea cliff up ahead of our walker. The status quo of the walker is altered at once because, witnessing this event, he can't simply walk on without doing something. His life is changed in that moment, and as we shall see, the lives of the other characters are also changed.

Let's take a complete look now at how all of this plays out when it's placed into the entire first scene in *Careless in Red*:

He found the body on the forty-third day of his walk. By then, the end of April had arrived, although he had only the vaguest idea of that.

Had he been capable of noticing his surroundings, the condition of the flora along the coast might have given him a broad hint as to the time of year. He'd started out when the only sign of life renewed was the promise of yellow buds on the gorse that grew sporadically along the cliff tops, but by April, the gorse was wild with colour, and yellow archangel climbed in tight whorls along upright stems in hedgerows on the rare occasions when he wandered into a village. Soon foxglove would be nodding on roadside verges, and lamb's foot would expose fiery heads from the hedgerows and the drystone walls that defined individual fields in this part of the world. But those bits of burgeoning life were in the future, and he'd been walking these days that had blended into weeks in an effort to avoid both the thought of the future and the memory of the past.

He carried virtually nothing with him. An ancient sleeping bag. A rucksack with a bit of food that he replenished when the thought occurred to him. A bottle within that rucksack that he filled with water in the morning if water was to be had near the site where he'd slept. Everything else, he wore. One waxed jacket. One hat. One tattersall shirt. One pair of trousers. Boots. Socks. Underclothes. He'd come out for this walk unprepared and uncaring that he was unprepared. He'd known only that he had to walk or he had to remain at home and sleep, and if he remained at home and slept, he'd come to realise that eventually he would will himself not to awaken again.

So he walked. There had seemed no alternative. Steep ascents to cliff tops, the wind striking his face, the sharp salt air desiccating his skin, scrambling across beaches where reefs erupted from sand and stone when the tide was low, his breath coming short, rain soaking his legs, stones pressing insistently against his soles . . . These things would remind him that he was alive and that he was intended to remain so.

He was thus engaged in a wager with fate. If he survived the walk, so be it. If he did not, his ending was in the hands of the gods. In the plural, he decided. He could not think that there might be a single Supreme Being out there, pressing fingers into the keyboard of a divine computer, inserting this or forever deleting that.

His family had asked him not to go, for they'd seen his state, although like so many families of his class, they'd not made any direct mention of it. Just his mother saying, 'Please don't do this, darling,' and his brother suggesting, with his face gone pale and always the threat of another relapse hanging over him and over them all, 'Let me go with you,' and his sister murmuring with her arm round his waist, 'You'll get past it. One does,' but none of them mentioning her name or the word itself, that terrible, eternal, definitive word.

Nor did he mention it. Nor did he mention anything other than his need to walk.

The forty-third day of this walk had taken the same shape as the forty-two days that had preceded it. He'd awakened where he'd fallen on the previous night, with absolutely no knowledge where he was aside from somewhere along the South-West Coast Path. He'd climbed out of his sleeping bag, donned his jacket and his boots, drunk the rest of his water, and begun to move. In midafternoon the weather, which had been uneasy most of the day, made up its mind and blew dark clouds across the sky. In the wind, they piled one upon the other, as if an immense shield in the distance were holding them in place and allowing them no further passage, having made the promise of a storm.

He was struggling in the wind to the top of a cliff, climbing from a V-shaped cove where he'd rested for an hour or so and watched the waves slamming into broad fins of slate that formed the reefs in this place. The tide was just beginning to come in, and he'd noted this. He needed to be well above it. He needed to find some sort of shelter as well.

Near the top of the cliff, he sat. He was winded, and he found it odd that no amount of walking these many days had seemed sufficient to build his endurance for the myriad climbs he was making along the coast. So he paused to catch his breath. He felt a twinge that he recognised as hunger, and he used the minutes of his respite to draw from his rucksack the last of a dried sausage he'd purchased when he'd come to a hamlet along his route. He gnawed it down to nothing, realised that he was also thirsty, and stood to see if anything resembling habitation was nearby: hamlet, fishing cottage, holiday home, or farm.

There was nothing. But thirst was good, he thought with resignation. Thirst was like the sharp stones pressing into the soles of his shoes, like the wind, like the rain. It reminded him, when reminders were needed.

He turned back to the sea. He saw that a lone surfer bobbed there, just beyond the breaking waves. At this time of year, the figure was entirely clothed in black neoprene. It was the only way to enjoy the frigid water.

He knew nothing about surfing, but he knew a fellow cenobite when he saw one. There was no religious meditation involved, but they were both alone in places where they should not have been alone. They were also both alone in conditions that were not suited for what they were attempting. For him, the coming rain – for there could be little doubt that rain was moments away from falling – would make his walk along the coast slippery and dangerous. For the surfer, the exposed reefs onshore demanded an answer to the question that asked why he surfed at all.

He had no answer and little interest in developing one. His inadequate meal finished, he resumed his walk. The cliffs were friable in this part of the coast, unlike the cliffs where he'd begun his walk. There they were largely granite, igneous intrusions into the landscape, forced upon ancient lava, limestone and slate. Although worn by time, weather and the restless sea, they were nonetheless solid underfoot, and a walker could venture near the edge and watch the roiling sea or observe the gulls seeking perches among the crags. Here, however, the cliff edge was culm: slate, shale and sandstone, and cliff bases were marked by mounds of the stony detritus called clitter that fell regularly to the beach below. Venturing near the edge meant a certain fall. A fall meant broken bones or death.

At this section of his walk, the cliff top levelled out for some one hundred yards. The path was well marked, moving away from the cliff's edge and tracing a line between gorse and thrift on one side and a fenced pasture on the other. Exposed here, he bent into the wind, and moved steadily forward. He became aware that his throat was painfully dry, and his head had begun to fill with a dull ache just behind his eyes. He felt a sudden bout of dizziness as he reached the far end of the cliff top. Lack of water, he thought. He would not be able to go much farther without doing something about it.

A stile marked the edge of the high pasture he'd been following, and he climbed it and paused, waiting for the landscape to stop swimming in front of him long enough for him to find the descent to what would be yet another cove. He'd lost count of the inlets he'd come upon in his walk along the undulating coast. He had no idea what this one was called, any more than he'd been able to name the others.

When the vertigo had passed, he saw that a lone cottage stood at the edge of a wide meadow beneath him, perhaps two hundred yards inland from the beach and along the side of a twisting brook. A cottage meant potable water, so he would make for that. It wasn't a great distance off the path.

He stepped down from the stile just as the first drops of rain fell. He wasn't wearing his hat at the moment, so he shrugged his rucksack from his shoulders and dug it out. He was pulling it low onto his forehead – an old baseball cap of his brother's with 'Mariners' scrolled across it – when he caught sight of a flash of red. He looked in the direction from which it had seemed to come, and he found it at the base of the cliff that formed the far side of the inlet beneath him. There, a sprawl of red lay across a broad plate of slate. This slate was itself the landward end of a reef, which crept from the cliff bottom out into the sea.

He studied the red sprawl. At this distance it could have been anything from rubbish to laundry, but he knew instinctively that it was not. For although all of it was crumpled, part of it seemed to form an arm, and this arm extended outward onto the slate as if supplicating an unseen benefactor who was not nor would ever be there.

He waited a full minute that he counted off in individual seconds. He waited uselessly to see if the form would move. When it did not, he began his descent.

I wrote this scene without identifying Lynley because the man's lack of identity poses a dramatic question: Who is this bloke? Other dramatic questions quickly follow: Why has he been walking for forty-three days? Why does he have so little with him? Why does he seem deeply depressed? Where is he? And those questions arise from the first three paragraphs. Both the tone and the information in those paragraphs set the sombre mood that is underscored bleakly in the fourth paragraph: *If he survived the walk, so be it. If he did not, his ending was in the hands of the gods.*

The fifth paragraph allows the reader a glimpse into his backstory and his family situation: a deeply concerned mother, a brother with addiction problems, a sister who with the words *'You'll get past it. One does'* reveals something of her own past. All the revelations serve the function of dramatic questions, asking the reader to wonder about this man, which is what dramatic questions are supposed to do.

The seventh paragraph onward establishes the setting more firmly, addresses the atmosphere, foreshadows things to come (the sight of the cottage), and sets the character up to witness – out of the corner of his eye – something red that appears to have fallen from a sea cliff. When that happens, he's faced with a decision: to walk on and pretend he saw nothing or to investigate what appears to be a body. His decision, of course, sets the rest of the story in motion.

All of this is planned in advance. Not the *way* everything will be revealed. That's the stuff of the running plot outline and the rough draft. But the *shape* of the scene and what it may contain are all determined by the next part of the process.

## Optional Exercise 1

Take one of the two headlines that I offered you earlier in this chapter:

### DOWRY: GIRL GOES THROUGH HELL

### WHY DID SYLVIA DIE?
### WOMAN AND BOY FACE HEARING TOMORROW
### IN GIRL'S TORTURE DEATH

Develop it into a plot kernel by asking yourself questions and then answering them. Then try to create from your answers a single sentence that encapsulates a writing project.

## Optional Exercise 2

Using your plot kernel, explain what the status quo is in the life of someone within the kernel. Using the plot kernel and the status quo of that character, explain what your primary event might be.

# CHAPTER 9

# Step Outlining

*What Happens Next?*

S
ometimes people look at outlining as a dreary way to rob the novel-writing process of all joy, taking from it not only moments of inspiration but also the exhilarating sensation of riding the current of an idea. However, I'd like to argue that outlining allows the writing to be suffused with all of this because the writer doesn't have to think about 'what's going to happen *now*?' and instead can immerse herself entirely in the world of language during which joy, inspiration, and riding that current of an idea all occur. For me, *that's* the fun part of writing. That's the joyful and most fulfilling part. To reach fun, joy and fulfilment, then, I'm willing to follow a process that I know from experience is going to get me there.

So far in this process I use, I've done my research, I've come up with a plot kernel, I've peopled the world of the kernel generically, I've peopled the world of it specifically, I've created all the characters in that world, I've chosen my settings, I know the status quo of every character, I've chosen the characters through whose viewpoints I'll tell the story, I've made my decision about where to begin and I've settled on what the primary event will be. So now it's time to begin the step outline.

This is the most difficult part of the process for me. I always dread doing it. *This* is where I deal with 'What's going to happen first?' and 'What's going to happen next?' It's never easy, but like everything else, there's a process to it.

First, I have to decide what is going to happen first to my characters – especially to the POV characters – once the primary event occurs *or* when the status quo is being demonstrated for the reader in advance of the primary event. What this requires of me as a crime novelist is the knowledge of each character's status quo, which is going to be disrupted, prior to the murder. I also need to know through whose eyes we are going to witness this disruption. A writer who is not creating a crime novel must attend to the same requirements. The only difference is that the primary event will probably not be a murder or other crime.

I generally begin this step-outlining process by listing all the possibilities on a sheet of paper which I've divided into columns. The columns are each headed by the name of a point-of-view character. For seven POV characters, I would therefore include seven columns. In these columns I put *whatever* comes to mind as something that will get the novel off the ground and give me a way to get into each character's individual story. Doing this is going to look like the example that follows but with a difference: at this point I'm not using the computer to generate ideas but merely jotting things down on a piece of paper under the names of the POV characters. Nothing, at this point, is written in concrete. (Actually, nothing at all is ever written in concrete when it comes to the creation of a novel.) I'm merely attempting to establish and disrupt the status quo. For some of the POV characters this might happen simultaneously; for other POV characters – unknowing as yet of the murder – I will only be establishing their status quo.

| LYNLEY | DAIDRE | CONSTABLE | CADAN | SELEVAN | KERRA | BEN |
|---|---|---|---|---|---|---|
| on path | returning to cottage | gets call | Lew back from surf | good to go home? | furious bike ride | liaison officer |
| sees body | | arrives; calls coroner | | | | |
| sees cottage | Polcare Cove | | doing something he's not supposed to be doing | surf shop? | altercation w/ Alan? | Dellen off her meds? |
| surfer? | heard from siblings? | OK to move the body? | | tells Tammy | arrives home | |
| | adopted brother? | takes pix | they're at odds, but why? | Will there? | | |
| | | calls for a detective | | Will has a thing for Madlyn | cops there | |
| | getting away from a colleague harassing her | suspicious re: Lynley | Cadan has been in trouble for drinking? | | | |
| | Lynley there | | was he supposed to do something he failed to do? | | | |
| | insists on seeing the body | | | | | |
| | go to Salthouse | | | | | |
| | caravan park on the way | | | | | |
| | goes to see Aldara | | | | | |

I hope you can see that when it comes to generating ideas, I'm not even *attempting* to create a list for the entire novel. I'm merely tossing around possibilities just to get myself going. Sometimes my ideas are in the form of questions to myself. Sometimes I'm giving myself alternative scenarios. The point is just to give myself *something* to work with when I begin to arrange scenes in a logical order that demonstrates causality. More on that in a moment.

Having come up with potential scenarios in the columns (and under each name I might have enough information for several scenes), I now am ready to create the step outline. This is something that I do on the floor of my office. I write either on index cards or – much more likely – on the blank side of pieces of previously used paper that I've cut down to the size of business envelopes. I still work in columns. What's different now is that I've put the names of my POV characters on pieces of scratch paper and I've placed them on the floor in a line. Hence, I'm now looking at individual papers on which are written:

**LYNLEY  DAIDRE  CADAN  CONSTABLE  SELEVAN  KERRA  BEN**

Referring to my general list of potential scenes from the example you've looked at, I now decide what will comprise an individual scene in that character's POV. For example, I might write, *Lynley on SWC Path; sees someone fall; weather turning bad; sees the cottage.* All of that gets written on the envelope-size piece of paper and placed beneath Lynley's name on my office floor.

Each time I select a scene from the list of potential scenes, I try to add details that will direct me when I get to the next stage of the process. All along, I'm trying to give myself enough ideas to fuel at least ten scenes. That's an arbitrary number that I decided upon years ago – God knows why – and if I can manage to step-outline fifteen or twenty scenes, I consider myself to be in the clover because those scenes will launch me into the next part of the process. For my type of novel, I'm aided by the fact that when a crime occurs, there's a certain logic to what *must* happen: the victim must be found, the police must be called, the victim must be identified, the medical examiner must check things out, the pathologist must come up with a cause of death, the family must be notified, etc.

Once I have my ten to twenty scenes on the floor – each of them under the name of the POV character through whose eyes those scenes will be written – I make certain that each one of them possesses causality. This means that the scene briefly described is going to *cause* another scene to happen somewhere along the line (not necessarily the very next scene) *or* that the scene contains a dramatic question that will eventually be answered. Thus, you can see that in the first scene, during which Lynley sees the fatal fall of Santo Kerne, he is placed in the position of having to do something about it: he can either tell himself he saw nothing and walk on or he can check to see if it is indeed an individual who fell and, if so, take the next step. So another scene will grow out of the scene that we've witnessed through his POV. Hence, that first scene contains causality. That scene also contains the dramatic questions mentioned in the previous chapter. So I've given myself a number of variables in one scene, and this will make future scenes easier to come up with.

The work I've done in advance of this part of my process will help me now in the creation of the step outline because I've given myself a wealth of information through which I can sift, and I'm not forced to manufacture anything on the spot. I already have the plot kernel, the characters, the analyses of the characters and the selected POVs. Contained in all of that is information that will show me where the areas of tension are and what the conflicts will be between characters.

Sitting on the floor of my office, then, I begin to pick up the lightly described scenes in the order that I see them playing out in the novel. As I do this, I try to make sure that I'm laying down dramatic questions throughout, I'm demonstrating causality, I'm answering dramatic questions, and I'm developing and maintaining tension, conflict and intrigue. I also try to make sure that I'm including nothing that will stall out the story. As my writing pal T. Jefferson Parker puts it, 'If your story stalls out on you, you've played your hand too soon.' Believe me, I've done that more than once.

. . .

So we have our ten to fifteen scenes put together in the order in which they will eventually appear in the book. We've used all our preliminary work to assist us in the creation of these steps. Things look good. Status quo is established, primary event occurs, dramatic questions are popping up all over the place. Tension and conflict are either present or promised. Now we're ready for the final step in advance of writing the rough draft: the running plot outline.

The running plot outline is a present-tense depiction of action or narrative that's going to show me how a scene will be shaped when I get to the rough draft. It also shows me where that scene will take place, what – if any – THAD will be used, and what format I'll be following. My purpose at this stage is to play with various options *now*: dramatic questions I might use, conflicts that might arise, tension that can be established or heightened. I do this so that when I'm writing the rough draft of the novel, I can enjoy the process of creating the narrative. Like a visual artist, what I've done for myself is sketch on canvas what I intend to paint, establishing the composition of the finished piece in advance. Having done that, I'm free to 'paint' with words. This will allow me to hone my skill, master my craft and display whatever talent for language I possess. It will also invite moments of inspiration during which I'm blithely typing along when, *wham!*, I'm hit with a great idea or the answer to a question that's been perplexing me (such as, How the heck is Lynley *ever* going to figure out who the killer is?).

By writing the running plot outline in a stream-of-consciousness fashion, I'm able to try out various options as I structure each scene. Using this method, I can talk to myself on the screen of the computer. This unlocks for me all the choices I have with regard to bringing a scene to life. I can include dialogue if I wish, and I can choose and describe various settings. I can also – if necessary – try out a different viewpoint if something in the outline doesn't feel right.

Note that I said 'if something in the outline doesn't feel right,' not, 'if I think something isn't working.' *Feel*, not *think*. There is a reason for this. As I develop the running plot outline for each of the scenes, I try to feel my body's energy ebbing and flowing. I will feel in my body the moment when I've hit on the correct structure of the scene. There's a surge within me that shouts 'Yes!' (Sometimes I even write *Yes!* in the outline.) During this time, I try to stay away from thinking, since inside my head is where the committee resides. Instead, I listen to my body because it will not lie to me. A *sinking* feeling tells me that I've gone in the wrong direction. A *singing* feeling tells me that I'm on the right track. (I do realise that it sounds a little woo-woo to be advising you to be conscious of your body's messages. But your body always knows what's going on in your world. Just as you feel your emotions and your passions, so can you feel the rightness and wrongness of your writing.)

Here, then, are the first five scenes of *Careless in Red* exactly as I wrote them in the running plot outline. You'll see that I toss around ideas on occasion, keeping some and rejecting others. My main purpose at the end of this part of the process is to give myself a structure and the information necessary to craft a fully developed scene.

## Plot Outline One for *The Summer Boy*

**DAY ONE**
**SCENE ONE (LYNLEY'S POV)**

This is Lynley's POV although the reader knows him only as 'he'. The novel begins: 'He found the body at four-ten in the afternoon on the thirty-sixth day of his walk' or words to that effect. He has been walking the coastal path since late February or early March and now it's

April. In the rare village he's come to, the daffodils are now done – although they were blooming magnificently at the start of his walk, the tulips are bending heavily on their stalks, the crocuses are flavouring the landscape with a variety of colours and people have started planting primroses. The hedgerows are coming back to life and soon the ubiquitous fuchsias, wildflowers in this part of the world, will be nodding along with foxglove on the verges. It's a time of rebirth for everything. Lambs in the fields and the whole nine yards. But not for him.

We learn that he's told his family that he will walk. That's all he's told them. He's determined that he will walk until he can walk no more. He'll recover, he'll slip and fall over the edge of a cliff, he'll die of exposure one night, he'll be set upon . . . it doesn't matter. He just needs to walk. That's all we know. That and the fact that his mother has asked him not to go and his brother is frightened for him, having never seen him in this state. So longtime readers will know it's Lynley and new readers will wonder what's going on. We won't know his name until he tells Daidre.

We learn what his walk has been like: the coldest March in more than fifty years. Wind, rain, sudden fog. He's on the coastal path and sometimes it has passed through a village but most of the time it's followed the cliffs, rising and falling into coves, skirting along the pillow granite (check) of X, between boulders of serpentine in X, finally coming to the culm coast: sandstone and shale and the blessed possibility of a step just too close to the friable edge and then . . . eternity. 'He would not do away with himself. He lacked the X for that. But if fate took a hand he would not protest. He'd sink over the side and into oblivion without a cry.'

He carries only a rucksack. He sleeps rough.

So I will begin with a combination of description and backstory blended together, alluding to his situation but not giving his name or what exactly happened. Then on the thirty-sixth day of his walk, he sees the body.

He sees the surfer first. He can't tell if it's a man or a woman because of the distance and because of the fact that the surfer is wearing a full wetsuit and a hood (ask Nigel or look in notes). He stops and watches but the person is just sitting there as if waiting for the tide to finish covering the reefs – fins of slate erupting from the sand – to provide him with a consistent shorebreak (check to see if that's correct). Right now, the waves are breaking choppily. The surfer is just beyond them, making no attempt to get a ride. (lingo)

Lynley is struggling up towards the top of a cliff. Very windy with the scent of salt water making the air feel heavy. The seabirds – kittiwake gulls – have taken to their cliff shelters and there they huddle, waiting for the storm. It feels like rain and the sky is uneasy with roiling clouds. The surfer is out of place but then so is he, Lynley thinks. Unquiet souls on an unquiet day.

There are no trees here, just gorse, rough grass, heather (check), and rock. What are his plans? The same as every day. To walk until he's completely exhausted. To sleep when he can walk no more and wherever he happens to find himself. He hasn't bathed or shaved in days. His clothes are filthy.

He reaches the top of the rising land. He stops to catch his breath. He looks down and sees he's come to a cove and he realises he has no idea what cove it is. There's a marker for the coastal path and he knows it will say the name of the place he's come to and how far the next place is, but he isn't interested as one place is the same as another just now and anyway the point is to walk. The point is exhaustion. The point is sleep. The point is sleep so deep that there are no dreams or, if there are dreams, he cannot remember them upon waking. Dreams are what he cannot tolerate. Dreams and the individuals who people them.

He sits. Does he eat? A piece of dried sausage that represents the

last of his food and an indication that he's going to have to work his way
inland to a community. But perhaps not today. He can go more than a
day without food. He's done so before. It's no trouble. But water? He's
thirsty but thirst is good. Thirst reminds him . . . of what? I don't know.
Except he sees a stream widening into a pool below and the pool drain-
ing into the Atlantic. He's been foolishly drinking from streams when
he's run out of water. He's got to stop doing that but somehow stopping
hasn't seemed important.

Anyway, let's not get carried away. He also notes a cottage, one lone
cottage up the road perhaps 250 yards from a sliver of beach that describes the cove. The beach itself is, like so many others he's seen, filled
with sharp-edged rocks and boulders that increase in size to great large
slabs as they approach the cliffs. There is very little sand to speak of.
The path he's on descends to this cove, which opens on the landward
side into a small glacial valley (check if this is possible) through
which the stream runs across a meadow. The path crosses this meadow
and then climbs the cliff on the other side. The cottage sits at the edge
of this meadow, across the stream from where Lynley is.

He thinks about going to the cottage to ask for water to fill his
canteen or whatever he has with him. Even if no one is home – and it
certainly looks deserted from this distance since there are no lights on
in the fading daylight and no car visible – he could perhaps get water
from a hosepipe.

He finishes his sausage and is aware of his thirst. He'll have to do
something about this. He rises to begin his descent. And this is when he
sees something lying on one of the great slabs at the base of the cliff. Not
lying as one would lie to get sun – had there been any sun – but crumpled in the torso with one arm extended across the slate as if supplicating an unseen benefactor. Lynley watches for a moment to see if this
body will move, knowing all along that it won't. He begins his descent.

## SCENE TWO (DAIDRE TRAHAIR'S POV)

Is Daidre just getting there from Bristol or has she been out for the afternoon? I would like Lynley to be suspicious of her. **So I'd like this to be written in a way that can be interpreted in several different ways.** I think she's come from Truro or wherever the hospital is that her natural mother is dying in. Or maybe she's not even in a real hospital but in the caravan with her husband and the 27-year-old twins. Yes. This is it. They've found Daidre in Bristol and they've come to tell her their mum is dying and she's gone to see her, the first time she's seen her since she was 13 years old. This is what she will lie about. **She will say she's come directly from Bristol, where she lives.** When Lynley says she has nothing with her, she bristles. This is her cottage. Why should she have something with her?

So, she arrives. How has she felt? Detached. She's telling herself that she should be feeling more, that she's less than human because she isn't feeling what she ought to be feeling. And she's heard that before: 'What's bloody *wrong* with you, Daidre? Stop holding back, for God's sake. Can't you see what you're doing to me? To us?' But there was no us. At least never for long. Just a thousand and one excuses why there could be a *you* and an *I* but nothing else.

The first thing she notices is that her cottage gate is standing open. Not just off the latch or ajar but completely open. She parks her car and gets out into the wind. Daylight is fading very fast because of the approach of the storm. She doesn't think much of the gate being open. She shoves it closed and inspects the latch. It doesn't look broken or even damaged. Someone must have come onto the property. She gets a pet carrier out of the car . . . except this makes her story look true, so maybe the otter lives there in a little colony??? Hmmm. Maybe she doesn't have an otter and someone else does? Or the otter is in Bristol?

Anyway, she looks at the cottage. She sees movement behind the glass. Someone is inside.

How did he get in? I would say he broke a window. Maybe part of the door is stained glass and he broke that? Or maybe there's a second door around the side of the building and he broke a pane of glass in that or next to that. Her reaction? She assumes it's some kid from Alsperyl, which is the nearest community or what goes for a community. She doesn't feel afraid but she does feel protective and exasperated. Maybe she even names a kid? Maybe she thinks it's Cadan. Maybe it's some kid she has a relationship with? Tammy? Hmm, this is possible. Maybe she's been something of a mentor to Tammy, but if Tammy is using this as a trysting place, she isn't going to be happy. Or could she think Aldara is there because Aldara has a key to the place. Why would Aldara need a key to the place? To meet Santo if she actually lives with Max. Hmm, this is quite nice. **So she thinks it might be Aldara. Or Santo waiting for Aldara.**

She goes to the door and that's when she sees a pane of glass is broken and then she's angry. She walks in.

Where is Lynley? This isn't a big cottage. I would say he's coming out of the bedroom. No lights are on because it isn't completely dark. She starts. Then she says, 'I don't know who you are or what you're doing here, but you are going to leave directly. If you do not leave, I shall become violent with you and I assure you, you do not want that to happen.' Then she switches on a light and she gets a good look at him. She said, 'Are you . . . You're injured. Where? May I help? I'm a doctor.'

I need to work in a description of him. He says, 'It's not me. I was . . . There's no phone here?' She says no. He asks if she has a mobile. She says no, not with her. She never brings a mobile with her. But I'm a doctor. Let me help you.

He says you can't help for this. There's a body on the beach. Up on the rocks. He's dead.

I broke in – I'm sorry. I'll pay for the damage – to phone the police.

She says to take her to the body. I told you I'm a doctor, she tells him. We're losing time in which we could save a life.

So he takes her to the beach. Now we have a description of the body. We also see he's a sea cliff climber. We also see that she knows who it is. We also see his rope and the carabiner it's tied to. They look up and the cliff soars above them some 200 feet. There's a depression in it where the sea has worn it away. An indication of what the tide can do. And the tide is rising.

She tells Lynley they're going to have to move the body. He says no! The police have to see it. They must phone for the police. Where's the nearest phone? She tells him to come with her.

They go to her car and she takes them to the Salthouse Inn, the only establishment for miles and miles around. It's a 13th-century inn that was used by travellers between X and Y (look on the map). They go inside. Daidre is known. She asks for the phone. She tells the publican Santo Kerne's had an accident. She says, 'This man found him.' And then to Lynley, 'What's your name? I don't know your name.'

He says Thomas. That's where the scene ends.

## SCENE THREE (CADAN ANGARRACK'S POV)

It seems to me that the POV will be Cadan and Lew will not be a POV character. So when the scene opens, where are we? Where does the family live? I see them living in one of the old houses in Victoria Road or even one of the houses in town on King Lane (check the map). Except I know the houses in Victoria Road have gardens and garages in the lane out back, so I'm best using that, I think. Is Cadan working on his trick bike when he hears his father's car? Is he training his parrot to do something? Is he in his bedroom and with the bird? Is Madlyn there? If he wants action, action, action and he's not getting any at the moment, he would be restless. He's been in trouble with his father for two things: not doing his job at the surfboard factory and getting hauled into the police station in Truro for being passed out drunk in the gutter. He's there to prove to his father that he can pull his life together because now he has a job at Adventures Unlimited. That's what he wants to report. His father is disgusted with him, however. Cadan has utterly let him down. Relationship with Cadan has always meant ceaseless change and change is what Lew Angarrack cannot handle.

I'd say that Cadan has recently ruined a surfboard that they were making. Or he failed to do something that he was supposed to do at the surfboard shop – like show up – and that did it for his dad. Lew is coping with a lot of stuff right now: Madlyn's state, Ione's demands and Cade's Peter Pan behaviour. He's utterly lost faith in his son. His journey is going to have to do with getting that faith back, although I'm not sure how it's going to happen.

So Cadan is there to tell him about his job. He's all excited because of what the job means: that he'll be able to do all the things he loves to do . . . once he does the maintenance work. And surely he will be able to show up for the maintenance work regularly if the excitement of all the activities is out there like a carrot.

So. What the hell is he doing? I would say he's eagerly riding the trick bike down the lane. He knows he presents a ridiculous sight: knees out to the sides and parrot on his shoulder, but he has no car to put the bike inside when he takes it to where he practises. And anyway he's not come from practice. He's come from Adventures Unlimited where he's just got a job. He'll have to ride this bike to work. But that's okay. Actually maybe what happened is that he crashed his car drunk driving and lost his licence. Where does he practise with the bike? In some empty swimming pool. At the town leisure centre where the swimming pool has been empty for years because there's no money to repair it. But that's not where he's been today. He's been at Adventures Unlimited. Although his father won't know that when he sees him. He'll assume Cade has been doing his trick riding. Bloody waste of time.

Cadan is riding along the lane to the back of the house when his father passes him. The surfboard is in the back of the car. Lew glances his way and looks disgusted. Cade isn't bothered because Dad won't be disgusted when he hears the news.

The THAD will be Lew washing off his stuff. He backs into the garage and unloads stuff and takes it into the garden: the board, his wetsuit, whatever else is in his kit (see notes from Nigel). Wetsuit, boots, gloves, hood. Board. He washes all this stuff off and hangs it over the line in the garden. He listens to what Cade has to say and his response is 'Where's your sister?' This sets them into a conflict. Don't you have anything to say about the job? Cadan asks his father. His father's question: How d'you intend to get there? On that thing? With a nod at the bike. Because you won't be using any car of mine. Not without a licence. Cadan says he'll walk if he has to. It's not that far. Or he'll ride the bike. He doesn't care what he looks like. He rode it there today, didn't he? And why the hell isn't his father happy or pleased or *whatever* that he got a job? That he's employed? That's what his father wanted, isn't it? Lew tells him that he *was* employed, he *had* a job. He cocked that up and he'll no doubt cock up this as well. Cadan will say that Working for you was always a stupid idea, Dad. We both know that. I'm not a detail person. I don't have the . . . I don't know . . . I guess I don't have the patience.

You want everything to be fun, Lew tells him. Life isn't fun. Cadan nods at the surfboard. 'And that's not fun?' he asks his father. For you? That's not fun. But no, I forget. It's about being a champion, isn't it? Always a goal in mind or forget about it.

There is nothing wrong with goals, his father tells him. And then again, Where's your sister?

How the hell do I know? Crying into her bloody soup as usual, Cadan tells him. When the hell is she going to pull herself together? Bloody hell, you'd think the world has ended. I could've told her . . . I *tried* to tell her. Man, she must get her moping gene from you.

There also needs to be mentioned why Lew was out surfing in this weather. The wind's rotten and the tide isn't right. Lew says he thinks better when he's surfing, and he needed to think. Cadan says he bets he knows what Lew had to think about.

So this scene lays out dramatic questions: Madlyn and what's wrong with her, Cadan's drinking and driving, Lew's troubles.

## SCENE FOUR (POV IS THE POLICE CONSTABLE)

This is the arrival of the local constable who is on patrol. He's stationed at the small three-man station in Casvelyn, and he's on patrol alone. Who is he? Police Constable (PC) Mickey Lynn. [I altered this character's surname later in order to name him after a friend.] He's twenty-eight years old and his ambition is to stay right there in Casvelyn, which he thinks is a great place to raise kids. He has one already, a two-year-old boy. He and his wife have a laissez-faire attitude towards raising him. Mickey is a surfer in his free time. He has no thoughts of going anywhere else as a cop and to this end, he likes to keep a low profile. He hates the thought of being transferred to another patch. This situation he's got – which is mostly about keeping order in the summer months and trying to stay awake in the winter months – is like a velvet coffin. And he hasn't got a single complaint about it. His wife works as well, as a teacher in the Casvelyn primary school.

He shows up, meeting Lynley and Daidre at Daidre's cottage. He wants to know who they are, and at first he assumes they're a couple although why he would is open to question as they couldn't look more different in their superficial appearance: clothing and grooming. But beyond that they have similar colouring. He alters his idea to assume they may be adult siblings.

Their names? Their identifications? Daidre says her name and hands over her driving licence. Lynley says his name. But he has no identification with him. Not a licence, not a thing. Lynn asks him what the hell he's doing wandering around without identification on him. This is wildly suspicious and he's going to have to do something to prove who he is. Yes, Lynley says, I do understand that. And you've got a plan, have you? the constable asks him. No, no plan, Lynley tells him. What's he doing out here without ID? Walking, Lynley tells him. Just walking.

The constable isn't happy with this. He isn't happy with anything that complicates his life. He tells them to take him down to the body. He's wearing a radio on his shoulder.

Down on the shore, he studies the sea before he looks at the body. Then he goes over to the body, but he tells Lynley and Daidre to stay where they are. He takes out a digital camera and takes pictures, not only of the body but of the rope and whatever else is there (check notes). Then he comes back to Lynley and Daidre. Or maybe he just makes the radio call from the body. Or perhaps the noise is too much there, so he has to go back to the shore where they are standing. He radios the police station and tells them two things: 1) Get the duty detective inspector out here and 2) Call the coroner and request permission to move the body although he doesn't say that directly so the reader will not know exactly why he's placing this call. The tide's coming in. And then he tells Lynley, I don't know who the hell you are, but when the coroner gives us the word, we'll have a job to do and I don't want you doing anything other than exactly what I tell you. Got it?

## SCENE FIVE (SELEVAN PENRULE'S POV)

What's happening when this scene opens? Is Selevan leaving the Salthouse Inn? Is he parking at the wharf and walking back to Clean Barrel Surf Shop? Is he entering the surf shop? Is he engaged in a THAD? He's a bitter man who thinks everything in life is a lesson to be learned and he's the one to interpret the lesson. So what does he see as the lesson with Santo's death? God's punishment, I would say. God's punishment on him for rejecting his granddaughter, although Tammy was never interested in him in the way her grandfather wanted her to be. In fact, perhaps he's invited Santo over because he's seen the effect Santo has on women and he hopes this will make her interested in men.

When Santo dies, he'll want Tammy to see that THIS is how her wonderful God works, he wants her to know. This is why you don't trust God and you trust only yourself because you sure as hell can't trust people.

So. He's got a message for Tammy and he can't wait to deliver it. I need to remember that they don't know if this is an accident, a murder, or a suicide. All the people know is that a body was found at the bottom of the cliff and Daidre murmured it was Santo. (Don't say his last name.)

His journey needs to be one of greater understanding about her. Of acceptance, support and agreeing with her vocation to be a nun. I decided that she wants to convert to Catholicism and be a nun and that's why she's been sent to live with her grandfather. Her parents can't do anything with her.

So. He is in the position of convincing her that she has no vocation, that she's a sexual being, and of proving to her that there is no God to serve. Thus he's anxious to tell her about Santo. Here's what your God does. Although he won't say as much. He'll tell her and he'll watch for her reaction. Because he's been hoping she has a thing for Santo.

He goes to Clean Barrel Surf Shop where she has a part-time job as a shop assistant. And he goes because he's there every day to take her home. He's been happy the three or four times that she's phoned and told him not to fetch her because Will is going to drive her home after they have a coffee (where he pours his heart out about Madlyn), but this is not one of those days. He goes into the shop. What's going on? They don't know about Santo. What are they doing? Will is showing some budding surfer one of the new boards from France but the kid wants to buy one of the cheaper Chinese boards. Or maybe they're getting ready to lock up for the night. Counting the money in the till. Will is bringing in the stuff that's outside: the hire board, the surfboards, the wet suits on sale. Tammy is closing up the till or maybe stuffing new brochures into a rack.

Selevan goes in. He tells them both about Santo. He's keen to see what Tammy's reaction is but he sees that she focuses entirely on Will. He can't figure this one out. He isn't getting from her the reaction he thought he'd be getting. He's done everything he can to encourage the relationship between her and Santo and nothing has happened. Maybe he assumes she's a lesbian. That's what it is, he tells himself. She can't admit that she's a lesbian.

Feel my way through this scene. Don't be hard on myself. The reader needs to see that there is something behind Will. The reader needs to learn that something is going on with Tammy. The reader needs to know she knew Santo. And what about Selevan? Has he told Santo not to come around any longer? Remember, Selevan is an angry and bitter man, but he's angry and bitter because of the decisions he himself made, not because of decisions that were forced upon him.

From looking at this running plot outline, the first thing you might notice is that the original title for the novel was *The Summer Boy*. It was only when I was writing the rough draft that I understood *Careless in Red* would be a better title because of its reference to Dellen Kerne's untreated bipolar disorder, crucial to the plot.

As you read the individual outlined scenes, you might also notice that I talk to myself, that I point out to myself areas that will need further research, and that I indicate where I think I will have to use lingo related to surfing. You'll also come across my use of $X$, $Y$ and $Z$ on occasion. This marks the spot where I might need a specific word that I don't want to stop and find just then, or it might indicate that I'll need to examine an ordnance survey map or a road atlas of Cornwall to complete a thought. You will also notice that there are places where I write *check this* in parentheses, or where I use bold type when I've come up with an idea that I definitely want to use. I say *definitely* because everything else contained in the running plot outline is subject to alteration when I get to the rough draft.

As you read the plot outline, you'll also come to scene four, which I've decided is going to be written in the POV of a police constable called Mickey Lynn. However, Mickey Lynn was not on the original character list, so there is no analysis of him. This appears to break a cardinal rule of How-Elizabeth-George-Creates-a-Novel. You're probably wondering if I stop everything and do an analysis of him. The answer is no. This is his only POV scene, and at the moment of creating the plot outline, I have no idea if he will appear in the novel again. So I give him an agenda, which is to stay in Casvelyn his entire life, and I make him a surfer as well as a police constable.

Through his eyes, the reader will be able to see things that, through Daidre's POV, the reader can't see. What I mean by this is that Daidre is used to her cottage, so it's not going to be described through her viewpoint, as she wouldn't be thinking of what it looks like as she approaches it during her scene. We see through her eyes only the things on the property that she must deal with, such as the gate which is partially open and the window that is broken. Similarly, we also now have an opportunity to see what she looks like since, as I've pointed out earlier, characters don't self-describe. Because the constable has never seen her before and he's never seen the unnamed man before, I now have an opportunity for a quick description.

The fifth scene sketches out an interaction among three of the characters:

Selevan Penrule, Tammy Penrule and Will Mendick. As you read it, you'll notice that I've already begun to make some changes from Selevan's character analysis, and the largest change has to do with Tammy. She's no longer as originally planned out. I've altered her to be a girl who wants to become a nun and who's been sent from Zimbabwe to live with her grandfather so that he can talk her out of it. Selevan's agenda in every scene he shares with Tammy will have to do with her belief in God, his own lack of belief in anything that he can't see or feel or taste or touch, his worries about her being a lesbian, his determination that she is not ever going to become a nun. You'll also note that at the end of the outline, I give myself a pep talk.

I'd like to stress here that the reason I *don't plot out an entire novel* before writing it is that I prefer to 'discover' the plot as I go along. I want to allow for moments of inspiration, for new ideas, for ways in which I might suddenly see how the subplots can twist and turn. I won't be able to do that if I attempt to plot out the entire book. Additionally, if I even tried to plot out the entire novel, I'd probably end up defeated – or at least terribly discouraged – by the effort.

Perhaps the most crucial part of plotting involves making sure that the scenes in the novel keep *opening* up the plot and the subplots. This is the only way to avoid dead ends. Examine the following partial scene between Tammy and Selevan Penrule:

'I've been talking to God,' Tammy said.

Now that was a real conversation stopper, Selevan thought. Straight out of the blue, like he hadn't been trying to make a point with the girl. He said, 'Have you, now? And what's God been saying back? Nice that he's got time for you, by the by, 'cause the bugger's never had time for me.'

'I've tried to listen.' Tammy spoke like a girl with things on her mind. 'I've *tried* to listen for his voice,' she said.

'His voice? God's voice? From where? You expecting it out of the gorse or something?'

'God's voice comes from within,' Tammy said, and she brought a lightly clenched fist to her skinny chest. 'I've tried to listen to the voice from inside myself. It's a quiet voice. It's the voice of what's right. You know when you hear it, Grandie.'

'Hear it a lot, do you?'

'When I get quiet I do. But now I can't.'

'I've seen you quiet day and night.'

'But not inside.'

'How's that?' He looked over at her. She was concentrating on the rain-streaked day, hedgerows dripping as the car skimmed past them, a magpie taking to the sky.

'My head's full of chatter,' she said. 'If my head won't be silent, I can't hear God.'

Chatter? he thought. What was the maddening girl *on* about? One moment he thought he had her sorted, the next he was flummoxed again. 'What d'you got up there, then?' he asked, and he poked her head. 'Goblins and ghoulies?'

'Don't make fun,' she told him. 'I'm trying to tell you . . . But there's nothing and there's no one that I can ask, you see. So I'm asking you, as it's the only thing left that I can think to do. I s'pose I'm asking for help, Grandie.'

Now, he thought, they were down to it. This was the moment the girl's parents had hoped for, time with her granddad paying off. He waited for more. He made a *hmph* noise to indicate his willingness to listen. The moments ticked by as they approached Casvelyn. She said nothing more till they were in town.

Then it was brief. He'd pulled to the kerb in front of Clean Barrel Surf Shop before she finally spoke. 'If I know something,' she said to him, her eyes fixed on the shop's front door, 'and if *what* I know might cause someone trouble . . . What should I do, Grandie? That's what I've been asking God, but he hasn't answered. What should I do? I could keep asking because when something bad happens to someone you care about, it seems like—'

'The Kerne boy,' he interrupted. 'D'you know something about the Kerne boy, Tammy? Look at me square, girl, not out of the window.'

She did. He could see she was troubled beyond what he had thought. So there was only one answer, and despite the irritations it might cause in his own life, he owed it to her to give it. 'You know something, you tell the police,' he said. 'Nothing else to it. You do it today.'

In this selection, several elements of plotting are brought into play. First, the relationship between Selevan and his granddaughter is addressed through the nature of their conversation and through its content. We see Selevan's exasperation with Tammy; we see Tammy's calm in the face of it. Second, their subplot is advanced through the planting of a dramatic question: *Now, he thought, they were down to it. This was the moment the girl's parents had hoped for, time with her granddad paying off.* As the writer, I know that this is all about Selevan's attempts to talk Tammy out of her vocation, but the reader doesn't know that. So *the moment the girl's parents had hoped for* plants the question about why Tammy's been sent to Cornwall. Finally, the plot is advanced in the scene as well. Tammy knows something and her grandfather tells her that she has to talk to the police. So the groundwork is laid for a future scene. Causality has been achieved.

A writer also opens scenes up by tightening tension between characters as they try to achieve their immediate agendas, by revealing details previously unknown to the reader, or by introducing another character with whom the POV character is in conflict.

Occasionally, though, I hit a dead end. That's just part of what happens when writing a novel. What I've learned over time is that the dead end is telling me one of three things:

I've followed a wild hare (i.e., a moment of plotting insanity disguised as inspiration).

I've gone off course in some way earlier in the novel (e.g., by having a character act in a way that is *out* of character and thus upsetting to the plot).

I've played my hand too soon (e.g., by giving out information too early in the book).

When any of these things occur, my solution is to back up in order to find the spot in the novel where I've gone wrong. Sometimes when I find it, I realise that I'm going to have to begin again and restructure the entire novel. (This happened for *Payment in Blood, In Pursuit of the Proper Sinner* and *The Punishment She Deserves.*) Sometimes when I find it, I see that I merely need to eliminate information that was handed out far too early in the book. (That happened in *For the Sake of Elena.*) Because I have a backup position formed by all my preliminary work, though, I generally can see fairly quickly what needs to be done to take care of the problem.

I'd like to stress once again that all of my preliminary work has everything to do with the seduction of my brain's natural tendency towards operating from the left side, which requires and responds to organisation. Creating the step outline in such a way as to be able to shuffle scenes around appeals to my brain's need for organisation. It assures my brain, 'Everything is under control here.' Once assured that all is well, my brain 'allows' its right side to be triggered through stream-of-consciousness writing, which produces the shape of the scenes in the running plot outline. Doing all of this prevents my committee – the members of which reside in the left side of the brain – from interfering in the creative process.

The most important part of novel writing is this, though: a great deal of it is about having or developing the ability to delay gratification. I see this as the key to success in just about anything we attempt and hope to become good at. In the case of novel writing, what this means for me is doing the tough stuff first and the fun stuff second. Better said, perhaps, it's all about doing what I *have* to do first and what I *want* to do second.

## Optional Exercise 1

Using your chosen headline and primary event from the Chapter 8 exercises – or material from something you're currently working on – attempt to create ten potential scenes that could later comprise the first ten scenes of your running plot outline. Then arrange those scenes in such a way that one scene is causally related to a scene that follows. Begin this merely with a simple list of scenes on a piece of paper (similar to what I've shown you in this chapter) and then assign each scene to a POV character.

## Optional Exercise 2

Writing in the present tense only, flesh out the first scene among your arranged scenes, using stream-of-consciousness writing. Feel free to try out ideas as you freewrite. Ask yourself: Where does this first scene take place? What are the details of that place? Is any other character present? Is there a buildup of tension? Are any dramatic questions laid down?

# CHAPTER 10

# Building the Scene

*Using Your Research*

We all approach just about everything in life differently, and for me, the process of writing a novel isn't about sitting down at the computer (or the legal pad or the notebook or the typewriter), banging out a first chapter, and hoping for the best. It's also not about getting in touch with the cosmos, or hoping that the spirit of Dorothy L. Sayers will speak through my fingertips. Should I attempt to write a novel that way, I would be placing myself under enormous pressure to create character, to establish status quo, to render a primary event, to create plot, to advance plot, to lay down dramatic questions, to answer dramatic questions, to heighten tension, to increase conflict, to showcase attitude – all at the same time.

I value every part of the process for its ability to assist me in the creation of a scene. Take a look at Images 23, 24 and 25.

This is one of the locations that I visited on my research trip to Cornwall. I knew about it from my preliminary research of place. From one of the books about Cornwall that I had acquired, I learned that there was a hut built into the side of a sea cliff outside of a hamlet called Morwenstow. I also knew from my reading that this hut had been built long ago by a vicar of the local church. Hut, cliff, vicar, hamlet – I had to check it out

IMAGE 23

because a hut on a cliff near a hamlet, built by a vicar or not, suggested a place where a scene in the book might occur.

I drove to Morwenstow and hiked from the church out to the South-West Coast Path: in the mud, along the side of a field of dairy cows, and towards the ocean, perhaps a quarter of a mile. When I came to the coast path, I discovered a set of steps hewn into the side of the cliff just a short distance from the field behind the church. These steps led down to yet another path above the ocean, and not far along this narrow trail, I came to the hut I'd read about. It had indeed been hewn out of the cliff, part of its structure supported by blocks of sandstone but most of it dug into the earth and supported inside by miscellaneous pieces of wood that had come, I believe, from wrecked ships. Inside, the hut had a bench that ran along three of the four walls, and on one of the walls someone had carved a

IMAGE 24

heart. Elsewhere people had carved their initials, but it was the heart that caught my attention.

IMAGE 25

When I saw the hut, its interior, and the heart, I knew that I would use this place in my novel. At that moment, I had no idea how I would use it or where I would use it, nor did I worry about it. But I knew that I *would* make it a setting for a scene at some point for no reason other than it was crying out to be part of my book. As things developed during the plotting and writing, the hut became the setting for two scenes. What follows is the first of them:

> The nearest village was a place called Alsperyl, which was also their destination. This comprised a church, a vicarage, a collection of cottages, an ancient schoolhouse and a pub. All fashioned from the unpainted stone of

the district, they sat some half mile to the east of the cliff path, beyond a lumpy paddock. Only the church spire was visible. Daidre pointed this out and said, 'St. Morwenna's, but we're going this way just a bit farther if you can manage.'

He nodded, and she felt foolish with her final remark. He was hardly infirm and grief did not rob one of the ability to walk. She nodded in turn and led him perhaps another two hundred yards where a break in the wind-tossed heather on the seaside edge of the path gave way to steps hewn into stone.

She said, 'It's not much of a descent, but take care. The edge is still deadly. And we're . . . I don't know . . . perhaps one hundred fifty feet above the water?'

Down a set of steps, which curved with the natural form of the cliff side, they came to another little path, nearly overgrown with gorse and patches of English stonecrop that somehow thrived here despite the wind. Perhaps twenty yards along, the path ended abruptly, but not with a precipitous cliff edge as one might expect. Rather, a small hut had been hewn into the cliff face. It was fronted with the old driftwood of ruined ships and sided – where such sides emerged beyond the cliff face itself – with small blocks of sandstone. Its wooden face was grey with age. The hinges that served its rough Dutch door bled rust onto pitted panels.

Daidre glanced back at Thomas Lynley to see his reaction: such a structure in such a remote location. His eyes had widened, and a smile crooked his mouth. His expression seemed to say to her, What *is* this place?

She replied to his unasked question, speaking above the wind that buffeted them. 'Isn't it marvellous, Thomas? It's called Hedra's Hut. Evidently – if the journal of the reverend Mr. Walcombe is to be believed – it's been here since the late eighteenth century.'

'Did he build it?'

'Mr. Walcombe? No, no. He wasn't a builder, but he was quite a chronicler. He kept a journal of the doings round Alsperyl. I found it in the library in Casvelyn. He was the vicar of St. Morwenna's for . . . I don't know . . . forty years, perhaps? He tried to save the tormented soul who did build this place.'

'Ah. That would be the Hedra from Hedra's Hut, then?'

'The very woman. Apparently, she was widowed when her husband – who fished the waters out of Polcare Cove – was caught in a storm and drowned, leaving her with one young son. According to Mr. Walcombe – who does not generally embellish his facts – the boy disappeared one day, likely having ventured too near the edge of the cliff in an area too friable to support his weight. Rather than confront the deaths of both husband *and* son within six months of each other, poor Hedra chose to believe a selkie had taken the boy. She told herself he'd wandered down to the water – God knows how he managed it from this height – and there the seal waited in her human form and beckoned him into the sea to join the rest of the . . .' She frowned. 'Blast. I've quite forgotten what a group of seals is called. It can't be a herd. A pod? But that's whales. Well, no matter at the moment. That's what happened. Hedra built this hut to watch for his return, and that's what she did for the rest of her life. It's a poignant story, isn't it?'

'Is it true?'

'If we can believe Mr. Walcombe. Come inside. There's more to see. Let's get out of the wind.'

The upper and lower doors closed by means of wooden bars that slid through rough wooden handles and rested on hooks. As she pushed the top one back and then the bottom one, and swung the doors open, she said over her shoulder, 'Hedra knew what she was about. She gave herself quite a sturdy place to wait for her son. It's framed in timber all round. Each side has a bench, the roof has quite decent beams to hold it up, and the floor is slate. It's as if she knew she'd be waiting for a while, isn't it?'

She led the way in, but then stopped short. Behind her, she heard him duck under the low lintel to join her. She said, 'Oh blast,' in disgust and he said, 'Now, that's a shame.'

The wall directly in front of them had been defaced and defaced recently if the freshness of the cuts into the wooden panels of the little building were anything to go by. The remains of a heart which had been earlier carved into the wood – no doubt accompanied by lovers' initials – curved round a series of vicious hack marks that now gouged deeply, as if into flesh. No initials were left.

'Well,' Daidre said, trying to sound philosophical about the mess, 'I suppose it's not as if the walls haven't *already* been carved up. And at least it isn't spray paint. But still . . . One wonders . . . Why do people do such things?'

Thomas was observing the rest of the hut, with its more than two hundred years of carvings: initials, dates, other hearts, the occasional name. He said thoughtfully, 'Where I went to school, there's a wall . . . It's not too far from the entry, actually, so no visitor can ever miss it . . . Pupils have put their initials into it for . . . I don't know . . . I expect they've done it since the time of Henry the sixth. Whenever I go back – because I do go back occasionally . . . one does – I look for mine. They're still there. They somehow say I'm real, I existed then, I exist even now. But when I look at all the others – and there are hundreds, probably thousands of them – I can't help thinking how fleeting life is. It's the same thing here, isn't it?'

'I suppose it is.' She ran her fingers over several of the older carvings: a Celtic cross, the name Daniel, B.J. + S.R. 'I like to come here to think,' she told him. 'Sometimes I wonder who were these people all coupled together so confidently. And did their love last? I wonder that as well.'

For his part, Lynley touched the poor gouged heart. 'Nothing lasts,' he said. 'That's our curse.'

Notice that the first paragraph exposes the reader to the setting, with the description coming from my notes and my photos of the place. Then the POV is established: Daidre is noticing Lynley's reaction.

The paragraphs that follow the establishment of viewpoint are my creation of the hut's history. The part about the vicar is true; the part about the widowed Hedra, her son, and the selkie comes from my imagination.

As Daidre explains to Lynley the hut's history, the scene advances with their entrance into the hut, where they see the carved heart that I myself saw. The appearance of the heart has been altered, however, as I move it from reality into the plot of the novel.

Lynley reflects briefly on his time as a pupil at Eton, where the carvings he mentions actually do exist. But his reflection is used to make a point he understands only too well: how fleeting life is, how it can all end in an instant as did the life of his wife.

So the research that initially led me to this location not only moved the plot forward but also provided me with details to incorporate in a scene to increase its verisimilitude. Since I had photographed the hut from the outside, from the inside, from the doorway, and from the approach along the path, I was able to create the scene more easily, with details that, I hoped, would make the place real for the reader. If they did what they're meant to do, the sensory details beyond sight – the smells and the sounds, for example – would heighten the mood and create the atmosphere between the two characters. Other scenes in the book would add to the reader's understanding of Cornwall as I introduced the flora, the fauna, the topography and the geology of the area.

. . .

A scene in a novel has several requirements, some of which are obvious to the reader and some of which are less so. In no particular order of importance:

The first requirement is the setting. As I've shown you, my settings are almost always places that I have seen and photographed. Using a real place is not, of course, a requirement for a scene. But using a real place works for me because I don't have to develop something out of my rather poor imagination and because the details of that place are right in front of me, the carved heart inside the cliffside hut being one example. Details make a setting real for the reader. While a superfluity of details can bog down a piece of writing, telling details that can be worked into the story will not.

The second requirement is the presence of one or more characters, and characters don't have to be humans. Consider the great white shark in *Jaws*, the horrors that haunt the hotel in *The Shining*, the car in *Christine*, the dinosaurs in *Jurassic Park*. In each case, these pseudo-characters put themselves into conflict with one or more of the human characters, and with stunning effect. As characters, they exist within the setting, and they appear in a scene with an agenda (such as the shark's desire to eat).

A character's agenda may apply to her ultimate end point in the novel, to the subplot she's featured in, or to the specific scene alone. For example, a character's agenda in a scene might be to seduce another character; it might be to vent anger; it might be to confront, to accuse, to excuse, to lie, to deny, or to do just about anything that the other character is not aware of when the scene begins. The POV character also will have an attitude that will colour how she looks at things.

The third requirement is that dramatic questions are present in the scene. They're either being laid down or they're being answered. If a dramatic question from a previous scene is being answered, there are also various ways in which this can be done. Half-truths can be given, partial information can be revealed, outright lies that wear the guise of answering a dramatic question might be told.

Conflict is present, either externally or internally. If the scene is using external conflict, it can be between two or more characters, between characters and their environment, or between characters and the situation in which they find themselves. The basic issue is that there are two or more opposing forces, both or all of them wanting something while someone or something stands in their way. For example, on the wedding night of two characters, an interruption in the middle of the celebration triggers open conflict when the lord and master of those two characters shows up to demand droit de seigneur. Or, a detective faces deep personal issues in his marriage because of time spent on the job. Or, a T. rex just wants to do his own thing when he escapes from his compound, which would be fine except his own thing involves eating the nearby humans who don't wish to be eaten. It's this opposition of intentions, desires and agendas that triggers the conflict and keeps it alive.

If, on the other hand, it's internal conflict that gives the scene its tension, the reader is going to see it in one of two ways. If it's the POV character's conflict, it may be demonstrated through her thoughts, speculations, reflections, decisions, indecisions and reactions to other characters. If it's the non-POV character's internal conflict, it may be demonstrated by what she says and does or by what she doesn't say or do. It's witnessing a character's internal conflict that encourages the reader to bond with that actor who is frequently mulling over a decision he must make or an action he must take. Shakespeare's soliloquies are often demonstrations of inner conflict, the most well-known of these being Hamlet's 'To be or not to be' soliloquy.

Consider the elements of scenic construction in the following selection:

Like so many beaches in Cornwall, this one began with boulders tumbled one upon the other near the car park. These were mostly granite, with lava mixed in, and the light streaks upon them gave mute testimony to the unimaginable former liquid nature of something now solid. Lynley extended his hand to help Daidre over them. Together they clambered carefully till they reached the sand.

'On its way out,' he told her. 'That would be my first piece of detection.'

She paused and frowned. She looked round as if to understand how he'd reached this conclusion. 'Oh yes, I see,' she finally said. 'No footprints, but that could be because of the weather, couldn't it? A bad time of year for the beach.'

'Yes. But look to the pools of water at the base of the cliffs.'

'Wouldn't they always be there?'

'I daresay. Especially this time of year. But the rocks that back them wouldn't be wet, and they are. The lights from the houses are glittering off them.'

'Very impressive,' she said.

'Elementary,' was his rejoinder.

They made their way across the sand. It was quite soft, telling Lynley they would need to take care. Quicksand wasn't unheard of on the coast, especially in locations like this one, where the sea ebbed a considerable distance.

The cove broadened some one hundred yards from the boulders. At this point, when the tide was out, a grand beach stretched in both directions. They turned landward when the cliffs were entirely behind them. It was an easy matter, then, to see the caves.

The cliffs facing the water were cratered with them, darker cavities against dark stone, like dusted fingerprints, and two of them of enormous size. Lynley said, 'Ah,' and Daidre said, 'I'd no idea,' and together they approached the largest, a cavern at the base of the cliff upon which the biggest house was built.

The cave's opening looked to be some thirty feet high, narrow and roughly shaped, like a keyhole turned on its head, with a threshold of slate that was streaked with quartz. It was gloomy within, but not altogether dark, for some distance at the rear of the cave dim light filtered from a roughly formed chimney that geologic action had aeons ago produced in the cliff. Still, it was difficult to make out the walls until Daidre produced a book of matches from her shoulder bag and said to Lynley with an embarrassed shrug, 'Sorry. Girl Guides. I've a Swiss army knife as well, if you need it. Plasters, too.'

'That's comforting,' he told her. 'At least one of us has come prepared.'

A match's light showed them at first how deeply the cave was affected at high water, for hundreds of thousands of molluscs the size of drawing pins clung to the rough, richly veined stone walls, making them rougher still to a height of at least eight feet. Mussels formed black bouquets beneath them, and interspersed between these bouquets, multicoloured shellfish scalloped against the walls.

When the match burned low, Lynley lit another. He and Daidre worked their way farther in, picking through stones as the cave's floor gained slightly in elevation, a feature that would have allowed the water to recede with the ebbing tide. They came upon one shallow alcove, then another, where the sound of dripping water was rhythmic and incessant. The scent within was utterly primeval. Here, one could easily imagine how all life had actually come from the sea.

'It's rather wonderful, isn't it?' Daidre spoke in a hushed voice.

Lynley didn't reply. He'd been thinking of the myriad uses a spot like this had seen over the centuries. Everything from smugglers' cache to lovers' place of assignation. From children's games of marauding pirates to shelter from sudden rainfall. But to use the cave for anything at all, one had to understand the tide because to remain in ignorance of the sea's acts of governance was to court certain death.

Daidre was quiet next to him as his match burnt down and he lit another. He imagined a boy being caught in here, in this cave or in another just like it. Drunk, drugged, possibly unconscious, and if not unconscious, then sleeping it off. It didn't matter at the end of the day. If he'd been in darkness and deep within this place when the tide swept in, he would likely not have known which way to go to attempt an escape.

'Thomas?'

The match flickered as he turned to Daidre Trahair. The light cast a glow against her skin. A piece of her hair had come loose from the slide she used to hold it back, and this fell to her cheek, curving into her lips. Without thinking, he brushed it away from her mouth. Her eyes – unusually brown, like his own – seemed to darken.

It came to him suddenly what a moment such as this one meant. The cave, the weak light, the man and the woman in close proximity. Not a betrayal, but an affirmation. The knowledge that somehow life had to go on.

The match burnt to his fingers. He dropped it hastily. The instant passed and he thought of Helen. He felt a searing within him because he couldn't remember what this moment clearly demanded that he remember: When had he first kissed Helen?

He couldn't recall and, worse, he didn't know *why* he couldn't recall. They'd known each other for years before their marriage, for he'd met her when she'd come to Cornwall in the company of his closest friend during one holiday or another from university. He may have kissed her then, a light touch on the lips in farewell at the end of that visit, a lovely-to-have-met-you gesture that meant nothing at the time but now might mean everything. For it was essential in that moment that he recall every instance of Helen in his life. It was the only way he could keep her with him and fight the void. And that was the point: to fight the void. If he floated into it, he knew he'd be lost.

He said to Daidre Trahair, who was only a silhouette in the gloom, 'We should go. Can you lead us out?'

'Of course I can,' she said. 'It shouldn't be difficult.'

She found her way with assurance, one hand moving lightly along the tops of the molluscs on the wall. He followed her, his heart pulsing behind his eyes. He believed he ought to say something about the moment that had passed between them, to explain himself in some way to Daidre. But he had no words, and even if he had possessed the language necessary to communicate the extent of his grief and his loss, they were not necessary. For she was the one to break the silence between them, and she did so when they emerged from the cave and began to make their way back to the car.

'Thomas, tell me about your wife,' she said.


The POV is established immediately with the words *telling Lynley*, and after this the setting is delineated. Its importance in the story – it's the place where a long-ago death occurred, which is critical to the motive for the murder in the book – asks for details so that the reader can fix the place in her imagination. Three of our five senses are used: sight, sound and smell.

The plot is touched on in Lynley's reflection upon the cave's various uses over the centuries, and his imagining exactly how the long-ago death probably occurred.

The tension in the scene comes from Lynley's brushing the hair off Daidre's face, which segues into his realisation regarding what this moment in the cave with Daidre Trahair could mean. This prompts the memory of Helen and his internal conflict of keeping her with him in every possible way or moving forward with his life, which he barely thinks he might one day be able to do.

His statement *'We should go. Can you lead us out?'* contains both the double meaning of her possibly being able to lead them away from this moment as well as out of the cave and the foreshadowing of a future relationship, which is reinforced with her reply, *'Of course I can. It shouldn't be difficult.'*

And then Lynley's additional inner conflict ends the scene: he ought to reveal to her the excruciating depth of his loss, but he can't even begin to find the words. And following upon that reflection on his part, Daidre's words signal the movement in their relationship: *'Thomas, tell me about your wife.'*

So what the scene contains turns out to be: place, and a description of place, including the sensory details of sight, sound and smell; reflections on the part of Lynley that demonstrate his inner landscape and that also serve to address the plot and the backstory of what will be revealed as the motive behind the murder of Santo Kerne; sexual tension between Lynley and Daidre; Lynley's inner conflict; and character development of both Lynley and Daidre.

All of that rose from my location research, as you can see in Images 26 and 27.

IMAGE 26

IMAGE 27

Image 26 depicts several of the cave openings that I saw when I was tramping along the beach. Image 27 is taken from inside the cave that I ended up using for the scene in the novel. I took other pictures inside as well. All the details contained in the description of the place were present in my photographs.

When constructing a scene, I try to be all people. I'm inside Lynley's head; I'm inside Daidre's reaction to Lynley's words. I attempt to create a narrative that propels the reader forward into the story's main plot and – if it can be done – into its subplots. The scene is there to advance the plot, but it doesn't do that at the expense of character.

If you make a second reading of the scene in the cave, you should also be able to see that the opening of the scene, taking in their initial conversation, allows their relationship to take a step forward. Their remarks to each other are light; they feel more comfortable in each other's company. My hope is that what passes between them in the scene will prompt the reader to continue, to find an answer to the questions 'What's going on with these two?' and 'Where will the story take their relationship?' Additionally, I hope to illustrate what's going on within Lynley: the conflict between his grief and his growing knowledge that life will go on, with or without his participation in it. Likewise, the reader has an opportunity to see that despite the mysteries surrounding exactly who Daidre Trahair is and what she's hiding, she appears to be a compassionate woman fully capable of reading another's suffering. And finally, the fact that a death occurred in this cave or a cave exactly like it reminds the reader that a crime story is also advancing. Dramatic questions are being answered regarding how one could become trapped in a cave such as this. At the same time dramatic questions regarding Lynley and Daidre are being asked.

## Optional Exercise 1

Using the scene for which you created a running plot outline in the previous chapter, now create the scene itself. Try to include in your scene all of the elements of scene setting, plot establishment and advancement, and character illustration that you can.

## Optional Exercise 2

Now examine the scene you've just written. What can you come up with as answers to the following questions?

What in your scene will encourage the reader to continue reading?
What personal qualities have you revealed in your characters?
How is your novel's plot being introduced or advanced?
What dramatic questions are being asked?
Are any dramatic questions being answered?

## Optional Exercise 3

Return to the scene in Chapter 2 between Tammy and Selevan Penrule. After reading it through, ask and answer the following questions: What is the conflict? What kind of conflict is it? Does it relate to the plot or to a subplot? What does the reader learn about Selevan Penrule? About Tammy? What dramatic questions are being asked?

# CHAPTER 11

# The Scene's Requirements I

*Openings and Plot Points*

A scene's placement in the novel helps me determine what specific needs it has beyond the general requirements of setting, character, dramatic questions, conflict/tension and causality. Every scene needs those elements. But there are certain scenes that have additional, *specific* requirements. Over the next two chapters, I'd like to examine these special scenes so that you can look at what those requirements are and how each example meets those requirements.

Opening scenes are tough because their number one requirement is to hook the reader. The writer has various tools to employ in order to hook, however: the promise of excitement or intrigue or conflict, an indication of theme, a problem that a character encounters, foreshadowing of things to come, the introduction of characters, the laying down of dramatic questions, and the primary event or the status quo or both.

If you review the complete opening scene of *Careless in Red*, which you can find in Chapter 8 of this book, you should be able to see a selection of specific elements.

Intrigue is established at once in the person of an unnamed man walking on the South-West Coast Path. He's been walking for forty-three days and is virtually unaware of his surroundings. Who is this man, and what's going on with him that he's out there largely unprepared for such a walk?

The first dramatic question appears in the last sentence of that first paragraph, contained in the words, *in an effort to avoid both the thought of the future and the memory of the past.* Specifically the reader's interest should be caught with *the memory of the past,* and her interest, one hopes, will be heightened by that incomplete information. It's my belief that this makes the opening much more powerful than it would be had I begun with Lynley's name and with what had previously occurred in his life to put him out there in this desolate place.

The theme is touched upon. One can recover or not recover from grief, and recovering is largely a matter of choice, grit and determination.

A problem is encountered later during this first scene: the unnamed man sees what he thinks might be a body at the base of one of the sea cliffs. Out of the corner of his eye, he's caught a flash of red that could well indicate someone's fall, but he isn't sure. Nonetheless, because it looks as if there is an outstretched arm at the bottom of the cliff, he decides to investigate since someone could be critically injured.

There is a foreshadowing of problems to come: if it is indeed a body (and this being a crime novel, we can assume it will be), he's going to have to do something about it.

His status quo has been given: he's a man walking and walking to get away from his memories. His status quo has also been disrupted by the primary event: he sees what he thinks may have been a body falling, and he also sees the result on the rocks below.

You might well ask if a writer has to have *all* of these elements in an opening scene. Of course not. Fashioning an opening scene isn't like checking elements off a list. (Intrigue? Got it. Foreshadowing? Check. Place, mood, atmosphere? Yes, ma'am.) But an awareness of them and their availability to you as a writer will help you avoid writing in the dark.

For me, the key to a strong opening is knowing my characters first and placing them into a real setting second. The plot kernel and the character analyses are going to serve me well now. The first tells me generally where I'm heading while the second advises me how the individual characters are going to react along the way.

Plot point scenes – sometimes called turning point scenes – have their own requirements. Before we get into them, though, I'd like to take a look at where they occur, because it's relatively simple: They occur wherever you want to put them. In your reading, though, you'll generally find them in three spots. The first is in the vicinity of one quarter of the way through the novel; the second is the midpoint of the novel; the third is at the three-quarter point. The crucial piece of information here is that, like virtually everything else related to the creation of a novel, nothing is set in stone. The only rules are 1) There are no rules, and 2) If it works, keep it.

The question is, how do you know when you need a plot point? The answer is, you need a plot point when the story slows or stalls and when a careful examination of what you've done so far tells you that the problem is *not* one of playing your hand (i.e., accidentally revealing something) too soon.

How, then, does one create a plot point – or turning point – scene? Raymond Chandler always said that you bring a man with a gun into the room. My husband used to say 'Kill someone else,' which is pretty much the same thing. But, actually, there are requirements of plot point scenes that can assist you in the creation of one.

Examine, if you will, the following plot point scene in *Careless in Red*:

It was, praise God or praise whomever one felt like praising when praise was called for, the last radiator. Not the last radiator as in the *last* radiator of all radiators in the hotel, but the last radiator as in the last radiator he would have to paint for the day. Given a half hour to clean the brushes and seal the paint tins – after years of practice while working for his father, Cadan knew he could stretch out *any* activity as long as was necessary – it would be time to leave for the day. Halle-fucking-lujah. His lower back was throbbing and his head was reacting to the fumes once again. Clearly, he *wasn't* meant for this type of labour. Well, that was hardly a surprise.

Cadan squatted back on his heels and admired his handiwork. It was dead stupid of them to put down the fitted carpet *before* they had someone paint the radiators, he thought. But he'd managed to get the most recent spill cleaned up with a bit of industrious rubbing, and what he'd not got up he reckoned the curtains would hide. Besides, it had been his only serious spill of the day, and that was saying something.

He declared, 'We are out of here, Poohster.'

The parrot adjusted his balance on Cadan's shoulder and replied with a squawk followed by, 'Loose bolts on the fridge! Call the cops! Call the cops!' yet another of his curious remarks.

The door to the room swung open as Pooh flapped his wings, preparatory either to making a descent to the floor or to performing a less than welcome bodily function on Cadan's shoulder. Cadan said, 'Don't you *bloody* dare, mate,' and a female voice said in concerned reply, 'Who are you, please? What're you doing here?'

The speaker turned out to be a woman in black, and Cadan reckoned that she was Santo Kerne's mother, Dellen. He scrambled to his feet. Pooh said, 'Polly wants a shag. Polly wants a shag,' displaying, not for the first time, the level of inapposition to which he was capable of sinking at a moment's notice.

'What is that?' Dellen Kerne asked, clearly in reference to the bird.

'A parrot.'

She looked annoyed. 'I can see it's a parrot,' she told him. 'I'm not stupid or blind. What sort of parrot and what's he doing here and what're *you* doing here, if it comes to that?'

'He's a Mexican parrot.' Cadan could feel himself getting hot, but he knew the woman wouldn't twig his discomfiture as his olive skin didn't blush when blood suffused it. 'His name is Pooh.'

'As in Winnie-the?'

'As in what he does best.'

A smile flickered round her lips. 'Why don't I know you? Why've I not seen you here before?'

Cadan introduced himself. 'Ben . . . Mr. Kerne hired me yesterday. He probably forgot to tell you about me because of . . .' He saw the way he was headed too late to avoid heading there. He quirked his mouth and wanted to disappear, since – aside from painting radiators and dreaming about what could be done to the crazy golf course – his day had been spent in avoiding a run-in precisely like this: face-to-face with one of Santo Kerne's parents in a moment when the magnitude of their loss was going to have to be acknowledged with an appropriate expression of sympathy. He said, 'Sorry about Santo.'

She looked at him evenly. 'Of course you are.'

Whatever that was supposed to mean. Cadan shifted on his feet. He had a paintbrush still in his hand and he wondered suddenly and idiotically what he was meant to do with it. Or with the tin of paint. They'd been brought to him and no one had said where to put them at the end of the workday. He'd not thought to ask.

'Did you know him?' Dellen Kerne said abruptly. 'Did you know Santo?'

'A bit. Yeah.'

'And what did you think of him?'

This was rocky ground. Cadan didn't know how to reply other than to say, 'He bought a surfboard from my dad.' He didn't mention Madlyn, didn't want to mention Madlyn, and didn't want to think *why* he didn't want to mention Madlyn.

'I see. Yes. But that doesn't actually answer the question, does it?' Dellen came farther into the room. She went to the fitted clothes cupboard for some reason. She opened it. She looked inside. She spoke, oddly, into the cupboard's interior. She said, 'Santo was a great deal like me. You wouldn't know that if you didn't know him. And you didn't know him, did you? Not actually.'

'Like I said. A bit. I saw him round. More when he was first learning to surf than later on.'

'Because you surf as well?'

'Me? No. Well, I mean I've *been*, of course. But it's not like it's the only . . . I mean, I've got other interests.'

She turned from the cupboard. 'Do you? What are they? Sport, I expect. You look quite fit. And women as well. Young men your age generally have women as one of their main interests. Are you like other young men?' She frowned. 'Can we open that window, Cadan? The smell of paint . . .'

Cadan wanted to say it was her hotel so she could do whatever she wanted to do, but he set down his paintbrush carefully, went to the window, and wrestled it open, which wasn't easy. It needed adjusting or greasing or something. Whatever one did to rejuvenate windows.

She said, 'Thank you. I'm going to have a cigarette now. Do you smoke? No? That's a surprise. You have the look of a smoker.'

Cadan knew he was meant to ask what the look of a smoker was, and had she been somewhere between twenty and thirty years old, he would have done so. His attitude would have been that questions like that one, of a potentially metaphoric nature, could lead to interesting answers, which in turn could lead to interesting developments. But in this case, he kept his mouth shut and when she said, 'You won't be bothered if I smoke, will you?' he shook his head. He hoped she didn't

THE SCENE'S REQUIREMENTS I                    251

expect him to light her cigarette for her – because she *did* seem the sort
of woman round whom men leapt like jackrabbits – since he had neither matches nor lighter with him. She was correct in her assessment of
him, though. He was a smoker but he'd been cutting back recently,
inanely telling himself it was tobacco and not drink that was the real
root of his problems.

He saw that she'd brought a packet of cigarettes with her and she
had matches as well, tucked into the packet. She lit up, drew in, and let
smoke drift from her nostrils.

'Whose shit's on fire?' Pooh remarked.

Cadan winced. 'Sorry. He's heard that from my sister a million
times. He mimics her. He mimics everyone. Anyway, she hates smoking.' And then again, 'Sorry,' because he didn't want her to think he
was being critical of her.

'You're nervous,' Dellen said. 'I'm making you that way. And the
bird's fine. He doesn't know what he's saying, after all.'

'Yeah. Well. Sometimes, though, I'd swear he does.'

'Like the remark about shagging?'

He blinked. 'What?'

'"Polly wants a shag,"' she reminded him. 'It was the first thing he
said when I came into the room. I don't, actually. Want a shag, that is.
But I'm curious why he said that. I expect you use that bird to collect
women. Is that why you brought him with you?'

'He goes most everywhere with me.'

'That can't be convenient.'

'We work things out.'

'Do you?' She observed the bird, but Cadan had the feeling she
wasn't really seeing Pooh. He couldn't have said what she *was* seeing
but her next remarks gave him at least an idea. 'Santo and I were quite
close. Are you close to your mother, Cadan?'

'No.' He didn't add that it was impossible to be close to Wenna

Rice Angarrack McCloud Jackson Smythe, aka the Bounder. She had never remained stationary long enough for closeness to be anywhere in the deck of cards she played.

'Santo and I were quite close,' Dellen said again. 'We were very alike. Sensualists. Do you know what that is?' She gave him no chance to answer, not that he could have given her a definition, anyway. She said, 'We live for sensation. For what we can see and hear and smell. For what we can taste. For what we can touch. And for what can touch us. We experience life in all its richness, without guilt and without fear. That's what Santo was like. That's what I taught Santo to be.'

'Right.' Cadan thought how he'd like to get out of the room, but he wasn't certain how to effect a departure that wouldn't look like running away. He told himself there was no *real* reason to turn tail and disappear through the doorway, but he had a feeling, nearly animal in nature, that danger was near.

Dellen said to him, 'What sort are you, Cadan? Can I touch your bird or will he bite?'

He said, 'He likes to be scratched on his head. Where you'd put his ears if birds had ears. I mean ears like ours because they can hear, obviously.'

'Like this?' She came close to Cadan, then. He could smell her scent. Musk, he thought. She used the nail of her index finger, which was painted red. Pooh accepted her ministrations, as he normally did. He purred like a cat, yet another sound he'd learned from a previous owner. Dellen smiled at the bird. She said to Cadan, 'You didn't answer me. What sort are you? Sensualist? Emotionalist? Intellectual?'

'Not bloody likely,' he replied. 'Intellectual, I mean. I'm not intellectual.'

'Ah. Are you emotional? Bundle of feelings? Raw to the touch? Inside, I mean.'

He shook his head.

'Then you're a sensualist, like me. Like Santo. I thought as much. You have that look about you. I expect it's something your girlfriend appreciates. If you have one. Do you?'

'Not just now.'

'Pity. You're quite attractive, Cadan. What do you do for sex?'

Cadan felt ever more the need to escape, yet she wasn't doing a single thing except petting the bird and talking to him. Still, something was very off with the woman.

Then it came to him at a gallop that her son was dead. Not only dead but murdered. He was gone, kaput, given the chop, whatever. When a son died – or a daughter or a husband – wasn't the mother supposed to rip up her clothes? tear at her hair? shed tears by the bucketful?

She said, 'Because you must do something for sex, Cadan. A young virile man like you. You can't mean me to think you live like a celibate priest.'

'I wait for summer,' he finally told her.

Her finger hesitated, less than an inch from Pooh's green head. The bird sidestepped to get back within its range. 'For summer?' Dellen said.

'Town's full of girls then. Here on holiday.'

'Ah. You prefer the short-term relationship, then. Sex without strings.'

'Well,' he said. 'Yeah. Works for me, that.'

'I expect it does. You scratch them and they scratch you and everyone's happy with the arrangement. No questions asked. I know exactly what you mean. Although I expect that surprises you. A woman my age. Married, with children. Knowing what it means.'

He offered a half smile. It was insincere, just a way to acknowledge what she was saying without having to acknowledge what she was saying. He gave a look in the direction of the doorway. He said, 'Well,' and tried to make his tone decisive, a way of saying, That's that, then. Nice talking to you.

She said, 'Why haven't we met before this?'

'I just started—'

'No. I understand that. But I can't sort out why we haven't met before. You're roughly Santo's age—'

'Four years older, actually. He's my—'

' – and you're so like him as well. So I can't sort out why you've never come round with him.'

' – sister's age. Madlyn,' he said. 'You probably know Madlyn. My sister. She and Santo were . . . Well, they were whatever you want to call it.'

'What?' Dellen asked blankly. 'What did you call her?'

'Madlyn. Madlyn Angarrack. They – she and Santo – they were together for . . . I don't know . . . Eighteen months? Two years? Whatever. She's my sister. Madlyn's my sister.'

Dellen stared at him. Then she stared past him, but she appeared to be looking at nothing at all. She said in a different voice altogether, 'How very odd. She's called Madlyn, you say?'

'Yeah. Madlyn Angarrack.'

'And she and Santo were . . . what, exactly?'

'Boyfriend and girlfriend. Partners. Lovers. Whatever.'

'You're joking.'

He shook his head, confused, wondering why she'd think he was joking. 'They met when he came to get a board from my dad. Madlyn taught him to surf. Santo, that is. Well, obviously, not my dad. That's how they got to know each other. And then . . . well, I s'pose you could say they started hanging about together and things went from there.'

'And you called her Madlyn?' Dellen asked.

'Yeah. Madlyn.'

'Together for eighteen months.'

'Eighteen months or so. Yeah. That's it.'

'Then why did I never meet her?' she said.

Plot point scenes contain new information, new facts, new agendas or new characters who will come 'onstage' to alter the direction of the narrative. In the example you've just read, Cadan is meeting Dellen Kerne for the first time. And for the first time, the reader has a chance to see Dellen in action with men, specifically what she does to throw them off guard.

Plot point scenes also contain discovery. The reader learns that Dellen has no idea that Santo was involved with someone called Madlyn Angarrack, despite what we know about Santo's erstwhile relationship with her.

Something occurs during plot point scenes to propel the story forward. Here, we see Dellen's attempt to seduce Cadan. We're learning that when she's in a bad mental state, she's nearly on autopilot when it comes to men. Seduction is part of how she copes with stress, and there's nothing more stressful than confronting the death of one's child. We can expect more to come from Dellen, and now we see the form it might take.

The writer can consider other options in the creation of plot point scenes as well.

First, she can have something occur that requires a new setting, launching the characters into a situation with which they have to contend. Taking a page from literary history, if we examine Jane Austen's *Sense and Sensibility*, we learn soon enough that the wife and daughters of the late Mr. Dashwood are contending with the revelation that they are now unwelcome in their own home, which has been inherited by Mr. Dashwood's son by a previous marriage and the son's rapacious wife. Therefore, they must and they do find a new place to live. In this entirely new setting, they meet the scoundrel Mr. Willoughby and the heroic Colonel Brandon.

Second, there can be a pivot in a scene that propels the action forward. A misunderstanding occurs; a heart is broken; a lie is believed. In Austen's *Pride and Prejudice*, Mr. Darcy proposes marriage to Elizabeth Bennett in the most teeth-grating, skin-crawling fashion imaginable. In anger, she very rightly refuses him. But in this process she insults Mr. Darcy, wounding him as much as he has insulted and wounded her. He leaves; she bursts into tears. In a few pages, however, she's going to learn something that will remove the veil from her eyes regarding Mr. Darcy, Mr. Wickham and her own family. This comes from a letter Mr. Darcy has written her, recounting his family's sad and painful history dealing with Mr. Wickham's talent for seduction. We have more information now, which is going to be extremely useful as the novel progresses.

Third, something can occur which requires a completely sudden change of setting (albeit not a permanent one as in the previous example). In *Pride and Prejudice*, Elizabeth Bennett has gone with her aunt and uncle to Derbyshire. There, at his family home – Pemberley – she is able to make peace with Mr. Darcy. It looks as if love might prevail, but all at once she receives a letter telling her that her sister Lydia has eloped with the scoundrel Mr. Wickham. Chaos reigns at Longbourn, her home. This necessitates her removal back to Longbourn post haste, quite possibly throwing to the wind her rapprochement with Mr. Darcy.

Finally, a THAD reveals something that also propels the action forward. In the scene with Cadan, everything Dellen does – from lighting a cigarette to petting the parrot – adds to our storehouse of knowledge about her. It also propels Cadan's later decision not to have anything to do with her, at least if he can hold on to that thought long enough to get some distance. In this scene as well, groundwork is being laid for future information. Seeing Dellen in action encourages the reader's belief in revelations that illuminate her character, her relationship with her husband and her conflict with her daughter.

## Optional Exercise 1

Using what you previously wrote addressing a character's status quo and the primary event which upsets the status quo, try your hand at creating the opening of a novel. In addition to either the primary event or the status quo, include two other elements that can be present in the opening of a novel (setting, outer landscape of character, inner landscape of character, THAD, etc.).

## Optional Exercise 2

Here's the first sentence: *Of the three objects, he chose the lantern.*

Using that sentence, create the opening scene of a novel. It can be as long or as short as you would like it to be, as long as it includes the problem, a dramatic question, and either the status quo or the primary event. It can include anything else as well.

# CHAPTER 12

# The Scene's Requirements II

*Climax and Denouement*

Everyone who has taken a literature class knows that novels require a climax. Lesser known, perhaps, is that there are two kinds: the narrative climax and the dramatic climax.

The first, the narrative climax, appears in *Careless in Red* within a scene in which Lynley goes to the small Cornish town of Boscastle to interview Niamh Triglia, the mother of the long-dead Jamie Parsons. Prior to this conversation, Niamh has been engaged in making crab cakes (the THAD), which she shares with Lynley during their conversation. This conversation leads up to the narrative climax. As the conversation begins in the example that follows, Niamh is the speaker:

'Francis and I – that's my late husband – were so similar to each other that we were often taken for brother and sister when we were younger.'

'You were married to him for a number of years, then?'

'Twenty-two years nearly to the day. But I'd known him before my first marriage ended. We'd been in primary school together. Isn't it odd how something as simple as that – being in school together – can forge a bond and make things easier between people if they see each other later in life, even if they haven't spoken in years? There was no period of discomfort between us when we first began to see each other after Jon and I divorced.' She scooped some aioli out of the bowl and handed it to him to do the same. She tasted the crab cake and pronounced it, 'Doable. What do you think of them?'

'I think they're excellent.'

'Flatterer. Handsome *and* well-bred, I see. Is your wife a good cook?'

'She's completely appalling.'

'She has other strengths, then.'

He thought of Helen: the laughter of her, that unrepressed gaiety, so much compassion. 'I find she has hundreds of strengths.'

'Which makes indifferent kitchen skills—'

'Completely irrelevant. There's always takeaway.'

'Isn't there just.' She smiled at him and then went on with, 'I'm avoiding, as you've probably guessed. Has something happened to Jon?'

'Do you know where he is?'

She shook her head. 'I haven't spoken to him in years. Our eldest child—'

'Jamie.'

'Ah. So you know about Jamie?' And when Lynley nodded, she continued by saying thoughtfully, 'I suppose we all carry some sort of scars from our childhood for this and that reason, and Jon had his share. His father was a hard man with set ideas about what his boys should do with their lives, and he'd decided that what they should do was science. *Very* stupid to decide your children's lives for them, to my way of thinking, but there you have it. That's what he did. Unfortunately, neither boy was the least interested in science, so they both disappointed him and he never let them forget it. Jon was determined not to be that kind of father to our children, especially to Jamie, and I have to say he made a success of it. We *both* made a success of parenthood. I stayed home with the children because he insisted and I agreed with him, and I think that made a difference. We were close to the children. The children were close to each other although strung along quite a bit in age. At any rate, we were a very tight and very happy little unit.'

'And then your son died.'

'And then Jamie died.' She set her knife and fork down and folded her hands in her lap. 'Jamie was a lovely boy. Oh, he had his quirks – what boy his age doesn't – but at heart he was lovely. Lovely and loving. And very *very* good to his little sisters. We were all devastated by his death, but Jon couldn't come to grips with it. I thought he would, eventually. Give it time, I told myself. But when a person's life becomes all about the death of another and about nothing else . . . I had the girls to think of, you see. I had myself to think of. I couldn't live like that.'

'Like what?'

'It was all he talked about and, as far as I could tell, it was all he thought about. It was as if Jamie's death had invaded his brain and eaten away everything that wasn't Jamie's death.'

'I've learned he wasn't satisfied with the investigation, so he mounted his own.'

'He must have mounted half a dozen. But it made no difference. And each time that it made no difference, he went just a bit more mad. Of course, he'd lost the business by then and we'd gone through our savings and had lost our home, and that made things worse for him because he knew he was responsible for it happening, but he couldn't get himself to stop. I tried to tell him it would make no difference to his grief and his loss to bring someone to justice, but he thought it would. He was *sure* it would. Just the way people think that if the killer of their loved one is put to death, that's somehow going to assuage their own desolation. But how can it, really? The death of a killer doesn't bring anyone *else* back to life, and that's what we want and can never have.'

'What happened to Jonathan when you divorced?'

'The first three years or so, he phoned me occasionally. To give me "updates", he said. Of course, there never were any viable updates to give me, but he needed to believe he was making progress instead of doing what he was really doing.'

'Which was?'

'Making it less and less likely that anyone involved in Jamie's death would . . . would *crack*, I suppose the word is. He saw in this an enormous conspiracy involving everyone in Pengelly Cove, with himself the outsider and them the close-mouthed community determined to protect its own.'

'But you didn't see it that way?'

'I didn't know *how* to see it. I wanted to be supportive of Jon and I tried to be at first, but for me the real point was that Jamie was dead. We'd lost him – *all* of us had lost him – and nothing Jon could do was going to alter that. My . . . I suppose you might call it my focus . . . was on that one fact, and it seemed to me – rightly or wrongly – that the result of what Jon was doing was to keep Jamie's death fresh, like a sore that one rubs and causes to bleed instead of allowing it to heal. And I believed that healing was what we all needed.'

'Did you see him again? Did your girls see him again?'

She shook her head. 'And doesn't that compile tragedy upon tragedy? One child died terribly, but Jon lost all four upon his own choice because he *chose* the dead over the living. To me, that's a greater tragedy than the loss of our son.'

'Some people,' Lynley said quietly, 'have no other way to react to a sudden, inexplicable loss.'

'I daresay you're right. But in Jon's case, I think it was a deliberate choice. In making it, he was living the way he'd always lived, which was to put Jamie first. Here. Let me show you what I mean.'

She rose from the table and, wiping her hands down the front of her apron, she went into the sitting room. Lynley could see her walk over to the crowded bookshelves where she extricated a picture from among the large group on display. She brought it to the kitchen and handed it over, saying, 'Sometimes photographs say things that words can't convey.'

Lynley saw that she'd given him a family portrait. In it, a version of herself perhaps thirty years younger posed with husband and four winsome children. The scene was wintry, deep snow with a lodge and a ski lift in the background. In the foreground, suited up for sport with skis leaning up against their shoulders, the family stood happily ready for action, Niamh with a toddler in her arms and two other laughing daughters hanging on to her and perhaps a yard from them, Jamie and his father. Jonathan Parsons had his arm affectionately slung round Jamie's neck, and he was pulling his son close to him. They both were grinning.

'That's how it was,' Niamh said. 'It didn't seem to matter so very much because, after all, the girls had me. I told myself it was a man-man and woman-woman thing, and I ought to be pleased that Jon and Jamie were so close and the girls and I were as thick as thieves. But, of course, when Jamie died Jon saw himself as having lost it all. Three-quarters of his life was standing right in front of him, but he couldn't see that. That was his tragedy. I didn't want to make it mine.'

Lynley looked up from his study of the photo. 'May I keep this for a time? I'll return it to you, of course.'

She seemed surprised by the request. 'Keep it? Whatever for?'

'I'd like to show it to someone. I'll return it within a few days. By post. Or in person if you prefer. I'll keep it quite safe.'

'Take it by all means,' she said. 'But . . . I haven't asked and I ought to have. Why have you come to talk about Jon?'

'A boy died north of here. Just beyond Casvelyn.'

'In a sea cave? Like Jamie?'

'In a fall from a cliff.'

'And you think this has something to do with Jamie's death?'

'I'm not sure.' Lynley looked at the picture again. He said, 'Where are your daughters now, Mrs. Triglia?'

At the point of a narrative climax, a decision is made by a character. This decision is going to affect the resolution of the novel. In this case, the decision is made by Lynley regarding a future action that he will take. He's asked for the photograph, and he's going to have an age progression done on it. The reader doesn't know this last part, of course. At least, not yet. But Lynley's request to keep the photograph signals to the reader that something's going on. The subsequent action that Lynley takes will direct the course of the novel, precipitate the climax, and lead to the resolution of the story I've been putting together.

The reader never needs to know the exact nature of a planned future action. Indeed, in this particular scene revealing that would have constituted asking a dramatic question and then answering that same question as well. By doing that, I would be playing my hand far too soon. So instead of saying anything more about the picture, I have Lynley veer slightly off course by asking Niamh Triglia where her daughters are. This, I hope, will direct the reader's thoughts to Daidre Trahair and all that she's been hiding from Lynley. Is she one of the daughters, all grown up now? Is she therefore somehow involved in what happened to Santo Kerne? That's where I want to place the reader's suspicions, keeping them away from the real killer of Santo, Jago Reeth – that is, Jonathan Parsons, who has been waiting all these years to avenge his son's death at the hands, he believes, of Ben Kerne. Thus, as soon as Lynley asks to take the photo with him, he's made some sort of decision. From this decision, the story is propelled forward.

Like plot point scenes, the narrative climax has a few requirements, one of which is the building of tension leading to some kind of revelation. In this scene with Lynley and Niamh Triglia, we find this within Lynley's growing understanding of the dynamics of the Parsons family as revealed by Niamh. The discussion leads her to fetch a photo of her family in order to make a point about Jonathan Parsons and his son. Their prior conversation makes this action logical.

There are various options available when you're thinking about the construction of the narrative climax.

First, you can consider *how* you want your scene to be constructed and what particular techniques of the writing craft you might use within your structure. You can try them out in the running plot outline. You can choose what seems most powerful:

Direct dialogue
Indirect dialogue
Amount of narration
The use of summary narration
The scenic form itself

Second, you can look at potential THADs. In this scene, Niamh's been making crab cakes. She shares them with Lynley. As the writer, I'm hoping this makes her more real to the reader and not just someone who's plopped conveniently into the story in order to give out information.

Third, you have a choice about conflict. Will there be some sort of conflict in the scene, leading up to the narrative climax? Will it be inner conflict or outer conflict? In this scene, the conflict comes from the revelation of the difficulties that led to the end of Niamh's marriage to Jonathan Parsons. There is no conflict – or even tension – between Niamh and Lynley.

. . .

The dramatic climax is the highest point of the drama the writer has been creating. Often, we think of the dramatic climax as a moment in which the adversaries face off through some kind of enormously exciting scene, such as a gunfight, a chase scene, a battle between groups of characters, etc., but this is the stuff of motion pictures and not necessarily novels. While a novel's dramatic climax can indeed be a scene of intense action, it's actually a moment in which *whatever* the writer has been leading up to finally happens.

Considering *Sense and Sensibility* once again, we find Edward Ferrars arriving at Elinor Dashwood's home and revealing that his *brother* was the person who married the loathsome gold digger Lucy Steele and not he. Elinor finally breaks down after holding it together through all her heartbreak and acting the part of pillar of strength for her mother and her sisters.

In the novel *Jaws*, we have an entirely different kind of climax. The men in the boat come face-to-face (or better said, they come face-to-teeth) with the great white shark in a kill-or-be-killed situation.

In my novel *In the Presence of the Enemy*, Sergeant Havers gets into a physical fight with the kidnapper of Leo Luxford in the crypt of an ancient castle where he has hidden the child.

My point is that in each of these cases, the novel has been leading up to this moment, and during this scene, you've got a lot to work with.

Tension should be building throughout the scene. It should build through dialogue, or it should build through a narrative of the ongoing action.

The conflict must reach its highest point.

Some kind of face-off needs to occur. Sometimes it's a physical confrontation; sometimes it's a psychological battle; sometimes it's the action of one character outwitting another.

A revelation is made.

A high point is achieved within the climactic scene itself. This is what I refer to as the bang within the bang. For example, the climactic scene in my novel *Payment in Blood* is Lynley's chase of the killer through the backstreets of Hampstead in London. The bang within the bang of that scene is the actual unmasking of the killer, who turns out to be someone Lynley did not at all expect to see, believing that someone else was responsible for the killings of Joy Sinclair and Hannah Darrow. In the climax of *Missing Joseph*, Lynley and St. James are in pursuit of Juliet Spence across moors in the snow. She's been unmasked as the killer, and in anticipation of this she has taken her daughter and made a run for it. The bang within the bang in this scene is an actual bang. Hiding inside a barn, Juliet Spence fires a gun that the reader has seen in her possession earlier in the novel.

Here is the dramatic climax from *Careless in Red*. The first thing you're going to notice is that nobody is running anywhere:

> Jago Reeth made it clear that he wanted Ben Kerne alone, with no hangers-on from his family present. He suggested Hedra's Hut for the venue, and he used the word *venue* as if a performance would be given there.
>
> Bea told him he was a bloody damn fool if he expected the lot of them to traipse out to the sea cliff where that ancient perch was.
>
> He replied that fool or not, if she wanted a conversation with him, he knew his rights and he was going to employ them.
>
> She told him that one of his rights was not the right to decide where their meeting with Ben Kerne would occur.
>
> He smiled and begged to differ with her. It might not have been his right, he said, but the fact of the matter was that she probably wanted him to be in a location where he felt easy with conversation. And Hedra's Hut was that location. They'd be cosy enough there. Out of the cold and the wind. Snug as four bugs rolled in the same rug, if she knew what he meant.

'He's got something up his sleeve,' was Sergeant Havers's assessment of the situation once they set off trailing Jago Reeth's Defender in the direction of Alsperyl. They'd wait at the village church for Mr. Kerne, Jago had informed them. 'Best phone the superintendent and let him know where we're going,' Havers went on. 'I'd have backup as well. Those blokes from the station . . . ? Got to be a way they can hide themselves round the place.'

'Not unless they disguise themselves as cows, sheep, or gulls,' Bea told her. 'This bloke's thought of all the angles.'

Lynley, Bea found, wasn't answering his mobile, which made her curse the man and wonder why she'd bothered to give him a phone in the first place. 'Where's the blasted man got off to?' she asked and then replied to her own question with a grim declaration of, 'Well, I wager we know the answer to that, don't we.'

At Alsperyl, which was no great distance from the Salthouse Inn, they remained in their respective cars, parked close to the village church. When Ben Kerne finally joined them, they'd been sitting there for nearly thirty minutes. During this time, Bea had phoned the station to give the word where they were and phoned Ray to do likewise.

Ray said, 'Beatrice, are you barking mad? D'you have any idea how irregular this is?'

'I've got half a dozen ideas,' she told him. 'I've also got sod all to work with unless this bloke gives me something I can use.'

'You can't think he intends—'

'I don't know what he intends. But there will be three of us and one of him and if we can't manage—'

'You'll check him for weapons?'

'I'm a fool but not a bloody fool, Ray.'

'I'm having whoever's out on patrol in your area head to Alsperyl.'

'Don't do that. If I need backup, I can easily phone the Casvelyn station for it.'

'I don't care what you can and cannot do. There's Pete to consider, and if it comes down to it, there's myself as well. I won't rest easy unless I know you've got proper backup. Christ, this is bloody irregular.'

'As you've said.'

'Who's with you at present?'

'Sergeant Havers.'

'Another *woman*? Where the hell is Lynley? What about that sergeant from the station? He looked like he had half a wit about him. For God's sake, Bea—'

'Ray. This bloke's round seventy years old. He's got some sort of palsy. If we can't take care of ourselves round him, we need to be carted off.'

'Nonetheless—'

'Goodbye, darling.' She rang off and shoved the mobile into her bag.

Shortly after she finished her phone calls – also telling Collins and McNulty at the Casvelyn station where she was – Ben Kerne arrived. He got out of his car and zipped his windcheater to the chin. He glanced at Jago Reeth's Defender in some apparent confusion. He then saw Bea and Havers parked next to the lichenous stone wall that defined the churchyard and he walked over to them. As he approached, they got out of the car. Jago Reeth did likewise.

Bea saw that Jago Reeth's eyes were fixed on Santo Kerne's father. She saw that his expression had altered from the easy affability that he'd shown them in the Salthouse Inn. Now his features fairly blazed. She imagined it was the look seasoned warriors had once worn when they finally had the necks of their enemies beneath their boots and a sword pressing into their throats.

Jago Reeth said nothing to any of them. He merely jerked his head towards a kissing gate at the west end of the car park, next to the church's notice board.

Bea spoke. 'If we're meant to attend you, Mr. Reeth, then I have a condition as well.'

He raised an eyebrow, the extent to which he apparently intended to communicate until they got to his preferred destination.

'Put your hands on the bonnet and spread your legs. And trust me, I'm not interested in checking to see what sort of cobblers you've got.'

Jago cooperated. Havers and Bea patted him down. His only weapon was a biro. Havers took this and tossed it over the wall into the churchyard.

Jago's expression said, *Satisfied?*

Bea said, 'Carry on.'

He headed in the direction of the kissing gate. He did not wait there to see if they were accompanying him. He was, apparently, perfectly certain that they would follow.

Ben Kerne said to Bea, 'What's going on? Why've you asked me . . . ? Who is that, Inspector?'

'You've not met Mr. Reeth before this?'

'That's Jago Reeth? Santo spoke about him. The old surfer working for Madlyn's dad. Santo quite liked him. I'd no idea. No. I've not met him.'

'I doubt he's actually a surfer although he talks the talk. He doesn't look familiar to you?'

'Should he?'

'As Jonathan Parsons, perhaps.'

Ben Kerne's lips parted, but he said nothing. He watched Reeth trudging towards the kissing gate. 'Where's he going?' he asked.

'Where he's willing to talk. To us and to you.' Bea put her hand on Kerne's arm. 'But you've no need to listen. You've no need to follow him. His condition to speak to us was to have you present and I realise this is half mad and the other half dangerous. But he's got us – that's

the cops and not you – by the short and curlies and the only way we're
going to get a word from him is to play it his way for now.'

'On the phone, you didn't say Parsons.'

'I didn't want you driving here like a madman. And I don't want
you like a madman now. We already have one on our hands, I believe,
and two would be overwhelming. Mr. Kerne, I can't tell you how far
out on a limb we are with this entire approach so I won't even go into
it. Are you able to listen to what he has to say? More, are you willing?'

'Did he . . . ?' Kerne seemed to search for a way to put it that
wouldn't make what he had to say into a fact he might have to accept.
'Did he kill Santo?'

'That's what we're going to talk to him about. Are you able?'

He nodded. He shoved his hands into the pockets of his windcheater
and indicated with a tilt of his head that he was ready. They set out
towards the kissing gate.

On the other side of this gate, a field provided grazing for cows, and
the way towards the sea edged along a barbed-wire fence. The path
they walked on was muddy and uneven, marked deeply by ruts made
from a tractor's wheels. At the far end of the field lay another field,
fenced off from the first by more barbed wire and accessed through yet
another kissing gate. Ultimately, they walked perhaps half a mile or
more and their destination was the South-West Coast Path, which
crossed the second field high above the sea.

The wind was fierce here, coming onshore in continuous gusts. On
these, the seabirds rose and fell. Kittiwakes called. Herring gulls replied. A lone green cormorant shot up from the cliff side as up ahead
Jago Reeth approached the edge. The bird dived down, rose, and
began to circle. Looking for prey, Bea thought, in the turbulent water.

They headed south on the coastal path, but within some twenty
yards, a break in the gorse that stood between the path and perdition

indicated a set of steep stone stairs. This, Bea saw, was their destination. Jago Reeth disappeared down them.

She said to her companions, 'Hang on, then,' and she went to see where the stone steps led. She was reckoning they were a means to get to the beach, which lay some two hundred feet below the cliff top, and she intended to tell Jago Reeth that she had no intention of putting her life, Havers's life and Ben Kerne's life at risk by following him down some perilous route to the water. But she found the steps went down only as far as fifteen of them could descend, and they terminated in another path, this one narrow and heavily grown on each side with gorse and sedge. It, too, headed south but for no great distance. Its conclusion was an ancient hut built partially into the face of the cliff that backed it. Jago Reeth, she saw, had just reached the hut's doorway and swung it open. He saw her on the steps but made no further gesture. Their eyes met briefly before he ducked inside the old structure.

She returned to the top of the cliff. She spoke above the sound of the wind, the sea and the gulls. 'He's just below, in the hut. He might well have something stowed inside, so I'm going in first. You can wait on the path, but don't come near till I give you the word.'

She went down the steps and along the path, the gorse brushing against the legs of her trousers. She reached the hut and found that Jago had indeed prepared for this moment. Not with weapons, however. Either he or someone else had earlier supplied the hut with a spirit stove, a jug of water and a small box of supplies. The man was, incredibly, brewing tea.

The hut was fashioned from the driftwood of wrecked ships, of which there had been countless numbers over the centuries. It was a small affair, with a bench that ran round three sides and an uneven stone floor. As long as it had been in this place, people had carved their initials into its walls, so they had the appearance now of a wooden Rosetta stone, this one immediately comprehensible and speaking both of lovers and of people whose internal insignificance made them seek an outward expression – *any* outward expression – that would give their existence meaning.

Bea told Reeth to step away from the spirit stove, which he did willingly enough. She checked it and the rest of his supplies, of which there were few enough: plastic cups, sugar, tea, powdered milk in sachets, one spoon for shared stirring. She was surprised the old man hadn't thought of crumpets.

She ducked back out of the door and motioned Havers and Ben Kerne to join her. Once all four of them were inside the hut, there was barely room to move, but Jago Reeth still managed to make the tea, and he pressed a cup upon each of them, like the hostess of an Edwardian house party. Then he doused the flame on the stove and set the stove itself on the stones beneath the bench, perhaps as a way of reassuring them that he had no intention of using it as a weapon. At this, Bea decided to pat him down again for good measure. Having put the spirit stove in the hut in advance of their arrival, there was no telling what else he'd stowed in the place. But he was weaponless, as before.

With the hut's double door shut and fastened, the sound of the wind and the gulls' crying was muted. The atmosphere was close, and the four adults took up nearly every inch of the space. Bea said, 'You've got us here, Mr. Reeth, at your pleasure. What is it you'd like to tell us?'

Jago Reeth held his tea in both hands. He nodded and spoke not to Bea but to Ben Kerne, and his tone was kind. 'Losing a son. You've got my deepest sympathy. It's the worst grief a man can know.'

'Losing any child's a blow.' Ben Kerne sounded wary. It appeared to Bea that he was trying to read Jago Reeth. As was she. The air seemed to crackle with anticipation.

Next to Bea, Sergeant Havers took out her notebook. Bea expected Reeth to tell her to put it away, but instead the old man nodded and said, 'I've no objection,' and to Kerne, 'Have you?' When Ben shook his head, Jago added, 'If you've come wired, Inspector, that's fine as well. There are always things wanting documentation in a situation like this.'

Bea wanted to say what she'd earlier thought: He'd considered all the angles. But she was waiting to see, hear, or intuit the one angle he hadn't yet considered. It *had* to be here somewhere, and she needed to be ready to deal with it when it raised its scaly head above the muck for a breath of air.

She said, 'Do go on.'

'But there's something worse about losing a son,' Jago Reeth said to Ben Kerne. 'Unlike a daughter, a son carries the name. He's the link between the past and the future. And it's more, even, than just the name at the end of the day. He carries the reason for it all. For this . . .' He gave a look around the hut, as if the tiny building somehow contained the world and the billions of lifetimes present in the world.

'I'm not sure I make that sort of distinction,' Ben said. 'Any loss . . . of a child . . . of any child . . .' He didn't go on. He cleared his throat mightily.

Jago Reeth looked pleased. 'Losing a son to murder is a horror, though, isn't it? The *fact* of murder is almost as bad as knowing who killed him and not being able to lift a finger to bring the bloody sod to justice.'

Kerne said nothing. Nor did Bea or Barbara Havers. Bea and Kerne held their tea undrunk in their hands, and Ben Kerne set his carefully on the floor. Next to her, Bea felt Havers stir.

'That part's bad,' Jago said. 'As is the not knowing.'

'Not knowing what, exactly, Mr. Reeth?' Bea asked.

'The whys and the wherefores about it. And the hows. Bloke can spend the rest of his life tossing and turning, wondering and cursing and wishing . . . You know what I mean, I expect. Or if not now, you will, eh? It's hell on earth and there's no escaping. I feel for you, mate. For what you're going through now and for what's to come.'

'Thank you,' Ben Kerne said quietly. Bea had to admire him for his control. She could see how white the tops of his knuckles were.

'I knew your boy Santo. Lovely lad. Bit full of himself, like all boys are when they're that age, eh, but lovely. And since this tragedy happened to him—'

'Since he was murdered,' Bea corrected Jago Reeth.

'Murder,' Reeth said, '*is* a tragedy, Inspector. No matter what kind of game of scent-and-chase you lot might think it is. It's a tragedy, and when it happens, the only peace available is in knowing the truth of what happened and having others know it as well. If,' he added with a brief smile, 'you know what I mean. And as I knew Santo, I've thought and thought about what happened to the lad. And I've decided that if an old broken-down bloke like myself can give you any peace, Mr. Kerne, that's what I owe you.'

'You don't owe me—'

'We all owe each other,' Jago cut in. 'It's forgetting that that leads us to tragedies.' He paused as if to let this sink in. He drained his tea and put the cup next to him on the bench. 'So what I want to do is tell you how I reckon this happened to your boy. Because I've thought about it, see, as I'm sure you have and sure the cops here have as well. Who would've done this to such a fine lad, I been asking myself for days. How'd they manage it? And why?'

'None of that brings Santo back, does it?' Ben Kerne asked steadily.

' 'Course not. But the knowing . . . the final understanding of it all: I wager there's peace in that and that's what I've got to offer you. Peace. So here's what I reckon was—'

'No. I don't think so, Mr. Reeth.' Bea had a sudden glimmer what Reeth intended, and in that glimmer she saw where this could lead.

But Ben Kerne said, 'Let him go on, please. I want to hear him out, Inspector.'

'This will allow him to—'

'Please let him continue.'

Reeth waited affably for Bea to concur. She nodded sharply, but she wasn't happy. To *irregular* and *mad* she had to add *provocative*.

'So here's what I reckon,' Jago said. 'Someone has a score to settle and this someone sets out to settle that score on the life of your lad. What sort of score, you wonder, right? Could be anything, couldn't it. New score, old score. It doesn't matter. But a form of accounting's waiting out there, and Santo's life's the means of settling it. So this killer – could be a man, could be a woman, doesn't much matter, does it, because the point is the lad and the lad's death, see, which is what cops like these two always forget – this killer gets to know your lad because knowing him's going to provide access. And knowing the lad leads to the means as well because your boy's an openhearted sort and he talks. About this and that, but as things turn out, he talks a lot about his dad, same as most boys do. He says his dad's riding him hard for lots of reasons but mostly because he wants women and surfing and not settling down, and who can blame him as he's only eighteen. His dad, on the other hand, has his *own* wants for the boy, which makes the boy roil and talk and roil some more. Which makes him look for . . . What d'you call it? A substitute dad . . . ?'

'A surrogate dad.' Ben's voice was heavier now.

'That would be the word. Or perhaps a surrogate mum, of course. Or a surrogate . . . what? Priest, confessor, priestess, whatever? At any rate, this person – man or woman, young or old – sees a door of trust opening and he – or she, of course – walks right through it. If you know what I mean.'

He was keeping his options open, Bea concluded. He was, as he had said himself, no bloody fool, and the advantage he had in this moment was the years he'd had to think about the approach he wanted to use when the time came for it.

'So this person . . . let's call him or her the Confessor for want of a better term . . . this Confessor makes cups of tea and cups of chocolate and more cups of tea and more cups of chocolate and offers biscuits, but more important offers a place for Santo to do whatever and to be whoever. And the Confessor waits. And soon enough reckons that means are available to settle whatever score needs settling. The boy's had yet another blowup with his dad. It's an argument that goes nowhere like always and this time the lad's taken all of his climbing equipment from where he's kept it in the past – right alongside Dad's – and he's stowed it in the boot of his car. What does he intend? It's that classic thing: I'll show him, I will. I'll show him what sort of bloke I am. He thinks I'm nothing but a lout but I'll show him. And what better way to do it than with his own sport, which I'll do *better* than he's ever managed. So that puts his equipment within the grasp of the Confessor and the Confessor sees what we'll call the Way.'

At this, Ben Kerne lowered his head. Bea said, 'Mr. Kerne, I think this is—'

He said, 'No.' He raised his head with effort. 'More,' he said to Jago Reeth.

'The Confessor waits for an opportunity, which presents itself soon enough because the lad's open and easy with his belongings, one of which is his car. This is nothing at all to get into as it's never locked and a quick manoeuvre opens the boot and there it all is. Selection is the key. Perhaps a chock stone or a carabiner. Or a sling. Even the harness will do. All four, perhaps? No, that likely would be – if you'll pardon the expression – overkill. If it's a sling, there's not a problem in the world as it's nylon or whatever and easily cut by shears, a sharp knife, a razor, whatever. If it's something else, things are a bit trickier, as everything else save the rope – and rope seems too bloody obvious a choice, not to mention too noticeable – is metal and a cutting device is going to be necessary. How to find one? Purchase one? No. That would be traceable. Borrow one? Again, someone's going to recall the borrowing, yes? Use one without the knowledge of the owner? That seems more possible and decidedly more sensible, but where to find one? Friend, associate, acquaintance, employer? Someone whose movements are intimately known because they've been watched just as intimately? Any of those, yes? So the Confessor chooses the moment and the deed is done. One cut does it and afterwards no sign is left behind because, as we've said, the Confessor's no fool and he knows – or she knows, because as we've seen, *she* is as possible as *he* when it comes to this – that it's crucial there be no evidence afterwards. And the beauty of it all is that the equipment's been marked with tape by the lad – or even by his father, perhaps – so that it can be distinguished from everyone else's. Because this is what climbers do, you see. They mark their equipment because so often they climb together. It's safer that way, climbing together, you see. And this tells the Confessor that there's little to no chance that anyone other than the lad will use this sling, this carabiner, this harness . . . whatever it was that was damaged because, of course, I myself don't know. But I've thought about it, and here's what I've come up with. The one thing the Confessor has to take care with is the tape used to identify the equipment. If he – or she, of course – buys more tape, there's a chance the new tape won't match exactly or can be traced back. God knows how, but there's that possibility, so the thing is to keep that tape usable. The Confessor manages this and it's quite a project because that tape is tough, like electrical tape. He – or she, of course, like I said – rewraps it just so and maybe it's not quite as tight as it once was but at least it's the same and will the lad even notice? Unlikely, and even if he does, what he's likely to do is smooth it down, apply more tape on top, something like that. So once the deed is done and the equipment's replaced, all that's left is waiting. And once what happens, happens – and it *is* a tragedy, no one doubts that – there's nothing really that can't be explained away.'

'There's always something, Mr. Reeth,' Bea said.

Jago looked at her in a kindly way. 'Fingerprints on the boot of the car? In the interior? On the keys to the car? Inside the boot? The Confessor and the boy spent hours together, perhaps they even worked together at . . . let's say it was at his dad's business. They each rode in the other's car, they were mates, they were pals, they were surrogate father and surrogate son, they were surrogate mother and surrogate son, they were surrogate brothers, they were lovers, they were . . . anything. It doesn't matter, you see, because it all can be explained away. Hair inside the boot of the car? The Confessor's? Someone else's? Same thing, really. The Confessor planted someone else's or even his own or her own because it can be a woman, we've already seen that. What about fibres? Clothing fibres . . . perhaps on the tape that marked the equipment. Wouldn't that be lovely? But the Confessor helped wrap that equipment or he or she touched that equipment because . . . why? Because the boot was used for other things as well – a surfing kit, perhaps? – and things would get moved round here and there and in and out. What about access to the equipment? Everyone had that. Every single person in the poor lad's life. What about motive? Well, nearly everyone, it seems, had that as well. So at the end of the day, there is no answer. There is only speculation but no case to present. Which the killer probably considers the beauty of the crime but which you and I know, Mr. Kerne, is *any* crime's biggest horror: that the killer simply walks away. Everyone knows who did it. Everyone admits it. Everyone shakes a head and says, What a tragedy. What a useless, senseless, maddening—'

'I think that's enough, Mr. Reeth. Or Mr. Parsons,' Bea said.

' – horror because the killer walks away now he – or she, of course – has done his business.'

'I said that's enough.'

'And the killer can't be touched by the cops and all the cops can do is sit there and drink their tea and wait and hope to find *something* somewhere someday . . . But they get busy, don't they? Other things on their plates. They shove you to one side and say don't ring us every day, man, because when a case goes cold – like this one will – there's no point to ringing, so we'll ring *you* if and when we can make an arrest. But it never comes, does it, that arrest. So you end up with nothing but ashes in an urn and they may as well have burnt your body on the day they burned his because the soul of you is gone anyway.'

He was finished, it seemed, his recital completed. All that was left was the sound of harsh breathing, which was Jago Reeth's, and outside, the cry of gulls and the gusting of the wind and the crash of the surf. In a suitably well-rounded television drama, Bea thought, Reeth would rise to his feet now. He would dash for the door and throw himself over the cliff, having at long last achieved the vengeance he'd anticipated and having no further reason to continue living. He'd take the leap and join his dead Jamie. But this, unfortunately, was not a television drama.

His face seemed lit from within. Spittle had collected at the corners of his mouth. His tremors had worsened. He was waiting, she saw, for Ben Kerne's reaction to his performance, for Ben Kerne's embracing of a truth that no one could alter and no one could resolve.

Ben finally lifted his head and gave the reaction. 'Santo,' he said, 'was not my son.'

Here, then, is where we've been heading all along: not only to the unmasking of Jago Reeth as the killer of Santo Kerne but also to his motive and to the revelation that Santo was not Ben Kerne's son. This doesn't mean, of course, that Ben did not love Santo. But that blood connection that Jago desperately wants is not there nor has it ever been.

The bang within the bang in the scene is contained in those final words: *'Santo was not my son.'* Jago didn't know this, but neither did the reader.

The options available to the writer in the construction of the dramatic climax are the same as they are for the narrative climax: how the scene itself is constructed, which can be played with in the running plot outline; the various elements of craft that can be used; the decision about the presence of a THAD; how a THAD can ratchet up the drama or reveal character; the choice of setting (and here you can see that I make my second use of that wonderful hut on the cliff outside of Morwenstow); and the presence and style of the dialogue.

When I reached this scene in the running plot outline for *Careless in Red*, I made the decision that legal justice would not prevail for anyone. The reader would have the satisfaction of knowing the identity of the killer, but the reader would also see that the killer was going to get away with it. For Jago Reeth, there would be no justice served – as he perceives justice served – through the death of Santo Kerne. He's been looking for a quid pro quo: Ben Kerne suffering the blood-loss as well as the lineage promised by a son; instead he's discovered he's not going to achieve it, as he learns that Santo wasn't Ben's son in the first place. All the years Jago Reeth waited and malevolently rubbed his hands together have come to nothing.

Finally, we have the denouement of the novel. I call this bringing all the balls down from the air without dropping any of them. In other words, it means bringing all the balls down in precisely the correct order so that the structure of the novel is tight to the end. In *Careless in Red*, the denouement comprises the final two chapters. During these final two chapters, what must happen is as follows.

The plot is itself resolved. This is the termination of the through line. In a crime novel, the identity of the criminal is revealed, and anything that needs to be sewn up by the detectives is handled.

Change has occurred in the lives or psyches of the characters. We see how they have been affected by what has gone on during the course of the novel. Or change has not occurred in the lives of the characters because they will not allow it. They've made a decision not to change. They cling to the self that has always worked for them.

Misunderstandings are clarified.

All the dramatic questions about the characters laid down in the course of the novel are resolved. (The only exceptions to this would be in the stories of the continuing characters, since over the course of the series itself, those questions will be answered.)

All the subplots are brought to a conclusion. The dramatic arc of each character's journey needs to end. Nothing can be left hanging at this point. So in *Careless in Red*, we're going to see some sort of resolution to Lynley's story of grief, to Kerra Kerne's story, to Bea and Ray Hannaford's story, to Madlyn's story, to Will Mendick's story . . . In other words, there are no loose ends at the novel's conclusion. Readers don't close the book and say, 'But what about . . . ?' because everything has been addressed. Some of the characters have changed because of what's gone on. Some remain as unchanged as they are untouched.

The denouement of *Careless in Red* was complicated by two facts: 1) Lynley wasn't present at the climax of the novel, and 2) The structure and placement of the final scenes had to be carefully considered in order to maintain tension until the story's conclusion. That means that partial information had to be given so that the reader would carry on to 'see how it all ends.'

It's in the cause of maintaining the reader's interest that the final three chapters of *Careless in Red* are constructed and placed as they are. Thus, we don't witness the entirety of Lynley's time with Daidre Trahair before the climax of the novel. Instead, that day he's spent with her is broken up and placed throughout the remaining chapters right up to the end of the novel. This playing out of the story with Daidre *felt* right to me in ways that dealing with her in a single long scene didn't.

We also have characters in the subplots whose stories need to be brought to a conclusion. As I deal with these subplots, I try to maintain the level of my writing so that not one of them is given short shrift. They've served to enrich the story and the reader needs to see and understand where they are at the story's end. To give the illusion that these are real people with real lives in a real world, not all subplots end happily. But it's my hope as I write that they all end in a way that the reader understands.

## Optional Exercise 1

Choose one of your favourite novels and identify its climax. Read from that point to the end and study how the writer created the denouement. Books I'd recommend considering are *Mystic River* by Dennis Lehane, *This Is How It Always Is* by Laurie Frankel, *The Monkey's Raincoat* by Robert Crais, *In Wilderness* by Diane Thomas and *Strange but True* by John Searles.

## Optional Exercise 2

Using the same book, look at the elements of craft that are included in the denouement. Choose one scene from the denouement and alter it with an element of craft such as:

Changing the POV
Creating or eliminating a THAD
Altering the POV character's attitude

## Optional Exercise 3

Using something of your own – perhaps from a manuscript that you've completed and are seeking representation for – choose one scene and do with it exactly what you did in Optional Exercise 2. Was this easier? Why? Was it more difficult? Why? How did it change your initial intentions for the scene?

# CHAPTER 13

# Structuring the Scene

*A Few Possibilities*

What I hope is that you, gentle reader, have begun to see that while writing a novel can indeed be all about sitting down, getting in touch with the cosmos, banging out a first chapter, and hoping that you can go on from there, the neophyte novelist can also end up in the hands of her critical mental committee. She can also end up encountering the enormous pressure of not knowing enough about any one element of the story. She can leave herself in a situation of not having a fallback position – i.e., any material that she can read and evaluate for its potential to stimulate more ideas.

Having looked at the many steps you can take to avoid what is commonly called writer's block but can be more easily expressed as 'What the hell do I do now?' our last exploration will be into a few ways that you can structure scenes. This structuring actually takes place in the running plot outline.

You'll recall that when you create a running plot outline from a step outline that you've put into order – addressing causality – you're writing it in a stream-of-consciousness fashion and in the present tense. This is going to allow you to try out various options for the structure of each scene. Remember that what you're doing is merely talking to yourself on the page (the page being the computer screen, the yellow tablet, the piece of paper in the typewriter, or whatever else you use in your writing life). This allows you to unlock all the choices you have with regard to bringing a scene to life.

During this talking-to-yourself-on-the-page, you're able to try out THADs, which you can frequently find in your character analyses. You can also try out dialogue. You can test your choice of point of view. All the time you're doing this, you can be in touch with your body, feeling for the moment when it tells you that you're on the right track with the choice you've made. When you've made the choices and have set upon the course of action that feels right to you, you'll then be able to mould a scene fully in the plot outline.

There are numerous approaches you can take when structuring a scene. I'm going to look at just three of them. Since I am a child of television and film, I'm a visual writer, and the name I give to my first technique is all about how things look on a television or a motion picture screen.

Thus, the first approach I consider when structuring a scene is what I call the Motion Picture Technique. Essentially, what the writer does with this technique is to go from place, to setting of scene, to action. Using the language of film, the writer uses an establishing shot, then dollies in, then cries 'And . . . action!' like a film director.

Here's an example directly from film, from the opening credits to the first scene of the wildly popular British programme *Downton Abbey*: the establishing shot shows us a huge great house in the distance along with part of a person and part of a dog walking towards it. Any shot of a landmark immediately sets place in the mind of the viewer, be it the Space Needle, the Eiffel Tower, the Sydney Opera House, London's Houses of Parliament with Big Ben next to them, or the Golden Gate Bridge. Nothing else is needed to tell the viewer where the ensuing scene is going to take place. In the case of *Downton Abbey*, we know we're on an English estate.

When the camera dollies in, we see a specific place within the general setting. In *Downton Abbey*, we might be in the servants' hall, the library, the drawing room, etc., and it doesn't matter if the scene is being filmed in a studio somewhere or in the house itself because the viewer makes the leap and understands where the ensuing drama is happening.

When the action begins, the characters interact. Someone comes into the room to speak to someone who is already there. Or someone comes into the room and begins to do something during which time someone else enters. Or a group of characters are already there in the midst of something. Whatever it is, it's action and it relates to the story being told.

Here is an example of the Motion Picture Technique being used in *Careless in Red*. We've seen some of this example earlier, but now let's look at it merely for the particular technique I've chosen to use:

> LiquidEarth stood on Binner Down, among a collection of other small-manufacturing businesses on the grounds of a long-decommissioned Royal Air Force station. This was a relic of World War II, reduced all these decades later to a combination of crumbling buildings, rutted lanes and masses of brambles. Between the abandoned buildings and along the lanes, the area resembled nothing so much as a rubbish tip. Disused lobster traps and fishing nets formed piles next to lumps of broken concrete; discarded tyres and moulding furniture languished against propane tanks; stained toilets and chipped basins became contrasting elements that fought with wild ivy. There were mattresses, black rubbish sacks stuffed with who-knew-what, three-legged chairs, splintered doors, ruined casings from windows. It was a perfect spot to toss a body, Bea Hannaford concluded. No one would find it for a generation.
>
> Even from inside the car, she could smell the place. The damp air offered fires and cow manure from a working dairy farm at the edge of the down. Added to the general unpleasantness of the environment, pooled rainwater that was skimmed by oil slicks sat in craters along the tarmac.

She'd brought Constable McNulty with her, both as navigator and note taker. Based on his comments in Santo Kerne's bedroom on the previous day, she decided he might prove useful with matters related to surfing, and as a longtime resident of Casvelyn, at least he knew the town.

The first paragraph comprises the establishing shot. The details of the place come from my research. I had learned that there was a disused airfield in St. Merryn, Cornwall, because I had an appointment there with a man called Adrian Phillips who owns and operates a business in that location, making surfboards. When I saw the airfield, I knew I would use it in the coming novel because it fairly begged to be used. So I photographed the location as I sought out the surfboard maker's shop. What appears in the novel, then, came from both my pictures and from the notes I took to record sensory elements.

My choice of point of view was Bea Hannaford's and the reason for this is simple: since she has never been to that location (which I moved to the part of Cornwall in which the story is set), she will notice things that would not necessarily be noticed from the viewpoint of someone who goes there often, unless what's noticed in the POV of someone who goes there often is used to establish that character's attitude or unless there has been a radical alteration to the place since the POV character was last there.

So we've had our establishing shot to allow the reader to see the setting, and now the camera is going to dolly in:

They'd come at LiquidEarth on a circuitous route that had taken them by the town wharf, which formed the northeast edge of the disused Casvelyn Canal. They gained Binner Down from a street called Arundel, off which a lumpy track led past a grime-streaked farmhouse. Behind this, the decommissioned air station lay, and far beyond it in the distance a tumbledown house stood, a mess of a place taken over by a succession of surfers and brought to wrack as a result of their habitation. McNulty seemed philosophical about this. What else could one expect? he seemed to say.

Bea saw soon enough that she was lucky to have him with her, for the businesses on the erstwhile airfield had no addresses affixed to them. They were nearly windowless cinder-block buildings with roofs of galvanised metal overhung with ivy. Cracked concrete ramps led up to heavy steel vehicle doors at the front of each, and the occasional passageway door had been cut into these.

McNulty directed Bea along a track on the far north edge of the airfield. After a spine-damaging jounce for some three hundred yards, he mercifully said, 'Here you go, Guv,' and indicated one hut of three that he claimed had once been housing for Wrens. She found that difficult enough to believe, but times had been tough. Compared to eking out an existence on a bomb site in London or Coventry, this had probably seemed like paradise.

When they alighted and did a little chiropractic manoeuvring of their spinal cords, McNulty pointed out how much closer they were at this point to the habitation of the surfers. He called it Binner Down House, and it stood in the distance directly across the down from them. Convenient for the surfers when you thought about it, he noted. If their boards needed repairing, they could just nip across the down and leave them here with Lew Angarrack.

They entered LiquidEarth by means of a door fortified with no less than four locks. Immediately, they were within a small showroom where in racks along two walls long boards and short boards leaned nose up and finless. On a third wall surfing posters hung, featuring waves the size of ocean liners, while along the fourth wall stood a business counter. Within and behind this a display of surfing accoutrements were laid out: board bags, leashes, fins. There were no wet suits. Nor were there any T-shirts designed by Santo Kerne.

The place had an eye-stinging smell about it. This turned out to be coming from a dusty room beyond the showroom where a boiler-suited man with a long grey ponytail and large-framed spectacles was carefully pouring a substance from a plastic bucket onto the top of a surfboard. This lay across two sawhorses.

After a paragraph that explains to the reader how we got to this moment in the novel, we begin to see more of the location in the second paragraph. This location narrows to one particular cinder-block structure, then narrows even more as the characters enter this structure. Ultimately it narrows to a single room and a single character within that room. We have the place where the scene will occur and a character who will be part of that scene. And now the action begins, and in the running plot outline I've already decided that a THAD is in order, one that I chose from having visited the

IMAGE 28

IMAGE 29

workshop of the actual surfboard maker and having watched him and his assistant in action. Images 28 and 29 were taken during my experiences at the settings depicted.

The gent was slow about what he was doing, perhaps because of the nature the work, perhaps because of the nature of his disability, his habits, or his age. He was a shaker, Bea saw. Parkinson's, the drink, whatever.

She said, 'Excuse me. Mr. Angarrack?' just as the sound of an electrical tool powered up from behind a closed door to the side.

'Not him,' McNulty said sotto voce behind her. 'That'll be Lew shaping a board in the other room.'

By this, Bea took it to mean that Angarrack was operating whatever tool was making the noise. As she reached her conclusion, the older gentleman turned. He had an antique face, and his specs were held together with wire.

He said, 'Sorry. Can't stop just now,' with a nod at what he was doing. 'Come in, though. You the cops?'

What I've done in structuring the scene is merely to go from a wide shot to a narrower shot, from larger to smaller, from general to specific. Another way of saying this is that I've gone from the general landscape to the specific setting to action within the specific setting.

A second technique of structure concentrates more on the THAD being used than on the setting in which the THAD is placed. Consider this partial scene:

On the south side of the building, a loading dock bore pallets of goods in the process of being removed from an enormous articulated lorry. Bea expected to find Will Mendick here, but the answer to another question pointed her over to a collection of wheelie bins at the far end of the dock. There, she saw a young man stowing discarded vegetables and other items into a black rubbish bag. This, apparently, was Will Mendick, committing the act of subversion for which Santo Kerne had created his T-shirt. He was fighting off the gulls to do it, though. Above and around him, they flapped their wings. They soared near him occasionally, apparently trying to frighten him off their patch, like extras in Hitchcock's film.

Mendick looked at Bea's identification carefully when she produced it. He was tall and ruddy, and he grew immediately ruddier when he saw the cops had come to call. Definitely the skin of a guilty man, Bea thought.

The young man glanced from Bea to Havers and back to Bea, and his expression suggested that neither woman fitted his notions of what a cop should look like. 'I'm on a break,' he told them, as if concerned that they were there to monitor his employment hours.

'That's fine with us,' Bea informed him. 'We can talk while you . . . do whatever it is you're doing.'

'D'you know how much food is wasted in this country?' he asked her sharply.

'Rather a lot, I expect.'

'That's an understatement. Try tonnes of it. *Tonnes*. A sell-by date passes and out it's chucked. It's a crime, it is.'

'Good of you, then, to put it to use.'

'I *eat* it.' He sounded defensive.

'I gathered that,' Bea told him.

'You have to, I wager,' Barbara Havers noted pleasantly. 'Bit tough for it to make it all the way to the Sudan before it rots, moulds, hardens, or whatevers. Costs you next to nothing as well, so it has that in its favour, too.'

Mendick eyed her as if evaluating her level of disrespect. Her face showed nothing. He appeared to take the decision to ignore any judgement they might make about his activity. He said, 'You want to talk to me. So talk to me.'

'You knew Santo Kerne. Well enough for him to design a T-shirt for you, from what we've learned.'

'If you know that, then you'll also know that this is a small town and most people here knew Santo Kerne. I hope you're talking to them as well.'

'We'll get to the rest of his associates eventually,' Bea replied. 'Just now it's you we're interested in. Tell us about Conrad Nelson. He's operating from a wheelchair these days, the way I hear it.'

Mendick had a few spots on his face, near his mouth, and these turned the colour of raspberries. He went back to sorting through the supermarket's discards. He chose some bruised apples and followed them with a collection of limp courgettes. He said, 'I did my time for that.'

'Which we know,' Bea assured him. 'But what we don't know is how it happened and why.'

'It's nothing to do with your investigation.'

'It's assault with intent,' Bea told him. 'It's grave bodily injury. It's a stretch inside at the pleasure of you-know-who. When someone's got details like that in his background, Mr. Mendick, we like to know about them. Especially if he's an associate – close or otherwise – of someone who ends up murdered.'

'Where there's smoke there's fire.' Havers lit up another cigarette as if to emphasise her point.

'You're destroying your lungs and everyone else's,' Mendick told her. 'That's a disgusting habit.'

'While wheelie-bin diving is what?' Havers asked.

'Not letting something go to waste.'

'Damn. I *wish* I shared your nobility of character. Reckon you lost sight of it – that noble part of you – when you bashed that bloke in Plymouth, eh?'

'I said I did my stretch.'

'We understand you told the judge it had to do with drink,' Bea said. 'D'you still have a problem with that? Is it still leading you to go off the nut? That was your claim, I've been told.'

'I don't drink any longer, so it's not leading me anywhere.' He looked into the wheelie bin, spied something he apparently wanted, and dug down to bring forth a packet of fig bars. He stowed this in the bag and went on with his search. He ripped open and tossed a loaf of apparently stale bread onto the tarmac for the gulls. They went after it greedily. 'I do AA if it's anything to you,' he added. 'And I haven't had a drink since I came out.'

The scene continues as Bea Hannaford and Barbara Havers go on with their questions and Will goes on with his wheelie bin diving. Will Mendick's character analysis establishes him as a freegan, so it was a simple matter to draw this quality from his analysis and decide what a freegan might be doing when encountered by the police. Hence, the THAD. The scene is from Bea Hannaford's POV, so the attitude is toned down from what it would be had I written it from Sergeant Havers's viewpoint.

The revelations Bea makes about Will Mendick's past in the course of the scene also come from his character analysis: the reader learns he has an anger problem and has committed assault and done time because of it. Also contained later in the scene is a dramatic question raised in Bea's mind when she refers to the fact that he's lying about something, as evidenced – to her way of thinking – in the colour of his skin, which flames more and more as he speaks.

Interspersing dialogue with the THAD in this scene serves the dual purpose of illuminating Will Mendick's character and avoiding a stretch of he said/she said. Additionally, it allows suspicions about him to build in the reader's mind as well as in the mind of the detectives interviewing him.

Sound versus Sight is another technique I use in writing a scene. Using this model, the scene I'm writing begins immediately with dialogue. This dialogue might comprise a single declaration, question, or exclamation made by a character or it might comprise a section of conversation between two or more characters, which goes on a bit. The dialogue pauses at a natural point, and then I indicate what the setting is or, perhaps, what the situation surrounding the conversation is. Having done that, I return to the dialogue and the crafting of the rest of the scene. The following is what Sound versus Sight looks like when it moves from the planning stage in the running plot outline to the actual scene:

'More than anything else, it's a question of balance,' was the declaration that Alan used to conclude. 'You see that, don't you, darling?'

Kerra's hackles stood stiffly. *Darling* was too much. There was no darling. *She* was no darling. She thought she'd made that clear to Alan, but the bloody man refused to believe it.

They stood before the glass-fronted notice board in the entry area of the former hotel. *Your Instructors* was the purpose of their discussion. The imbalance between male and female instructors was Alan's point. In charge of hiring all of the instructors, Kerra had allowed the balance to swing to females. This was not good for several reasons, according to Alan. For marketing purposes, they needed an equal number of men and women offering instruction in the various activities and, if possible and what was highly desirable, they needed *more* male than female. They needed the males to be nicely built and good looking because, first of all, such men could serve as a feature to bring unmarried females to Adventures Unlimited and, second of all, Alan intended to use them in a video. He'd lined up a crew from Plymouth to take video footage, by the way, so whatever instructors Kerra came up with also needed to be onboard within three weeks. Or, he supposed – thinking aloud – perhaps they could actually use actors . . . no, stuntmen . . . yes, stuntmen could be very good in making the video, actually. The initial outlay would be higher because stuntmen no doubt had some sort of scale upon which they were paid, but it wouldn't take as long to film them because they'd be professionals, so the final cost would likely not be as high. So . . .

He was absolutely maddening. Kerra wanted to argue with him, and she had been arguing, but he'd matched her point for point.

He said, 'The publicity from that *Mail on Sunday* article helped us enormously, but that was seven months back, and we're going to need to do more if we're to begin heading in the direction of the black. We won't be *in* the black of course, not this year and probably not next, but the point is, we have to chip away at debt. So everyone has to consider how best to get us out of the red.'

*Red* did it for her. *Red* held her between wanting to run and wanting to argue. She said, 'I'm not *refusing* to hire men, Alan, if that's what you're implying. I can hardly be blamed if they're not applying in droves to work here.'

'It's not a question of blame,' he reassured her. 'But, to be honest, I do wonder how aggressive you're being in trying to recruit them.'

Not aggressive at all. She couldn't be. But what was the point in telling him that?

She said, with the greatest courtesy she could manage, 'Very well. I'll start with the *Watchman*. How much can we spend on an advertisement for instructors?'

'Oh, we'll need a much wider net than that,' Alan said, affably. 'I doubt an ad in the *Watchman* would do us much good at all. We need to go national: advertisements placed in specialised magazines, at least one for each sport.' He studied the notice board where the pictures of the instructors were posted. Then he looked at Kerra. 'You do see my point, don't you, Kerra? We must consider them as an attraction. They're more than merely instructors. They're a *reason* to come to Adventures Unlimited. Like social directors on a cruise line.'

Here we see the speaker – Alan, boyfriend to Kerra Kerne and, like her, an employee of Ben Kerne's project Adventures Unlimited – making a simple declaration, followed by a question. We have Kerra's reaction to it, so we know at once we're in her point of view. We also have a taste of her attitude towards the entire subject of hiring more men. Additionally, a dramatic question is implied: Why *isn't* Kerra – whose job it is to staff the hotel and to hire the instructors for various athletic activities – hiring more men? The word *red* tells us something about her fears, but it will be only later that we completely understand why she's reacting as she does.

When I'm constructing a scene like this – or any scene, really – I have various options for inclusion. I can choose to use a THAD, as I did with Will Mendick searching for food past its sell-by date behind the supermarket. I can create action that's related to the place where the characters are, such as – had I wished to use it – the Gloucester Old Spot owned by Aldara at the cider farm being thrown a basket of bruised apples to gobble down. I can demonstrate a character's state of mind through a moment of reflection on her part. I can advance the story through a character's inner speculation about something related to the plot or subplot. I can lay down or answer dramatic questions. I can display a character's attitude through her actions, reactions, words and thoughts. All of these are tools to be used. While they might elongate a scene, they also reflect aspects of the story I'm telling and hence are a vital part of what I try to do when I create a crime novel.

I call the next structure Present-Past-Present. To create this type of scene, I begin the action in the real time in which it's going to play out. While I'm writing the opening of the scene in real time, I'm waiting to feel the logical point at which I can stop, back up, and deal with how-did-we-get-to-this-moment. Let's look at the example in parts.

Lynley didn't approach the cottage at once because he saw immediately that there was probably going to be no point. She didn't appear to

be at home. Either that or she'd parked her Vauxhall in the larger of
the two outbuildings that stood on her property in Polcare Cove. He
tapped his fingers against the steering wheel of his hired Ford, and he
considered what his next move ought to be. Reporting what he knew to
DI Hannaford seemed to top the list, but he didn't feel settled with that
decision. Instead, he wanted to give Daidre Trahair an opportunity to
explain herself.

Despite what Barbara Havers might have thought once they parted
at the Salthouse Inn, Lynley had taken her comments to heart. He *was*
in a precarious position, and he knew it although he hated to admit or
even think about it. He wanted desperately to escape the black pit in
which he'd been floundering for weeks upon weeks, and he felt inclined
to clutch just about any life rope that would get him out of there. The
long walk along the South-West Coastal Path hadn't provided that escape as he'd hoped it would. So he had to admit that perhaps Daidre
Trahair's company in conjunction with the kindness in her eyes had
beguiled him into overlooking details that would otherwise have demanded acknowledgement.

When this scene begins, we're immediately with Lynley at the cottage
in the present time of the novel. We also learn what has taken him there:
what Barbara Havers said to him earlier. He's reflecting on this as he sits
there staring at Daidre's cottage, and his thoughts lead logically to his conclusion that he might be overlooking some things about her that he wouldn't
overlook were the person to whom the details applied not Daidre Trahair.
The last sentence of that paragraph takes us ineluctably to a consideration
of those details, which he's gathered in a previous moment in the novel, one
that the reader has no clue about yet:

He'd come upon another of those details upon Havers's departure earlier that morning. Neither pigheaded nor blind when it came down to

it, he'd placed another phone call to the zoo in Bristol. This time, how-ever, instead of enquiring about Dr. Trahair, he enquired about the primate keepers. By the time he wended his way through what seemed like half a dozen employees and departments, he was fairly certain what the news would be. There was no Paul the primate keeper at the zoo. Indeed, the primates were kept by a team of women, headed by someone called Mimsie Vance, to whom Lynley did not need to speak.

Another lie chalked up against her, another black mark that needed confrontation.

What he reckoned he ought to do was lay his cards on the table for the vet. He, after all, was the person to whom Daidre Trahair had spoken about Paul the primate keeper and his terminally ill father. Per-haps, he thought, he had misinterpreted or misunderstood what Daidre had said. Certainly, she deserved the chance to clarify. Didn't anyone in her position deserve as much?

That section puts us back in the past, as indicated by the use of the past perfect *he'd come* in the first sentence. But note that what I've created isn't a flashback because it's not a fully rendered scene. It is merely laying out for the reader what led up to the moment during which Lynley finds himself at Daidre's cottage. Once that's been established, the scene goes back to pres-ent (or real) time in the book:

He got out of the Ford and approached Daidre's cottage. He knocked on the blue front door and waited. As he expected, the vet was not at home. But he went to the outbuildings just to make sure.

The larger one was empty of everything, as it would have to be for a car to be accommodated within its narrow confines. It was also largely unfinished inside and the presence of cobwebs and a thick coating of dust indicated that no one used it often. There were tyre tracks across the floor of the building, though. Lynley squatted and examined these. Several cars, he saw, had parked here. It was something to note, although he wasn't sure what he ought to make of the information.

The smaller building was a garden shed. There were tools within it, all of them well used, testifying to Daidre's attempts to create something gardenlike out of her little plot of land, no matter its proximity to the sea.

He was studying these for want of studying something when he heard the sound of a car driving up, its tyres crunching on the pebbles along the verge. He was blocking her driveway, so he left the garden shed to move his vehicle out of her way. But he saw it wasn't Daidre Trahair who'd arrived. Rather it was DI Hannaford. Barbara Havers was with her.

Here we're back to real time and we see what Lynley is doing in real time. So I've started us out at the cottage, backed up to explain how we arrived at this point, created a bridge to the information from the past that Lynley has gleaned and been affected by, and then moved the scene forward. Then Havers and Hannaford arrive, and the scene moves on:

Lynley felt dispirited at the sight of them. He had rather hoped Havers would have said nothing to Bea Hannaford about what she'd uncovered in Falmouth although he'd known how unlikely that was. Barbara was nothing if not a pit bull when it came to an investigation. She'd run over her grandmother with an articulated lorry if she was on the trail of something relevant. The fact that Daidre Trahair's past *wasn't* relevant would not occur to her because anything odd, contradictory, quirky, or suspicious needed to be tracked down and examined from every angle, and Barbara Havers was just the cop to do it.

Their eyes met as she got out of the car, and he tried to keep the disappointment from his face. She paused to shake a cigarette out of a packet of Players. She turned her back to the breeze, sheltering a plastic lighter from the wind.

Bea Hannaford approached him. 'She's not here?'

He shook his head.

'Sure about that, are you?' Hannaford peered at him intently.

'I didn't look in through the windows,' he replied. 'But I can't imagine why she wouldn't answer the door if she were at home.'

'I can. And how're we coming along with our investigation into the good doctor? You've spent enough time with her so far. I expect you've something to report.'

Lynley looked to Havers, feeling a curious rush of gratitude towards his former partner. He also felt the shame of having misjudged her, and he saw how much the last months had altered him. Havers remained largely expressionless, but she lifted one eyebrow. She was, he saw, putting the ball squarely into his court and he could do with it what he would. For now.

The scene continues. It's full of conflict and tension because once Hannaford leaves, Havers gets down to the crux of the matter with Lynley: Daidre Trahair has lied to them regarding any number of topics and the fact that Lynley hasn't grilled her about her lies or, what's worse, even reported her lies to Hannaford suggests to Barbara that Lynley's conclusions about Daidre are suspect, having been influenced by what he's been through. The shooting death of his pregnant wife and the agonising decision he had to make to turn off her life support weigh so heavily on him that he cannot hope to think clearly, not yet. So there is suspicion between them; there is distrust; there is misunderstanding; there is emotional risk. Thus, the scene ends up being not just about how-we-got-to-this-moment but also about Lynley's uncertainty regarding his feelings for Daidre Trahair, Havers's concern about how his feelings in general might be clouding his vision, and Hannaford's concern that Lynley keeps failing to do what she has instructed him to do. In addition to this, there is misdirection for the reader. And finally, there is also the revelation – unknown to the first-time reader of a Lynley novel – that Lynley had to make the decision to take his wife off life support.

Using this Present-Past-Present structure also allowed me to telescope a scene through quick summary. I'm not presenting a fully realised scene in which Lynley talks to people at Bristol Zoo. But I'm giving the reader necessary information all the same. That's how this particular structure works.

There are other ways of structuring scenes as well. The only limits to the ways in which a scene is structured are the limitations within the writer's mind. The purpose of the running plot outline is to give yourself an opportunity to play with various scene constructions so that you can see which of them best serves the purpose of the scene you're creating.

In making your choice of construction or in playing with various types in a search for the one that feels right, you merely have to keep in mind:

The point of view from which the scene will be rendered

The details that the POV character would notice

Whether a THAD will be effective in the scene and your choice of THAD

The need for conflict, tension, agendas and attitude

What information – played out in the scene – will serve the story best

## Optional Exercise 1

Choose one of the techniques of structuring a scene presented in this chapter. Create a scene featuring two characters and include the elements mentioned in the final paragraph of this chapter.


## Optional Exercise 2

Using the scene you've just created, now alter the POV character so that an entirely different attitude is revealed.

# CHAPTER 14

# Revising

*Being Your Own Editor*

By now, I've put in month upon month on the process, so when I reach the finish line I give myself a few days to decompress in order to clear my mind. Then I sit down and take a critical look at the novel because I've never considered anything I've written as something finished after the first draft. What I want to do at this point, then, is evaluate the novel for its strengths and weaknesses.

Initially, I read the manuscript in as few sittings as possible. When my books were shorter, I could do this in one eight-to-ten-hour day. As they became longer, I had to increase the time it would take to read everything. But in any case, I do this first reading in as few sessions as I can manage because I want to keep the story, its plot, its subplots, its theme and its characters as fresh in my mind as I can, and I couldn't do that if the reading of the manuscript took me several weeks of interrupted time. So I go into my office, close the door, and emerge for meals (during which I still read the manuscript). Doing it like this, I've found it's easier for me to find the faults that I otherwise might miss.

While I'm reading, I'm using Post-its on the manuscript with notes referencing whatever it is on that particular page that I need to look at and evaluate later. I'm also making lengthier notes on paper that I keep next to the manuscript as I read. But even these lengthier notes aren't much more than 'I might need to back off the overt emotion from Lynley' and so on.

Following this method, I can generally tell if there are problem areas, repetitions, inconsistencies, too much of something, too little of something else. I can note if words or phrases have been overused. I can see if a subplot isn't necessary. Most of the time, I can also see if something is lacking: for example, a scene may need a fuller description of place, a more character-specific THAD, a different THAD entirely because too many people are doing the same thing (like cooking or eating). All of this is noted on the aforementioned piece of paper that I keep next to the manuscript as I'm reading.

Then I get more serious. Having completed my as-quickly-as-I-can initial reading, I now read each subplot on its own. To do this, I first remove all subplots from the manuscript, having identified them with mini Post-its of various colours. Going from start to finish on each individual subplot, I look at the arc of this story, since a subplot, while thematically unified with the rest of the novel, must tell a full story as well. This is the point at which I'm evaluating whether an entire subplot will stay or meet its fate on the cutting-room floor. I ask myself if the subplot truly meets the needs of the novel. I ask myself if the subplot adds to the reader's understanding of place, character and theme.

I then generate an editorial letter for myself. It's going to take me some time to do the second draft of the novel, so I want to know what my objectives are and I want to remember these objectives throughout my creation of a second draft.

When I turn from this information-gathering step, I generate a second draft of the novel by working directly on the first draft. I won't put anything into the computer until the second draft is completed. During this part of my process, I cut and paste when necessary, I slash anything that seems prolix, unnecessary, or overwrought. If the novel needs to be restructured, now is when I do it, moving things around should they need to be placed at a different point in the book. When I've taken this manuscript revising as far as I can without someone offering an opinion on it, I put all the changes that I've made into the computer, and I print another copy of the manuscript.

This copy is going to go to my longtime cold reader. She is a former teaching colleague who is not a writer but rather a passionate book lover who reads dozens of novels every year. What makes her an exceptional cold reader is that she has absolutely no axe to grind: personal, professional, literary or otherwise.

I don't hand over the manuscript with the message 'Do what you will.' I want to direct her reading in a way that will be helpful to me when it comes to creating the third draft. So I give her two sets of material that will guide her reading.

One set she reads in advance so that she'll know what I'm looking for from her. Examples might be 'Mark any spot where your interest is flagging' or 'Mark every place where you suspect someone of something.'

The other set I give to her in a sealed envelope. She opens this envelope immediately upon finishing the novel. Now she sees the questions that I feared might influence her reading if she'd had them in advance. These are questions like 'I think I have too many Barbara Havers scenes. What do you think?' or 'I had trouble describing the market square in Ludlow. Have I given you enough information so that you can picture it?' She answers these questions with the novel still fresh in her mind.

From what she's written I create another set of revisions, which will be narrower in scope than those that arose from my editorial letter to myself. As before, I work directly on the manuscript, which my cold reader has returned to me. From this I ultimately generate a third draft, and it is this draft that I send to my editor.

Why go through all this? you might well ask. I go through it because once I've sent the novel to my editor, I want to spend as little additional time on it as possible. I want my editor's letter to me to be very brief, suggesting minor adjustments only. I want to be finished with the book because, frankly, after all the work I've put into it, the novel holds virtually no charm for me. I also go through all of this because I'm a perfectionist. I take enormous pride in my work, and when I show it to someone – particularly to my editor – I want it to represent the best I can do. Handing off a rough draft and telling my editor, 'You figure out what to do with it,' isn't who I am.

That begs the question, does someone need to be a perfectionist to follow and maintain the process that I've described in this book? Nope. But by trying various ways of approaching novel writing, all creators of fiction can develop a process that works for them.

I expect you know the drill and the drill is discipline. People can give all kinds of advice and make all sorts of recommendations when it comes to writing a novel. But none of these are going to be helpful if the potential writer lacks self-discipline. Self-discipline is all about being willing to delay gratification. It's all about doing what you have to do or need to do first and doing what you want to do second. All successful people know this. The luckiest among them find that what they have to do, what they need to do, and what they want to do combine to lead to the same thing: the joy of living a creative life.

# CHAPTER 15

# Routine

*After All, It's Still a Job*

Sometimes people are curious about how a writer schedules her day in order to get her writing done, and this brief chapter will show you how this one writer does it. I would love to have nothing else to do but my writing, but that isn't the case for me and it's probably not the case for you either. The question is, how does someone get anything done when there are endless calls upon one's time?

This is how I do it: I work to a daily schedule, and it's a simple one.

Alarm goes off at 4:50 a.m., and I attempt to drag myself out of bed. Sometimes I manage it at once. Other times I just can't manage it. But in either case, I eventually put on my workout clothes and ride the Exercycle, then do weight training.

Showered, dressed, and otherwise looking presentable, I head with my dog to my office, which is about a ten-minute drive from my house. Once there, as I'm eating breakfast, I draw up my schedule for the day. This will include my writing, a period of studying Italian, dealing with email, dealing with snail mail, running errands and going to appointments.

My schedule is arranged so that I can do my writing in the morning. Depending on what part of the process I'm dealing with, I either write to a specific page count (five pages a day when I'm doing the rough draft; fifty pages a day when I'm doing the second draft), I write to a particular object-ive (two character analyses or ten step-outlined scenes or two running-plot-outlined scenes), or I write to a timer. Sometimes what I'm doing is organisational work prior to the writing process: organising all my photographs, reading research that I've pulled off the Internet, looking for books on a topic that will be handled in the novel, creating a particular setting (such as the boarding school in *Well-Schooled in Murder* or St. Stephen's College at Cambridge University in *For the Sake of Elena*). But in any case, I keep my commitment to the schedule and get that work done.

I take very few breaks, mostly because I'm writing in an isolated and largely silent location. I might get up and walk around; I might go outside onto the balcony and look at the view; on rare occasions I might walk down to the local coffee house and have a latte.

If I travel to another location, my writing goes with me. In advance of anything else I do on the trip, I do my writing, generally quite early in the morning. For the length of time that I'm writing an individual novel, I write five days a week. I take weekends off. I also take off the Fourth of July, Thanksgiving Day and Christmas Day.

Weekends are a time to spend with my husband, to relax, to read, to see friends, to go out to dinner, to go to the theatre or to concerts, to have ad-ventures, to try out new activities, to explore the Pacific Northwest, to take the dog to dog parks or to other spots she'll enjoy.

Following this schedule, I end up writing a novel.

Someone I used to teach with once said to me rather sneeringly, 'Well, *that* doesn't sound like fun,' when I explained to him what my writing life was like.

I responded by saying that skiing is fun, riding roller coasters is fun, boogie boarding is fun, shopping with girlfriends is fun . . . but I don't re-quire my career to be fun. I require it to be challenging and deeply satisfy-ing. For me, fun is ephemeral. Satisfaction generally is not.

# Afterword

Good writing generally evolves from three sources: a knowledge of the elements of craft (something I covered in my first writing book, called *Write Away*), the extensive reading of the works of well-respected writers from various genres, and an enormous amount of practice. If creating a novel were easy, everyone would be doing it. The fact that it's not easy, the fact that it requires talent, knowledge, perseverance, discipline and passion, gives most people pause, especially if their interest is based on *having written* a book rather than on actually *writing* a book. Sometimes a would-be writer discovers that she really is only interested in seeing her work in print, between hard covers, with her photo on the back flap. This is a tough position from which to begin, since most people who attempt to write don't become published writers at all. But for those for whom writing is a psychological and emotional necessity as well as a way of life, the more they know about the craft itself, the more they practise, and the more they work to develop a process that benefits them, the better the chances of finding someone willing to take a chance on them in the world of publishing.

So I encourage you to develop a process. I hope you see that novels don't just come out of nowhere, springing fully formed onto the page. Every writer has some sort of way of getting to the finish line, and that way is that particular writer's process.

Elizabeth George
Seattle, Washington

# Recommended Reading

I believe that a whole lot of what constitutes good writing can be developed through *exposure* to good writing, almost like osmosis. I always tell my writing students to read *up*, never to read down. There's no point to reading something that's badly written or written with less skill and artistry than you yourself currently possess. If you read something wretched or just clumsily written, all that will do is make you wonder how that person became a published writer while you're still battling in the trenches. Forget about that author and others like her. The point is to develop yourself as a writer, not to wonder about anyone else.

Towards that end, here are some books that I recommend for various reasons:

## SENSE OF PLACE

*Broken Harbour* by Tana French
*Rose* by Martin Cruz Smith
*A Stained White Radiance* by James Lee Burke
*Our Lady of the Forest* by David Guterson
*The Magus* (original version) by John Fowles

*Wildfire at Midnight, The Moonspinners* and *This Rough Magic* by Mary Stewart

*The Dogs of Winter* and *Tijuana Straits* by Kem Nunn

*Cold Mountain* by Charles Frazier

*A Tale for the Time Being* by Ruth Ozeki

*The Island of Sea Women* by Lisa See

*The Wolf and the Watchman* by Niklas Natt och Dag

## NARRATIVE VOICE

*Disobedience* by Jane Hamilton

*The Trespasser* by Tana French

*Shining Through* by Susan Isaacs

*Penmarric* by Susan Howatch

*The Collector* by John Fowles

*A Perfect Spy* by John le Carré

*The Dawn Patrol* by Don Winslow

*Sula* by Toni Morrison

*The Remains of the Day* by Kazuo Ishiguro

*Telling the Bees* by Peggy Hesketh

*One Hundred Years of Solitude* by Gabriel García Márquez

## ALL-AROUND GREAT

*In the Lake of the Woods* by Tim O'Brien

*Possession* by A. S. Byatt

*The French Lieutenant's Woman* by John Fowles

*Atonement, On Chesil Beach* and *Enduring Love* by Ian McEwan

*Waterland* by Graham Swift

*Mystic River* by Dennis Lehane

*Beloved* by Toni Morrison

*The Constant Gardener* by John le Carré

*We Are All Completely Beside Ourselves* by Karen Joy Fowler

*The Time Traveller's Wife* by Audrey Niffenegger

*The World According to Garp* and *A Widow for One Year* by John Irving

*The Blind Assassin* by Margaret Atwood

## ADORED CLASSICS

*East of Eden* by John Steinbeck

*To Kill a Mockingbird* by Harper Lee

*Persuasion, Sense and Sensibility* and *Pride and Prejudice* by Jane Austen

*Desperate Remedies, Far from the Madding Crowd* and *The Mayor of Casterbridge* by Thomas Hardy

*Middlemarch* by George Eliot

*Light in August* and *Absalom, Absalom!* by William Faulkner

The Anne of Green Gables series by L. M. Montgomery

The Poldark series by Winston Graham

And of course, there are others. Those I've listed above are right off the top of my head.

There are thousands of books well worth reading in order to expose yourself to good writing. I encourage you to seek some of them out.

# Acknowledgements

Ten writing students from around the world were instrumental in the process of my putting together this book. They met me in Chianti, Italy, under the auspices of Minerva Education, and there they became my willing guinea pigs upon whom I tried out the material. I'm grateful to them as well as to many other writing students who have seen portions of this material over the years.

I'd like to thank the people at Trident Media Group for their unfailing support: my literary agent, Robert Gottlieb, who believed in this project from the moment I explained it to him; tech wizards Nicole Robson and Caitlin O'Beirne (cocktails at Sun Liquor once again the next time you're in town), Dorothy Vincent and Sulamita Garbuz. I'd also like to thank my online guru, Cindy Peterson, who manages to throw many balls into the air at once and unfailingly catches them all.

At Viking Books, I am indebted to my editor/publisher, Brian Tart, for his support and his insight into what would make *Mastering the Process* a better tool for writers; to associate editor Amy Sun; to editor-in-chief Andrea Schulz; to Lindsay Prevette and Shannon Twomey from publicity; to

Mary Stone and Molly Fessenden from marketing; and to Alan Walker from higher education and marketing.

The combined knowledge, resources and enthusiasm of all these people were and are invaluable to me.

Elizabeth George

Seattle, Washington

July 31, 2019

## An invitation from the publisher

Join us at www.hodder.co.uk, or follow us
on Twitter @hodderbooks to be a part of
our community of people who love the very
best in books and reading.

Whether you want to discover more about a book
or an author, watch trailers and interviews, have the
chance to win early limited editions, or simply browse
our expert readers' selection of the very best books,
we think you'll find what you're looking for.

And if you don't, that's the place to tell us what's missing.

**We love what we do, and we'd love you to be a part of it.**

www.hodder.co.uk

 @hodderbooks

HodderBooks

HodderBooks